Groundwork

Groundworks
by Doug Rucker
Layout by Helane Freeman

Doug Rucker
Vilimapubco
Malibu, CA
ruckerdoug@gmail.com

Printed in the United States of America

Library of Congress Control Number: 2018900304

ISBN 978-0-9996811-1-4

First Edition
10 9 8 7 6 5 4 3 2 1

TABLE OF CONTENTS

MALIBU OFFICE

DORR & OTHER JOBS

1960 – VIVEKA

CHAMBER, WORK & PLAY

Foreword

It is my belief we create memories to suit our survival and comfort needs at the time of remembering. That we rarely recall the truth on what took place, but based on those events, we rearrange, reorganize, embellish and change our recollections in the way we need or want them to be. These new remembrances and images then become the reality forming the basis of our new actions. What follows is my truth. I can readily accept the idea that it wasn't the same truth to another. Forgive me if I have left anything out or have not seen or expressed what might be another truth.

Doug Rucker

Groundwork

DENVER

RIDE TO DENVER

On the sleeper to Denver I had the opportunity to think about my life. Looking back, I was a socially naive 22-year-old, five foot seven inch, somewhat athletic guy with suitcase and architectural degree. I was anxiously traveling west to Denver, a romantic place about which I knew nothing. Thrills welled up within me knowing I was now seeking my personal way, this time totally on my own. Life and the world were out there. I prayed for good things to come. I reminded myself I had health, education, $500.00, and my greatest asset, youth.

Through the train window vast plains of corn, wheat, oats, soybeans, and rye swept past in broad patterns. I never knew the fields were so big. I'd brought a snack in a paper bag from home and finished it soon after we'd dived into the trestle bridge and click-click-clicked across the Mississippi. On the other side, the steady but softer clicking was hypnotizing and reassuring. We passed through Cedar Rapids and Des Moines and when it darkened, I climbed through the curtains into my sleeper bunk and dozed wakefully through the traveling night. As I slept we passed Council Bluffs and Omaha and crossed the Missouri River, then Lincoln and the mysterious dark plains of Nebraska and Eastern Colorado. In the morning I sat in the diner car next to the window, ordered some breakfast and watched the endless morning desert with tufts of evenly spaced sage, sweep past. Within and hour we came sliding into the big city, Denver.

Chuck Shutner and his three-year-old daughter, Peggy, met me at the station and took me to their Arvada home.

1 - Helen, Peggy and Chuck Shutner, Arvada.
Doug's 1937 Chevrolet in background.

Aunt Helen, who was Chuck's wife and Mother's younger sister, had been in a tuberculosis sanitarium for several years prior to moving to Denver. Recovering still in the Arvada Sanitarium, she was allowed to visit home on special occasions. At the moment she was confined and on the following day we went to the sanitarium to see her. Nephew and aunt were joyfully reunited.

I stayed with Chuck and Peg for a few days while I looked in the paper for jobs and made calls to Denver architects for work. Almost immediately I found the University of Colorado in Boulder was looking for some one to do simple drafting. I applied, got the job, and rented a small one-room apartment usually occupied by students attending the University of Colorado.

*2 - Helen and Chuck's house at 4430 Eliot Street, Arvada.
Peggy off to school.*

BOULDER JOB

My place of work was light and efficient. My table with drafting machine was more or less isolated. I had a view out the window to other buildings and the bright green of the campus. My boss seemed friendly and soon I was tracing remodeled toilet rooms for the University. I traced the new men's toilet with three stalls, four urinals and three lavatories, a mirror and a place for paper towels. I traced the new women's toilet, which had about the same fixtures, but more stalls and no urinals. I felt educated. I was entering the man's world. Now I knew what was in women's toilets. I was drawing them, for gosh sake, a big step for me. Perhaps, even a milestone of sorts, and sort of saying good-bye to *naive*.

After work I looked over the University of Colorado, found the pool, the track, the stadium, the men and women's dorms. I climbed the mountains and viewed the college town from the heights, walked the down town area, found the sports and ski shops, the markets and theater. In the evening, I bought food, hung my minimum wardrobe in the small closet and checked my funds again before laying down to sleep.

During the two weeks stay in my Boulder room, two songs sung by Frankie Laine stick in my mind and even now mark my aloneness.

The Cry of the Wild Goose:

My Heart knows what the wild goose knows
      and I must go where the wild goose goes!
Wild goose, brother goose, which is best,
      a wanderin' fool or a heart at rest?
etc.

and *Ghost Rider's in the Sky:*

And all at once in a cloud of dust
the red-eyed ----I saw
running down a ---
and up the lonely draw
Yippee-ay-yo! Yippee-ay yayyy!
Ghost riders in the sky.

DENVER JOB

*T*he University job was not what I had in mind. My plan was to get experience under a bona fide architect doing business under his own name in a *small* office. I thought I would learn more than getting stuck in a *large* office forever doing window and door details or some other boring job.

At the University I was not working directly under anyone. I had a boss but he was not around much. I had to figure things out alone with little confidence to do so.

I kept my eyes open and continued making calls into downtown Denver. After two weeks I discovered what I considered to be the last available job in any category in the Denver area. It was a junior draftsman's job for an 80-year-old Church of Divine Science Architect named, Eugene G. Groves. His office was located on the fifth floor of an old brick building at 17th and California Street in Downtown Denver. *(Now replaced with a high-rise.)* He made his reputation doing elliptical domes and employed one licensed architect and three *would-be* architects. I was offered the position of a junior member and accepted.

Groves was a large, elderly man, almost totally bald except for a well trimmed white fringe of hair circling over his ears and to the back of his neck. He was the butt of a joke in the office. The guys said his head matched his initials, EGG. He had silver rimmed glasses and confident, clipped speech and his heels clicked on the hardwood floor as he moved through the office in his neat gray suit and expensive, though worn, patent leather shoes.

When he sat in his private office his presence was felt throughout the drafting room. The peasants put their heads down and elbows up and worked in the silence. All that could be heard was clicking of drafting machines and sometimes the tearing of sketch paper. As time went on I discovered he didn't come in very much and the office mellowed into sitting with arms folded, mundane conversation, ribald jokes and working tedium. The veteran's read him like a book and knew his schedule, but to me, where he was remained a mystery.

I don't think he hired me because he wanted to educate the younger generation. I think he hired me because I had come from a reasonable university; I looked sincere and appeared naive enough that he might sell me on his strange architectural designs. I was also desperate and willing to be paid $39.00 for a 40-hour week.

It may have been he was unable to find draftsman from the area because of his reputation. Others said he thought of himself as a modern day *Brunelleschi,* doing elliptical domes instead of circular or hexagonal. *Brunelleschi* designed the hexagonal dome of the famous Florence Cathedral in Italy using steel reinforcing in a concrete bond beam to prevent the dome's spreading and breaking under it's own weight. I suspect they didn't want to work for him because the local draftsman were well aware of his idiosyncratic ideas and thought him too estranged from contemporary architectural thought to work for him.

But for me, this was the only job in town and was at least suitable for one of my more important goals; *a small office in which I could get preliminary experience under a private architect; one in which the principal architect could confirm my employment under his supervision as required by the State Licensing Board.*

DENVER MUSIC APARTMENT

I rented an apartment on Grant Street, near the State Capital building in downtown Denver in which most of the inhabitants were devoted to the study of music.

3 - Doug in front of Colorado State Capitol Building, Denver, 1976.

The music building made it easy to do something I'd always wanted to do. I'd take piano lessons from Mary *something-or-other* who had a studio apartment in the building. Mary was a semi-attractive female with glasses, about 33 years old and one leg a few inches shorter than the other. She was very pleasant and we sat side by side at the piano bench during my lesson while she showed me special fingering techniques. Since I was to learn *classical* piano, doing slow scales perfectly was absolutely necessary. I remember holding my wrists straight and several inches above the keyboard and arching my fingers so they touched the keys, lightly and vertically like Jose Iturbi. I remember learning to *slip the thumb under* while playing scales, which put it in the position to strike, firmly and squarely on the next key.

I played the standard stuff, like Minuet in G by Bach, and although it was natural for me to *memorize* music, I was learning to *read* music. I did my scales faithfully, *hiding my thumbs,* while I worked two to three hours a day after my architectural job.

In September, just before I was to quit my Groves job and go to Tucson, Mother made the following notes in her journal:

"Doug took us to see his room at 1115 Grant Street. It is located in the Fine Arts Building, which houses music studios of all sorts. Doug has a very large room in the basement. It isn't anything fancy but is apparently comfortable enough. The dominating object is a fine sounding grand piano, which is placed near the center. Doug played a Beethoven Sonatine for us and we really were surprised at the progress he's made in the short time since he started lessons. I would have enjoyed hearing more but felt that the others were restless. Besides, it was well after lunch time and everyone was hungry."

As I read this notation I am bothered again that Mother called a halt to listening to me play the piano in favor of her guests, whom she assumed were hungry. I took it that Mother was not interested in whether I could play the piano or not. At that time I wanted her approval. Cutting me short was denying it.

Looking back, I see that I attacked the piano as a way of escaping social life. It worked for a while, too. For three months I practiced like a trooper and was swiftly gaining on the music, until I ran out of gas. I realized my life consisted of drafting and piano interspersed with laundry, food, and lunch hours and not much else. Something inside me said to stop.

WORK

My board on the fifth floor in downtown Denver was at right angles to one side of a corner window with a view of the entire drafting room and the street below. I could sight across the street to windows of other tall buildings. Sometimes we could see beautiful young business ladies passing back and forth across their windows.

*4 - View of California and 17ᵗʰ Streets from window of Grove's
downtown Denver office. Photo courtesy of Don Wiederspan and
Chuck Hazlewood.*

Chuck Hazlewood, a 25-year-old, good looking, athletic, blond draftsman, befriended me and patiently answered my architectural questions. He had been in the Naval Air Corps, was married with one child and as Chuck says, *"admired feminine pulchritude."* If this could be considered a fault, I ignored it. We became good friends. A more experienced draftsman was a 30-year-old married person named Don Wiederspan who had been in the U.S. Coast Guard. Paul Graves, a thin person with glasses and former U. S. Army man, I came to know as Grove's long-time right hand man. He was in charge of the office when Groves was out. Occasionally a part time draftsman joined us.

Though Groves's office, considering it as a whole, was not without benefit, nevertheless, it was not my first choice. I remember tracing the floor plan of some big clunky looking building in ink! After that, I did whatever I was required to do but I don't remember what. Some people say you mentally block what you don't like. The architectural work was unsatisfying to me in every way but I needed office experience and this seemed all that was available to me in 1950. It is no wonder I blocked what I was doing there.

HAZLEWOOD

Chuck soon became someone I could like and trust. He complimented me when he came to know me better, saying I had many good qualities but needed more experience with girls. He called me *a diamond in the rough.*

During our lunch hour we'd walk along the busy downtown streets of Denver packed with shoppers, young and old, and other white-collar workers out to lunch. While walking and talking, I was sometimes surprised to find I was speaking to air. Then I'd notice Chuck had quickened his pace to get a better look at some beautiful young lady.

Despite admiration of *"pulchritude,"* he was careful to be discrete and was at all times a gentleman.

Hazlewood and Wiederspan introduced me to a rather sophisticated, somewhat taller, young blond girl who worked nearby. She was quite beautiful and available. I lacked the courage to ask her for a date, which drove the two married men up the walls.

"How can you be so stupid? They asked. *There she is, literally asking you to go out, and you won't give her a tumble. You're crazy!"* and they'd moan and roll their eyes and slap their foreheads. Chuck was the most sensitive to my feelings and didn't choose to embarrass me further. He knew I was concerned about my shyness and that it would take me some time to improve.

One time the four of us were having coffee in the downstairs coffee shop and something was said to the affect about the young lady riding horses and I commented, *"---but, she's certainly good in the saddle!"* I thought this was funny, but the sophisticated lady took it as a sexual reference and was insulted. I came away thinking, what did I do?

5 - Daughter, Chuck and Mary Ann Hazlewood.

Chuck and I went swimming at the man-made lake with the diving platform, the buoyed rope, the life guard, the park crowded with picnicking mother's and their children. We threw our blankets on the grass and went swimming, always with an eye for same-age girls. The only trunks I had were bright orange Speedo, *muscleman, racing trunks* that were given to me by Don Clooney, a former Illinois swimming mate. I liked the trunks because they felt good on me while swimming. However they were not *cool*. All male swimmers in Denver wore boxers. I knew Speedo's were not considered *cool* but wore them anyway and justified to myself that once some one saw me swim, they'd see I was *entitled* to wear orange, Speedo, *muscleman,* unsuitable, racing trunks. So I swam around the raft and back and forth and up and down and way out to the center of the lake, showing my great speed and agility to prove that, even though I wore glow-in-the-dark-muscleman trunks, I was - *cool*. I was a *dork* proving I was not a *dork*.

By meeting guards and competitive swimmers and talking to them about racing, I decided to compete in the upcoming summer Rocky Mountain Swimming Champ-ionships. I got seconds and thirds and anchored a winning pick-up relay team. My experienced swimming ability was evidence of my *diamond* side, not part of the *rough*.

In good time Hazlewood and I started playing early morning golf. First we went to the driving range and I learned to hit a few balls. After several sessions, we agreed to try nine holes. I can remember awakening at 5:00 AM and getting to the course by 6:00 AM and playing until 7:00 AM, then having breakfast and getting to work by 8:00 AM. Though I could belt the little white ball quite far for my size and age, nevertheless, my scores were in the middle 50's for 9 holes. Chuck recently wrote me a letter. I had asked him to comment about old times for my 70th birthday. I'd like to quote:

"Dear Doug,   *January 3, 1998"*
"Congratulations, --- etc. (One paragraph.)"
"Do you recall when we worked for Eugene Groves, way back in '49 and '50? Wow, that was almost 50 years ago! You were my swimming coach and we would rush over to the YMCA for a quick dip during lunch hour. (Hour and a half. I think we gouged Groves a bit.) I still recall how you were trying to get me to do the porpoise swimming motion without using my arms. Dumb me thought I could also dive like a porpoise, hands at my side, head first, Went straight to the bottom, banged my head and

didn't know which way was up. Fortunately, a body floats."

"How about those early, before dawn mornings when we would get 9 holes of golf before going to work. That was at Overland Golf Course here in Denver. Then there was that small lake on the second hole where we were sure the bottom was filled with balls. One afternoon we sneaked on to the course with two pillowcases under our arms. You, being the natural fish, jumped in, only to find this pool was just waste deep. However you went underwater and began throwing golf balls out to me, which I put in the pillowcases. As we were about to fill the sacks, a couple of the maintenance men spotted us. They came over to claim the balls, and demanded we empty the sacks. I threw some of the balls into the dry ground by the pond and they, still being wet, collected a layer of dirt. The guys said, "Well, they don't look so good, you can keep those, but get out and don't ever come back!" We used those balls for years."

"When we played golf I recall telling you that in order to make the ball pop up you must hit down on it (drive it into the ground) and take a divot in front of the ball. You thanked me many times for that concept."

"Remember when you decided to take up trumpet playing? You were living in a boarding house up on Grant Street, but they wouldn't let you practice in the house, so you would go out and sit in your car on the street to practice. I don't think that lasted too long." (More letter ----)

"Some of the fellows that I went to college with (those that are left) play golf regularly and one of them is Don. He also worked with us at Groves' office. He said to remember him to you. He recalled how we put signs in the window for the girls who worked in the building across the street. After making contact with them we sometimes met them for coffee. There was a particularly nice on that we lined up for you. Do you remember dating her? Those were the days!"

"Congratulations,
Chuck Hazlewood"

DATE

*W*hile I was working, my aunt Helen, even though she was confined to a sanitarium, arranged for me to double date a friend of hers who had a car. In 1950 I was 22-1/2 years old and didn't have a car, nor did I know how to drive.

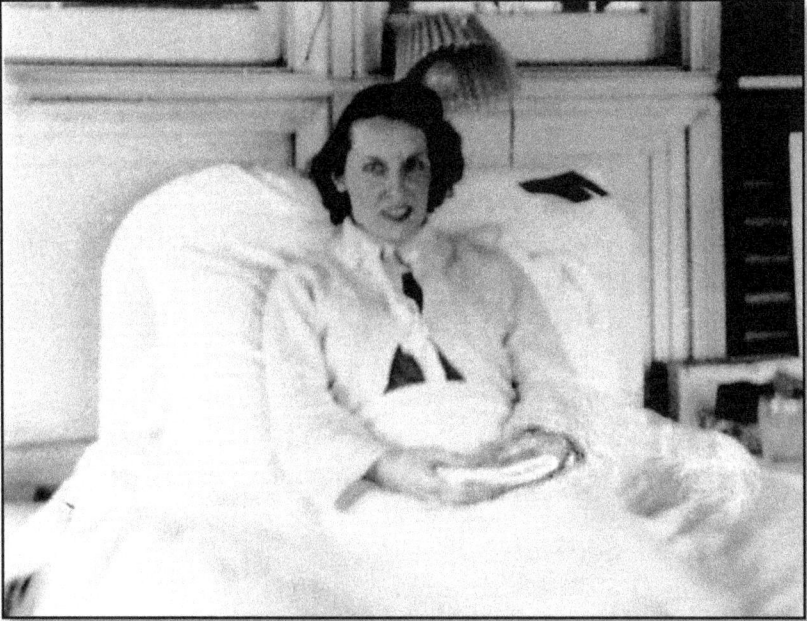

*6 - Helen as she appeared to me in the sanitarium. Photo from an
earlier confinement in another sanitarium.*

My date was to be 19 year Tina who was in Denver for two weeks
apparently trying to get over a break-up with a boy friend she'd had in
Kansas City. I had two dates with her, both of which felt to me like a
replay of my Prom graduation date. I was nervous, excited, I wanted
to go but didn't. I was adolescent. Coming home in the back seat on
a second double date, we kissed. That is, she *French kissed* me. I didn't
know what to do next.

Helen was amused when she asked later, *"Is Tina teaching you
things?"*

I have a hunch my naiveté was not a secret and Helen had set Tina
up to *shake the tree.* And shake it she did!

CAR

*F*ive months into my Denver work, Chuck Shutner, Helen's husband
and my uncle by marriage, decided it was time for me to have a car.
He knew of one coming up for sale and asked me to look into it. A

friend of his had owned it and he knew it to be a good car. It was a 1937, four door Chevrolet and would cost me $200.00. Not bad for a 13-year-old car. *(See car in background, Photo #1, page 2)*

Chuck Shutner helped me give it a test drive and sold me on it. It didn't take much. I bought it and drove it around the alleys and back streets and residential neighborhoods for a few days and practiced my left turn, right turn and stop hand signals and studied the booklet in preparation for the driving and written test.

The morning of the test arrived. I took the written and felt I'd done all right and then the test person, a sturdy man in open shirt with notebook, asked me to take the drivers seat.

"Pull out of the driveway and make a right turn." He said.

I did and we drove straight for a while, then we came to a stoplight and I had to make a left turn. We drove for 5 or ten minutes into the country, and then he had me stop. I had to back into a place, pull out, make a right hand turn signal and drive back toward the DMV testing station. I think I remember only a few groans from the test person but certainly nothing that would compliment my ability. On returning, suddenly the engine sputtered and coughed. I panicked and gave it some gas. The engine coughed to a start again, then sputtered to a disbelieving silence as the car continued to roll down hill. I pulled onto a gravelly shoulder and we bumped to a stop. One of my worst nightmares had come true. During my first driving test at the age of 22-1/2 years old, I'd run out of gas!

The formerly quasi-friendly inspector got out, slammed the door and said, *"When you get a car that can go all the way, let me know!"* and stalked back to the DMV.

I must have walked for some gas. In any event, I got the car back to Chuck Shutner, told him the story and returned the next day, terrified I'd meet the same inspector. Fortunately I didn't and with tank full, passed the second time.

Now I had a car and a license and all the thrills and dangers of that machine. I took it everywhere, drove in the mountains, drove in the neighborhoods, drove downtown and experienced a sense of freedom I'd never felt before. The possibility of real dating as a bona fide young suitor became a reality.

ARMY PHYSICAL

I received a U. S. Greetings in the mail. I was to high tail myself to a beaurocratic office on the outskirts of town with about 90 other white-faced victims and take another Army physical. This came as a shock. I'd already been there and done that. However, the Korean War was beginning. I will quote from my *Timetables of American History* book:

President Truman authorizes the use of U. S. Forces in Korea, following the invasion of South Korea by North Korean troops. A naval blockade of Korea is ordered.

It was intended I go to Korea and fight, most likely in hand to hand combat. I was worried but went to the physical where again I had to strip, have a digit poked up my butt and balls examined. They tested my heart, urine, hearing, eyes, balance, coordination, and so forth. Shortly before we finished a Sergeant made an announcement. *"Those who would like Officers Training should report to Room X for a written test."* Assuming being an officer might be more interesting and earn me more money, I went to Room X and took the three-hour multiple-choice test.

Being recently from the University and used to being tested, I finished in my normal state of panic and anxiety.

Following the mental test was the physical one for high blood pressure. Yes, my blood pressure was 190/94 and again I was joyfully disqualified for armed service.

OTHER DATES

Somewhere I met a young lady my age whose face and hair was pretty in a large, coarse sort of way. She was overweight in all the right places and as naive as I. We went to a couple of shows and one night I parked under the trees in front of her apartment and we talked and listened to the radio which, by one o'clock AM, was becoming less audible until it became completely silent. My battery had run down! Embarrassed, I walked home and fudged around the following morning to get the darn thing re-charged.

The date with the somewhat coarse beauty went nowhere but it gave me just a little more experience with the opposite sex. I learned that some young girls, like some young boys, could have the benefits and deficiencies of being both ingenuous and artless. Perhaps I was not the only naive person in the world. My type was the *guileless* date.

Chuck had a friend who was quite a cool guy. He was about 26 or 27 and had been around. He loved the ladies and dated often. With a good sense of humor, he was attractive and athletic - a gentle kind of guy with working hormones. He got a date with Mary, the lady Hazlewood and Wiederspan had tried to fix me up with, and Mary got me a blind date.

On the way to the show in my friend's car, I tried to be cool, too. My brain was racing and I tried to think of smart, funny, remarks and not let anything go by without making what I thought to be a funny or weird or hysterical comment. I experimented with a new personality. This time I was going to be different. I was funny, I was strange, I was weird, and I was *cool!* I thought maybe the way to maturity was to be *weird*.

We went to the show and when we got back to one of the girls apartments, my cool friend began kissing his date, leaving me alone with mine. I suppose he was expecting me to do the same with my date. I kissed her a few times but being so reticent, excited, and anxious and without confidence, I didn't want to take the date any farther. The girl was nice but I didn't know her and she didn't know me. She was kind of a *female thing* and I was kind of a *male thing*. I felt like a jerk and remained nerdy and boring and politely affectionate, until everybody gave up and my cool friend and I returned to our apartments. That date was a bust but it was at least another attempt to get familiar with the opposite sex. What I learned? *If you don't care about the person, it's no fun.*

PARENTS VISIT

*I*n September Dad and Mother drove out with from Chicago with my grandmother, Momo, Dad's brother, Ralph and his wife, Gert, to visit the Shutner's and me.

7 - Marguerite, Momo, Phil, Helen, Gert and Ralph.

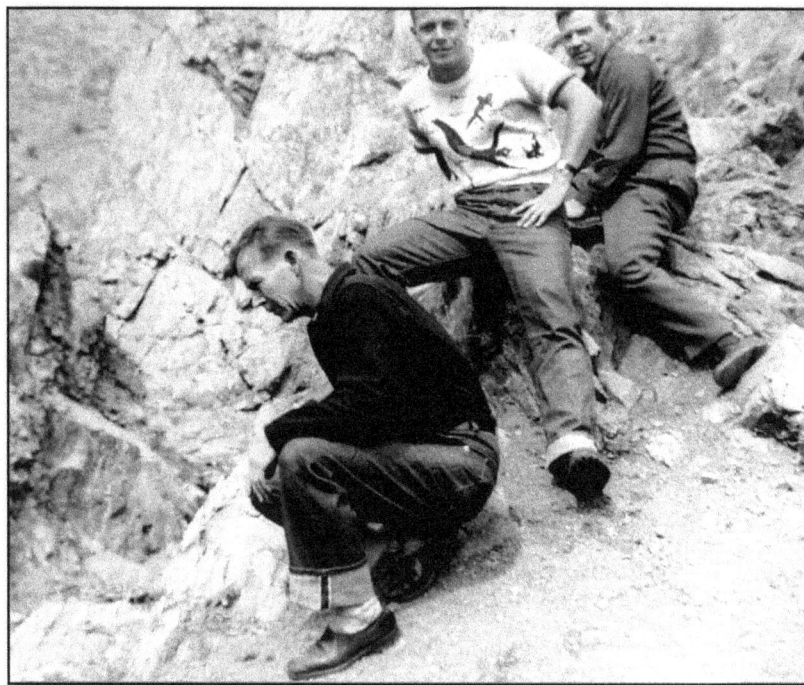

8 - Phil, Doug and Ralph descending the Rockies.

9 - Ralph and Gert on rock.

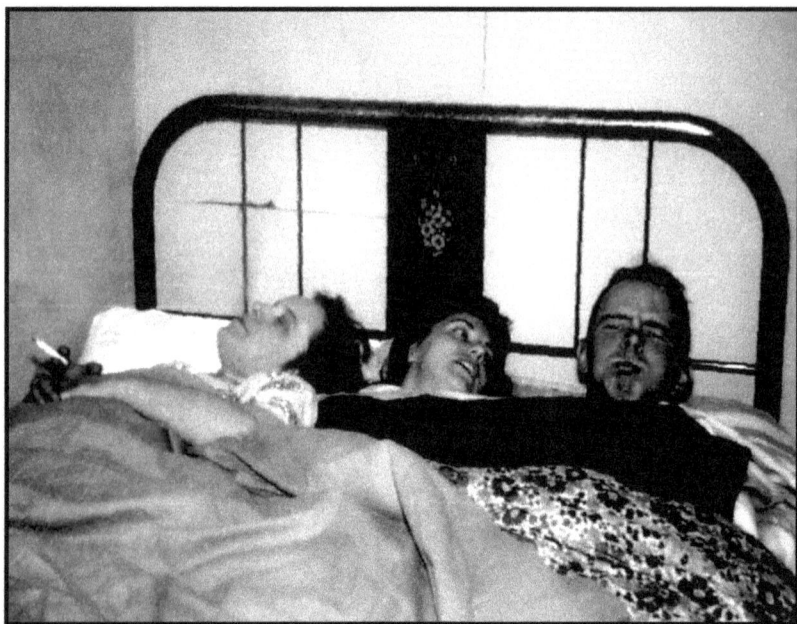

10 - Marguerite (Mother) in bed with newlyweds.

11 - Buffalo Bill's grave.

12 - Family reunion. Denver.

13 - Father and son being nerdy.

14 - Doug with fishing pole.

15 - Mother and Dad.

Mother's younger sister, Marguerite and her daughter, Marjory with her new husband, Wallace Harrison, visited, too. Wallace had a very responsible job as head of the Refrigeration Department for the Armor Meat Packing Company in Fort Collins.

We turned the visit into a family reunion. While they were here, we visited Buffalo Bill's grave on top of Lookout Mountain above Golden, the mining city of Blackhawk, Evergreen Park, Poudre Canyon, and Red Rock's Amphitheater.

SHRINER PARTY

I continued to do *I don't know what* at work. The occasional part time worker guy turned out to be a cartoonist as well as draftsman. *A pornographic cartoonist for the illegal underground market!* One evening, when all the draftsman were gone, I opened his drafting table drawer and found several of his original drawings. It was extremely titillating for a person with my lack of experience and seeing his cartoons turned me on to such an extent that it occupied a permanent spot in my brain for years.

I'd been frightened by the college homosexual person saying I couldn't go through life sexless. I'd have to make a choice. I had been deeply unsettled as to what that choice might be. Was I homosexual or a heterosexual? It was not fun. Due to my long standing sexual denial and what appeared to be social apathy, I was now awake enough to be terrified of the ridiculous thought that I might be a be homosexual. The thought had never occurred to me and, though I have nothing against gays, the idea was the *last* thing I would have wanted or could have expected. Finding that I could be turned on by pornographic cartoon girls and learning more about the subject, I became hopeful that masturbation might be OK - even healthier rather than bad for you. My confidence was bolstered and my deepest fears were being relieved.

Chuck Hazlewood took me a step further down the path. He invited me to a Shriner party on a particular Friday night. I had heard of the Shriner's and had seen their odd tasseled hats and heard some of their strange names, *Royal Order of the This or That, or Grand High Something or Other,* but had no idea what a Shriner party was. Chuck gave no indication.

When we arrived at a rented hall that evening Chuck showed our tickets and we entered a large space with a bar in one corner, which was surrounded by Shriner's drinking, smoking, and laughing. The room was crowded with a hundred or so animated, middle aged gentlemen dressed in suits, ties, slacks, and open collared shirts. A few had gold or red or green tasseled hats and they chatted with un-tasseled members. Most were laughing or talking loudly or blowing smoke and grinning while telling ribald jokes. Feeling free without their wives, they were noisily making merry in an atmosphere charged with expectation.

A long platform, six feet wide and three feet high, extended from a doorway at the end of the hall to about the center of the room and at the appointed time a Master of Ceremonies materialized under the meager spotlight and announced the evening's entertainment to outrageous hoots, whistles and applause. It dawned on me we were going to witness a live strip show.

So that's what a Shriner's party was - a strip show.

I was shocked but knowing Chuck, this thing sort of figured. In any case, Chuck wasn't going anywhere, the Shriner's weren't going anywhere, the strippers were already paid for, and so I wasn't going anywhere, either. In 1950 most of the country was without TV and definitely without X-rated movies. It was a time 20 years prior to the birth control pill, the sexual revolution, and legal adult movies. Strip shows, which were just this side of common, were the main substitute. I was 22, my street-wise brother, Dave, was 18. Many other young men of Dave's and my age had already been to strip shows. A 22-year-old was supposed to be a man. I tried to see my attendance as a helpful growth experience.

With dramatic announcements of their exotic names, three or four girls, one after the other, danced down the runway swinging their hips in exotic movements and tossing their wild manes, all dressed in costumes almost imperceptible. The M C encouraged the audience to applaud loudly and told us the girls danced with more spontaneity and less inhibition if properly appreciated. The audience went crazy with clapping, whistles, and lusty noise. The girls were pretty, though I would more accurately describe them as skimpily clad middle-aged women. Their performances and encores lasted about an hour.

For the finale, however, the organization brought out a stunning 30-year-old professional stripper, a brunette called Snow who went all the way and blew the Shriner's minds. They appreciated her as much as was humanly possible. I must say she was well tipped. In the midst of the standing out of their minds group, silent me got an education. The images were seared into my brain and I am reminded of a saying, "*The soft putty of my mind awaits your great sculpture!*" The soft putty of my mind now danced with naked girls to the exclusion of all other thoughts. Eye opener? I think so!

When I returned to my little apartment with the grand piano and decided relief was indeed healthy and necessary. I was learning new things.

EARLY SKIING

September was getting colder. The Arapaho slopes were receiving their first snow and I decided to go skiing. I don't know with whom I went, probably Chuck Hazlewood or my uncle, Chuck Shutner. Both the Chucks wanted *the flatland Chicago boy* to experience the *slopes*. I had never skied before but soon was trying on, if you can believe it, clip-on skis. Clip-ons were attached to work boots soles like the ancient 4-wheel roller skates were fastened to shoes. We turned a skate key. I had no ski clothes because there weren't any in 1950 but wore dark blue Levi's.

At the bottom of the beginner's slope, after skiing all day I looked back and noticed blue streaks all over the hill I was using. I wondered how they got there. I'm sure others wondered, too, until I realized that my new Levi's were losing dark blue color on the snow. As I fell and slid down the slope, I was dyeing the snow blue. Thereafter, my new skiing name was *The Blue Streak!*

On another weekend skiing trip, I was shushing down small slope and falling whenever I lost balance, then getting up and shushing, and falling down again all the way to the bottom. Skiing straight down the slope was all I could do. My friend urged me to go twice as high up the hill and try *traversing* the slope. I did as he suggested and practiced *traversing* as he showed me. I *traversed* in one direction then turned and tried to *traverse* in the other direction. Unfortunately, I couldn't make it all the way around and gravity and my shushing habit took over and I found myself again hurtling straight down the slope, trees flashing, skis bouncing, snow swirling in a blur as I hurtled, out of control, down the slope.

The wind whistled in my hair and cooled my legs through wet Levi's and tears from the cold wind formed in my eyes, as I gained speed. I was helpless with fright. I didn't know how to snowplow. Looming before me was a long line of skier's waiting for the lift. Skiers stretching 50 yards to left and skiers 50 yards to the right with a solid looking log-cabin clubhouse behind. I was not only to injure the innocent but also break a leg on the building.

I leaned desperately to the left to try to turn myself parallel to the line. At the last moment both skis began to bite into the snow leaving a spray in the alarmed faces of those waiting for the ski lift. I traveled swiftly along the line, seeing each face zip by, 66, 67, 68, etc. Eventually, I passed the crowd and, because the snow began to rise, came to a stop. I glanced around rather proudly, took a deep breath, and fell down.

DENVER RECAP

*T*he eight months I stayed in Denver were important to me. I entered my first two jobs, got two new apartments, bought a car, got my driver's license, learned to ski and play golf, continued swimming competition, made important social inroads and began to resolve a difficult personal problem.

There came a time when I knew instinctively that Denver wasn't my place. If I were to analyze it, I would say, *working for Groves was the pits!* I enjoyed Hazlewood, but, yes! Groves was just too set in his ways. As a member of the Church of Divine Science, he had the audacity to proclaim I would never leave his office. I understood it was unacceptable in his religion, and therefore in himself, to permit negativity to enter his Scientifically Religious Mind. I was secretly flattered that he wanted to keep me, but my inner reaction was, *"No blinking way will you hold me against my will! You've got something to learn, Groves! If it's mind over matter, we'll see whose got the real mind! Me, of course!"* Why was I so vehement? I don't know. After all, I was a lad with just eight months experience. Why should he care one way or the other if I left?

16 - Doug at Grove's drafting table. Photo courtesy of Don Wiederspan and Chuck Hazlewood.

His philosophy was lost on me. I felt he didn't understand the younger generation nor did he understand contemporary architecture. I had come from the University of Illinois that was largely under the influence of one of the three great Architects in the world, Mies Van Der Rohe. His modern use of steel and glass heavily influenced the Illinois teachers and students. I had read several books by Frank Lloyd Wright and had seen publications of his work and had had many discussions with fellow students about his gifts to the architectural world. I had read Le Corbusier, *Towards a New Architecture*, and had more than a nodding acquaintance with the French painter-architect.

I had just finished 4-1/2 University years studying *Architectural History*. I knew about Brunelleschi's dome and what a futile thing it was to base your practice on domes, whether elliptical, or not, and then think you were God's gift to the architectural world. Also, I had seen many copies of, and even subscribed to editor and owner, John Entenza's slim Southern California avant-garde magazine called, *Arts and Architecture*.

Entenza wanted to publish the work of young Architect's, artist's, musician's and poets while they were making their mark. Entenza loved the underdog and things on the cutting edge. He had faith in the future of the arts and published the fresh works of young professional artists such as Thornton Abell, Craig Ellwood, J. R. Davidson, Richard Neutra, Pierre Koenig, Charles Eames, Killingsworth, Brady and Smith, Quincy Jones and Don Emmons, of whom all were working in the new 50's *post-and-beam style*. I wasn't a complete dummy! I *did* have a degree from a University and wanted something better for myself. Let's face it, for design advancement; Groves's office was injurious.

I'll give Groves's credit, though. He believed in what he was doing, so much so that he was still practicing at 80 years of age in 1950. That means he was born in 1870 and probably opened his office about the turn of the century. Think of it! When he was 10, Rodin did *The Thinker*. When he was 25, Marconi invented the wireless. When 35, the Panama Canal was finished and Einstein proposed relativity and developed the formula, $E=MC2$. When 52, the Titanic hits the iceberg. When 57, Doug Rucker is born on the same year that Lindbergh flew the Atlantic.

What he believed he was doing, the spirit in which he did it, the length of time he practiced it, and his dedication to architecture was remarkable. He was devoted to his religion, The Church of Divine Science. I don't know what a Divine Science person believes, but I observed his positive attitude and single mindedness when it came to a project or employee. He cared for himself. He wore clean suits, a white shirt and tie; he polished his shoes and combed the sides of his balding head. In his own mind, he was being the best individual of which he was capable. I have no doubt that in his prime he was a powerful worker and sales person, one of great self-respect, a mover and shaker. I think that if I were 50 years younger, I might have been proud to work in his office. He had an invincible personality and was someone with whom to be reckoned.

Architecture had passed him by and he was no longer in his prime. I wonder how he died, because I don't think that he could admit to death. While I was in his office, he never talked to me, rarely said hello, nor did we ever discuss his philosophies of architecture or personal life. He was a figurehead, and though I was glad to get away, in many ways, I admired him.

TUCSON

TRIP TO TUCSON

At 22 years old, I had 8 months experience in an authentic architectural office of which I was not particularly proud. I had done the Denver skiing, swimming, golfing and dating and run out of interest for the piano. I asked about other jobs, but couldn't find the enthusiasm to make a real try.

There was one successful architect in Denver, William Muchow, who graduated from Illinois University ten years or so earlier than I. He headed his large firm and it was said he did good contemporary work. Drafting in his office with intelligent supervision might have been a possibility. I didn't pursue, nor did I analyze myself about it. I probably thought he wouldn't have hired me anyway, or I was afraid of failure if I were to work in a *good* office. My youthful spirit was calling me away from Denver and to the southwest.

News came from Chicago that brother, Dave, not only had become the President of his Senior Class, but had also won a football scholarship to the University of Arizona at Tucson. Suddenly the lust for new adventure invaded my soul. I would drive my new 13-year-old Chevy across country and as I wandered aimlessly toward California, visit Dave at Tucson. I gave my two weeks notice and thanks to Chuck Hazlewood and the guys in the office and expressed my appreciation for the help and hospitality to the Shutner's. On October 3rd, 1950 I drove off in my '37 Chevy with $200.00 in my pocket calculated only to last as long as it would. I left it to faith. I'd find another job when the money was gone. The $200.00 would at least get me to Tucson. My plans were not definite. I wasn't conscious of it, but in those days I was searching for myself. I wouldn't know who I was until I found me. I was a guy not through with sports, not through with adolescence, partially age appropriate, afraid of life, anxious to do the right thing for my future, full of promise, shy, yet equipped with most of the right stuff. I was everything and nothing - an assembly of contradictions and loaded with promise and hope for a good future. I was doing the next thing, a healthy, educated pawn of feelings and fate, going on guts and desire, hoping to get lucky. I was anxious about failure while being afraid of success and desirous of long delayed female relationships.

Early October found me in my '37 Chevy pushing through the misty dawn toward Colorado Springs. The tall silhouette of Pike's Peak was projecting deep into the Rocky Mountain sky to my right and I felt lonely. At the same time my spirits were high with adventure and I relished the car ride across Southern Colorado, New Mexico and Arizona to see Dave.

By the end of the first day I was well into New Mexico and probably slept in my car near Albuquerque. The following day I passed through one of the most beautiful canyons I had ever seen. Close to the Petrified Forest near the little town of Holbrook, Arizona, I wound down the Northern slopes through enormous outcroppings of tan and red-colored boulders shaded by pine trees. Clumps of brush dipped into the Little Colorado River. The view across this immense canyon that swirled in a seemingly arbitrary westerly path toward the Pacific was illuminated by the afternoon sunshine. Dark shadows accented the sand-colored rock formations that penetrated bright green foliage. The black bridge spanning a silvery river at the bottom was breathtaking and the highway traveling up the other side was a silent adventure in steep walls, perilous drops, a tunnel or two, hair-pin turns and pink walls of rock. For a moment in time, I met no cars. This colorful, miracle canyon in the desert was all mine.

Late in the evening on the second day I reached the East Stadium Dormitory where Dave and the football players were staying. I was welcomed by Dave and introduced to the fellow players as Doug, older brother of Dave, former college swimmer and high school football player, and the between-jobs graduate of the University of Illinois in Architecture. Dave got me something to eat and found me a bunk with some of his football mates in the University dormitory. I was to be a guest for the night, but as I later found out, my two-month stay at the University would be divided into three parts. *(a) Respected older brother. (b) Fairly respected older brother. (c) Non-respected older brother.*

DAVE

*E*xcept for a few brief trips home and from the little information written about him in Mother's letters, I didn't know a thing about Dave during his high school years. My head was in the books or drafting room. What might have been *free time* was taken up with a meal job. Dave had all the makings and I'm not surprised little brother was a star,

Dave was devoted to music and athletics in high school. He graduated with eleven letters, the most awarded in Austin's, and perhaps any high school's history. He'd competed in track, running the 100-yard sprints and relays and for four years in a row either placed in or won the City's pole vault championship. His best jump was ten feet six inches with an aluminum pole.

Dave also lettered for three years in swimming. His events were the 50 and 100-yard freestyles and anchoring both the 4-man and 3-man medley relays. In his senior year he won his ice skating letter by placing in the City championships and during his spare time, and I use the term *spare time* jokingly, he played trumpet while leading the Austin High School jazz band at school dances. To top off his musicianship and athleticism, he was elected Senior Class President.

I didn't notice Dave as a shy person in Arizona University. Attractive to girls, he was quite able to able to reciprocate their flirtations and compared to anybody and particularly compared to me, he was acting age appropriate. Dave had grown. I'd stayed adolescent.

17 - Brother Dave in practice, Austin High School football team.

18 - Austin High School's December, 1949 Class Officers: Center, Dave Rucker, President. Left to right, Sid Smith, Bob Morrissey, Burt Anderson, Angie Trentadue.

While still a University freshman, Dave seemed to overflow with confidence, if not ego. He played the trumpet for beer in Nogales, the Mexican border town 60-miles south of Tucson. It was the weekend get-way spot for the more adventurous Arizona students, particularly the football players. I suspect this was so because it possessed fewer moral values than the city of Tucson. I could never have gone into a bar in any town, and particularly that town, and played trumpet for beer.

19 - Dave Rucker, 1949

Dave recognized my being uncomfortable in the world, yet didn't apologize for me in front of his teammates. Through good times and bad he treated me with pride and respect. Though four years older, I felt, looked and acted like a younger brother. I felt the dork and saw Dave as Mr. Cool. Often times I had to remind myself I had an Architectural degree from the University of Illinois, one of the finest architectural schools in the country.

RESPECTED OLDER BROTHER

*T*he following day I met the coach and while Dave was attending classes, checked out the University. It was beautiful, clean and looked well funded. Lots of well-dressed pretty girls attended and it appeared most would be graduated with a Liberal Arts degree and a husband. I learned the University was rated outstanding in some subjects, like music and theater, and had a lesser standing in other subjects. Some called it a play University, but this was only partially fair. There were many intelligent students of both genders seeking a serious education.

I was invited to eat breakfast, lunch and dinner at the training table. This I enjoyed, since it cost me nothing and it seemed no problem for the University. They were paying for the food. There were many huge, lumbering, youngsters playing football that ate at the training table like you'd expect them – double and triple helpings, lots of milk, atrocious table manners, laughter, off color jokes, teasing, stories about what happened on dates, camaraderie, friendship and an abundance of enthusiasm for physical life and fun. These antics were familiar to me. I had known football players, having played with them in high school and having followed them as a spectator at Illinois. I found these jocks to be more of the same and felt at home.

I spent two weeks or so as the Honored Guest, though toward the end of the two weeks it was more just Guest. While Dave was in class, I drove around town and into the outskirts of Tucson and discovered the department stores and went swimming in the University pool. I was becoming more popular with some of Dave's teammates, not because of my scintillating personality, but because I had a car, if an ancient one, and they wanted to double date.

Dave was playing fullback and working hard. He was one of the smaller members on the team being 5-feet, 9-inches tall and 185-pounds, but he was a four-threat man. He could run, block, punt and kick extra points. I attended a couple of practice games before the official start of the season. Dave performed well.

FAIRLY RESPECTED OLDER BROTHER

*A*fter two weeks the coach passed the word down to Dave, *"Would your brother mind working at the training table while being a guest?"* I wouldn't mind at all. I was staying in my East Stadium Dorm bunk at night. I had the free run of the campus all day. I had no work to do. I went to the pool, watched the practices, occasionally went to the show, but generally hung out. Why shouldn't I ladle food, clean up tables and wash dishes? I'd been a darn good waiter and dishwasher in college. In fact I could have graduated with a degree in waitering and dishwashing. I wouldn't mind at all.

Dave, in the Music School, would frequently make the 60-mile trip to the Mexican border with a few of his musician friends and play the trumpet with his combo in the cafes and bars in Nogales. He had those adventures, but I never went with him.

Instead I sometimes went hiking in the mountains with a couple of friends. We climbed around in the hot sun in shorts, tennis shoes and shirts. I became familiar with Saguaros, scorpions, lizards, and watched for big western rattlesnakes. One time we visited a player's friend's house in the desert. I remember the hacienda on a hot Sunday with a sloping red tile roof supported on arches and a sparkling blue swimming pool among the palm trees.

One time, Dave and I were swimming in the University Pool and I tried a few 2-1/2 somersaults off the three-meter board. Almost got them in, too.

We went to see one of the new movies with Fred Astaire, Red Skelton, Vera Ellen and Debbie Reynolds, called *Three Little Words*. One song from the movie was the Boop Boop A-doop, song. I remember the words:

I wanta be loved by you,
Just you and no body else but you.
I want to be loved by you,
Lo-o-o-oved! Boop Boop A-doop.

I couldn't aspire
to anything higher
than to fill a desire
to make you my own.
Bump Bump E dump,
Boop Boop A-doo.

And another nostalgic tune which is still one of my favorites, *Where Did You Get That Girl?*

Where did you get that girl?
Oh, you lucky devil!
Where did you get that girl?
Tell me on the level!

Have you ever kissed her?
Has she got a sister?
If she has then,
Lead me to her, mister!
Gee, I wish that I had a girl.
I'd love her; I'd love her,
Oh goodness how I'd love her.

If you can find another,
    I'll take her home to Mother.
Where? Where?
Where did you get that girl?

By the time the next two weeks went by I was out of money. Phil Rutkowski, a tall, dark and good looking right-tackle convinced me to stay a few more weeks until the beginning of Christmas vacation. At that time, I could drive him back to his home in San Diego and stay with his parents until I found a job. This sounded good to me because if I had a place to live, facing life wouldn't be as difficult. I had to figure a way to hang in for three more weeks.

NON-RESPECTED OLDER BROTHER

Along with this invitation came the announcement that the University and the Coach would no longer need my services at the training table. I was not informed about the sleeping arrangements at East Stadium Dorm, but assumed that privilege had also been discontinued.

What did I do? Well, there were four more games to be played at home and I was told I could get a job selling ice cream, popcorn and cokes. I took the job and for the next four games put on my white apron and matching Coke hat and marched up and down the aisles shouting, *"Popcorn! Coca Cola! Ice Cream!"* I served them and threw them along the aisles and had money passed down and change returned, spectator-to-spectator. My work prevented me from seeing most of the games, but I was able to pick up living money.

I continued to sleep in the Dorm by getting up early and arriving late. At training table breakfast, occasionally a player would take an extra helping of roll, or small carton of milk, or a couple of extra pieces of bacon and deliver them to me in the morning. More than once my morning meal was furnished by the players albeit a little cool and a might second hand.

In the evening, the same thing occurred. Some of the more caring players would ask for seconds or thirds and fold them in a napkin and smuggle them out of the training mess hall to feed me. I was freeloading! I felt discouraged and disheartened. I kept my spirits up by remembering that I really *intended* to get a job.

DOUBLE DATE

One of my friends asked if we could go on a double date. He didn't have a car and wanted to use mine. His friend fixed me up with a girl named Rita Riggs. We had seen each other somewhere - around the pool or on campus. We double dated and this gave me the opportunity to work on my shy-with-girls problem. Unfortunately, having only had six months of driving experience, I was driving poorly. My passengers didn't realize this, but driving at night in an unfamiliar town while being distracted by conversation in the car was difficult. I got lost. It was dark. The sky was overcast. I was in the desert. I could no longer see lights of the city. We finally drove around until someone recognized a highway and we made it home.

I regret not getting to know Rita Riggs better and have always wondered what good things might have happened between us. She moved home to Santa Ana after graduation and later became chief costume designer for a major television studio. Afterward she was head of the costume department for a motion picture organization and I was able to see her name in the television credits for many years following.

CHANCE AT A REAL JOB

One day, in a fit of hunger and despair, I put on my best clothes and went to an architect's office in downtown Tucson to search for a job. I had heard the architect was an Illinois graduate and hoped he would hire an alumnus. I applied for the job with his secretary and surprisingly, a couple of days later I got a call from her. The architect wanted me to come in for an interview.

I entered a well-designed reception room and was ushered immediately into an obviously architect-designed office. There were pictures of modern structures on the walls and a contemporary architectural model or two sitting around. His office and demeanor spoke of him being mainstream and contemporary, certainly not another type like Eugene G. Groves. He asked of my experience. I told him of the Colorado University job and my work with Groves. He asked about Illinois. I answered with capable knowledge because it seemed I was just there. I must have looked youthful, but could see he was interested.

He put his fingertips together, elbows on the table and gazed directly at me. I returned his gaze. He said, *"If you take this position, I would want your serious and continuous effort. I don't want part time help. Are you ready to settle down and become serious about Architecture?"*

What ran through my head was, *(1) I've got this job! There goes my trip to San Diego with Rutkowski. (2) I wanted to see the Pacific Ocean, smell it's soft air, go swimming, sailing and fishing in the salt water. (3) It is terribly hot in Tucson and I'm far from a large body of water. (4) I would learn a lot here and could play at the University. (5) If I start in Tucson I will be stuck here permanently. (6) I want to move on.*

I said, *"No, sir. I don't think I'm ready to be serious about architecture in Tucson."*

He looked at me for a short time before realizing I was too immature to make such a momentous decision. He understood I was not ready to learn what he had to teach. It had become obvious to him I was too young and working through too many other pressures and problems. He raised his shoulders in a dismissing gesture and said, *"I'm sorry."*

I left wondering what I had done. Here I was offered a choice architectural job from an alumnus and refused to take it. I had been challenged on being serious about architecture and rejected a fast way to get there. This was the perfect small office I'd said I was looking for, and he was plainly a congenial boss doing contemporary work. My unconscious organism was having a field day.

No one seemed to think this was much. Rutkowski was pleased that I was still going to take him to San Diego. In fact he'd invited a girl friend along. Be it known, another young football player would accompany us and we'd be four going to San Diego in my 4-door, '37 Chevy. My decisions were now made. I would hang on for one more week and drive with my friends to San Diego.

WHAT I LEARNED AT TUCSON

I had my adventure traveling. Other than my friend, Hazlewood, I was easily able to forget Denver and my job with Groves. I enjoyed being around campus life again, this time with a car and little else to do. In my relationship to brother Dave and his teammates, I felt young and inexperienced.

College football players can be a wild bunch. Most of them were at the University because of superior playing ability and there was no lacking of ego in their group. Wherever they went they all were used to and demanded respect.

The players, including Dave, were physically healthy, self centered, socially wise young supermen, easily playing and dating. Because I was older and had a degree and 8 months of experience, I deserved respect, too, but my joblessness and freeloading position plus my newness and awkwardness in driving and discomfort in dating made it hard for me to be their equal. I learned my same problems were still with me.

With my problems, however, I brought a highly moral attitude that people liked. I didn't lie, curse, drink, smoke or steal. I could be trusted by anyone, which was probably obvious. I got along well with everyone because I was relatively non-judgmental. To some, these were pleasing personality traits. To Phil Rutkowski, who also valued these things, I was a definite plus and why he could be sure I would get along with his family in San Diego. I was aware my good traits were with me as well.

20 - Dave – Third row from bottom, first person.
Phil Rutkowski – extreme upper right.

SAN DIEGO

TRIP TO SAN DIEGO

Through Toltec, Casa Grande, Gila Bend, Aztec and Mohawk we traveled 250-miles to Yuma, the latter half along the Gila River, and descended from the Tucson elevation of about 6,000-feet to the Yuma elevation of 3,000 feet. With Phil and his female acquaintance in the back seat and his ball-player friend and me in the front we did well in *the good old downhill car,* the '37 Chevy.

At Yuma we crossed the now not so mighty Colorado River and entered California. We were going to travel another 150 miles, parallel to the U. S. Mexican border through Hotville, El Centro, Plaster City, Jacumba and Descanso, to San Diego. Unfortunately, Descanso, which is about 25-miles from San Diego, is at an elevation of close to 6,000 feet. Going up another the 3,000-foot grade with the three extra people and their luggage was too much for the heart of the old Chevy. She was not *the good old up hill car* and started to steam and cough and lose power. We had to pull off the road several times, but were so close to Descanso and anxious to arrive home and there was no place to get repairs and they would be costly and all of us were broke. We decided to gear down and go for it. When the car finally rattled and popped into Descanso, we let it cool down then practically coasted and used the brakes to the eastern section of San Diego and Phil Rutkowski's home.

RUTKOWSKI FAMILY

Phil was a strapping, smart College sophomore tackle with a great future in both business and football. Georgia, his fifteen-year-old sister, was a bright high school student. Mrs. Dona Rutkowski was a big-boned woman with thick, dark, salt-and-pepper hair. Deeply inhaling her beloved cigarette, it was her habit to squint through her bifocals to keep smoke out of her eyes before giving a considered answer. She had a generous heart and volunteered as a teacher of Arts and Crafts to Junior High students. Mr. Tom Rutkowski was slightly shorter than his wife and a man of good nature retired from the Navy. Tom smoked a pipe while reading every page of the morning newspaper and had opinions he voiced whether you wanted him to or not. After enjoying another cup, he'd perform some late morning yard work, or take nap, or make comments without removing his pipe. The whole family had a positive attitude, a good sense of humor, and held an optimistic view for everyone. I immediately liked them and it wasn't long before I viewed Mrs. Rutkowski as a substitute mom and her house as a home away from home.

Their house was a plain, well-kept tract house in eastern San Diego. Mrs. Rutkowski was the boss. She ran the show with a cigarette and kindly clenched iron fist. I was welcomed, appreciated, and respected, and everyone looked on me with interest. It was my job not to impose myself, but to show I was responsible as well and get out there fast and find a job. First I had to observe the Christmas Holidays with Tom, Dona, Phil and Georgia because job-hunting during the holiday season would not have been productive.

The Rutkowski's had an extra room for me with a bunk bed and I was glad to occupy a room of my own. I selected the lower bunk and when I fell into it, became aware of how good it was to be with a loving family and at least honestly frecloading, again.

Shortly Phil had to return to school and I settled down with the Rutkowski's and Georgia. When the proper Monday in January came along, I went into San Diego and asked for a job at the architectural firm of Kistner, Curtis and Wright, who were exclusively doing schools. I was elated when they agreed to hire me at $2.00 an hour and I was thrilled at having my salary doubled by just coming to

California. The Rutkowski's took hope as well. I was proving not to be a flake. My idea was to stay with them until I had enough money to rent an apartment. I would also need another car. The '37 Chevy was losing lots of oil. It had lost its compression and was unable to run up to normal speed. For the time being I would have to limp along.

KISTNER, CURTIS AND WRIGHT

The drafting job was in downtown San Diego on the second floor of the *Spreckle's* sugar building. A personnel manager hired me and showed me that I was to work in a large drafting room with windows along one side facing the city street. It had about six or seven drafting tables with about twelve draftsmen on each side of a center aisle. In the middle of the room on one side, taking up the position of one or two tables, were material files and active working drawings storage. From the drafting room one could go into a public hall, which led to bathrooms, the structural, mechanical and electrical engineers office and separate rooms for Mr. Curtis and his private secretary.

The firm of Kistner, Curtis and Wright had an office in the Los Angeles area, as well. Kistner and Wright operated there. Curtis handled the San Diego area.

There were three persons important to me in this firm, the *Foreman* of the entire operation of KCW, who was not a licensed architect, the *Designer,* a licensed California architect, and an inexperienced *Draftsman* who was an Army Student.

It was the policy of the U. S. Government under the G. I. Bill to pay for the Armed Forces person's education in return for defending our country. Basically, the government paid Kistner, Curtis and Wright for the *Army Student's* drafting time. KCW got the *Army Student* free.

Why did they hire me? Perhaps they needed a junior guy to help with the unappealing work. You could look at it that they got two of us for a buck an hour. In some way it made sense to them.

I enjoyed the slightly older *Army Student* because we could identify with each other. We were both inexperienced and misery loves company.

The *Designer* guy was 32 years old and married with two small kids. He had a sense of humor, was mildly talented and with his genial attitude, we hit it off. The thing we each had in common was our liking for design. I was able to discuss the overall workings of his projects in more detail than with his fellow draftsmen.

When *Foreman* walked in all heads went down and elbows went up. Short, overweight, dressed in slacks and open shirt with belt straining lightly against his stomach, *Foreman* carried an authority no one in the firm had the courage to attack. He evidently had come from *hard-work-in-the-trenches* school and probably had been a seasoned contractor for ten years or more before he took his present job. *Foreman* would walk slowly from desk to desk checking each draftsman's work radiating energy such that everyone was aware of his presence or lack of it.

There were numerous projects in the KCW office. One was the new San Ysidro Junior High School. Another was the classroom addition to the Chula Vista High School. Whatever the project, all the details had to be drawn including site, landscape, structural, architectural, heating, mechanical, electrical, roof, cabinet, door and window plans. Afterward the specifications had to be meticulously written. Rows of mysterious different colored reference catalogues were stacked neatly and authoritatively on shelves. Twenty draftsmen moving their drafting machines and pencils seemed to know what they were doing. How was a young student going to grasp all there was to know. It was overwhelming. I talked to my *Army Student* friend and we commiserated. I was given door and window details on a current project with reference drawings to follow. Essentially, I was copying them from one sheet to another. I didn't know what my lines meant, probably something about windows and doors and how they fit into openings. So began the learning process of the profession.

SKIN DIVING

During Easter vacation, Phil Rutkowski came home for two weeks and introduced me to some of his buddy's and asked me to join them for skin diving. Though I had been to Fort Lauderdale in Florida and swum in the ocean there, this was the first time I had ever swum in the Pacific. I took to it easily. Early in the morning off Pacific Beach

Cove three of us went skin diving, me for the first time.

Few people in early 1951 went scuba diving. The tanks had just been invented and were not in common use, so everyone was skinning it, usually without snorkels. Snorkels are used mostly for viewing the ocean floor from the surface, but are problematic for deep dives that require sustained activity like collecting abalone or spear fishing.

On an overcast day at Pacific Beach the water was clear and cold with mild surf conditions. We each had an abalone iron, called *ab iron,* which in those days was cut from a slightly curved, hardened steel Ford automobile spring leaf. The guys gave me instructions on how to dive, look around, and follow them to see how getting Abs was done. Abalone were hard to see but if I saw one I should use my *ab iron* to pry it off.

I put on my fins, rubbed spit in the face-glass as instructed by the other two, and waded into the water. A breaker came in and I suddenly found myself lying face down, braving the cold and salty water. The first shock was alarming, but the dark swirling scenery below quickly captivated me and I lost consciousness of my discomfort. Dark green eelgrass moved in with the surge then out again like long, loose hair. Brown Kelp stems rose vertically at a slight angle, their flowing leaves drifting effortlessly in the advance and retreat of the swell. As I kicked farther out, the bottom deepened and I saw it covered with various shaped colored stones with vegetation in varied greens. An occasional massive boulder rose from the sea bottom, it's black and brown surface surprising and discomforting to see. The undersea outcropping seemed a warning from primordial times. Then in the deeper eelgrass and upright Kelp, backlit tan against the lighter surface, I became aware of strange live orange creatures hovering and occasionally twisting and turning, the Garibaldi fish, eight to ten inches long! They examined me, tilting their bodies and eyeing this strange intruder.

Garibaldi are so beautiful and loved by the Southern California people they are protected by the State Fish and Game Act. Other living creatures could also be seen, orange star fish, black and purple sea urchins, and gently curved, brown, sea cucumbers, to name a few. The dark beauty of the under-sea richly moved me.

We stayed out for an hour and I was lucky to come in with three sizable abalones. The guys thought this pretty good and said, *"Most first divers can't even spot an abalone, let alone actually get one."*

BARBER OF SEVILLE

I finally collected enough money to rent an apartment and offered this to Mrs. Rutkowski. She suggested that if I so chose, I could pay her a small amount of rent and continue saving for a car. I could pay more attention to Georgia, who needed to learn social graces and perhaps take her to a movie.

I decided to accept her offer and took Georgia to the movies once. Though I was the older man of 23 and she the younger woman of 15, we were socially matched and went to see the motion picture, *The Barber of Seville.* Tito Gobbi, Italy's Pavarotti, was the star in 1951. We loved the show and thought it outstanding. They sang arias so easily. Later I learned singers in motion pictures usually lip-sync their own songs, which enables them to focus more intently on acting. I guess I wasn't *too* bothered.

RIPPING PLASTER

*O*ne day *Foreman* asked *Army Student* and me if we'd like to do some demolition work on a vacant store building. We'd be paid time-and-a-half and could work Saturday's, if necessary. We leapt at the chance and at 8:00 AM one bright Thursday morning found ourselves in front of a two-story brick building with floor to ceiling store windows. We wore Levi's, white T shirts and tennis shoes, and were given a couple of crow bars and instructed to remove all the interior plaster from the first floor of the store building.

We eagerly set to it and after a couple of hours were sweating into the dusty work. We'd begin a wall by striking and penetrating the interior plaster with our hooked three foot steel crow bar using our body weight to rip down through plaster and wood lath to the floor. It made a shattering noise and clouds of dust would sweep over our noses and into our mouth. The next day we protected ourselves with red bandanas wrapped just under our eyes, but then our eyes were so bombarded with plaster dust we could hardly see. The dust required much blinking and wiping of faces and our shirts stuck to our backs with perspiration. After finishing one area, we'd move to the next stud and repeat the breaking and removal.

21 - Doug at Rutkowski house during time of ganglion removal.

When a wall was sufficiently ripped with many long vertical openings we'd use the other end of the crow bar to pry off sections and pull random nails. Sometimes we'd break stubborn sections with a construction hammer. When all bare studs were exposed we'd start the other side of the wall and so on until the day was finished. We continued this for three days and on Monday returned to our drafting.

Later in the week a lump on the right side of the middle finger of my right hand annoyed me. It was sufficiently uncomfortable that *Foreman* recommended the company doctor see it. It was a ganglion, a watery lymph that fills the tissue surrounding a strained tendon. I injured myself working too hard and too long with the crow bar.

The doctor asked if my hands were particularly necessary to

me. I told him they were and he gave me special treatment, a local painkiller with a 1-1/4" long incision. He then removed the liquid and tissue, sewed me up, and gave me a couple of pain pills.

That evening in my bunk bed, I resolved not to take a pain pill but about 2:00 AM I was unable to sleep and took one and went back to sleep. My surgery healed well in a few weeks and all I carry with me now is the story and the scar. *(A tiny San Diego adventure.)*

PUNTA ABANDA

A couple of Phil Rutkowski's diving buddies invited me to go spear fishing and abalone hunting at Punta Abanda. The Punta, or Point, is a narrow peninsula projecting 4 or 5-miles into the ocean below Ensenada. Ensenada is 50-miles down the coast from Tijuana to the Mexican border town. They wanted to take my '37 Chevy 80-miles into Mexico. In 1951, no one would want to take their car into Mexico because the two-lane paved roads were narrow enough to be accident-prone and off-road driving was car suicide. You had to be prepared to lose your car, or at least your suspension system, and have a back-up position for returning to the border.

But I didn't know any better and my car was not that terrific and accompanying two experienced divers familiar with Mexico made me think nothing much could go wrong.

The drive past Ensenada on the two-lane highway to the Point went without effort. We talked diving and laughed and had sandwiches until we turned off the paving onto the dirt road. If you have been on a Mexican dirt road, my description isn't necessary. Shall we say it was so tortuous as to be dangerous to the kidneys?

When your front left tire was in a hole, your right rear tire was on a hill, only to reverse itself in the next 20-feet. Try keeping that up for 10-long miles, which took you an hour, because the best time you could make was 10-miles-an-hour. Try it while breathing dust, scraping through toyon bushes, willow trees, live oaks, chamise, and wooly blue curls. Try it while rattling around inside the car, head hitting the roof, guts plunging seat-ward, your body striking alternate sides of the car and often crossing stony, water filled, barrancas. Two of us were slightly seasick when we finally came to the end of the point.

It was cloudless and warm about 10:00 AM and a gentle swell was rolling in from the west and breaking onto the rocks over the point. We had the rest of this delightful day to enjoy the beauties of underwater diving in the ocean to the south. There was a northerly cove and a southerly cove. The end of the Point was out of the question, the ocean too deep and surf too high. Our preference was the protected coves. We looked at the beautiful northerly cove, with the surfacing of a few kelp beds, but one test of the water, told us it would be too cold. While my friends were deciding whether or not to go in, I tried the southerly cove. Faceplate and fins donned and one fist grasping a rope around a floating inner tube, I gingerly entered the deep water about five-feet off shore. I stepped down steep underwater rocks to allow my body to be slowly accustomed to the freezing temperature. It was so cold I couldn't feel my lower half.

I decided to go for it and dropped chest and faceplate into the water, only to suddenly leap out, pulling myself atop the inner tube. My body had gone into an involuntary state of panic and usurped my will. Breathing was forced and abnormally rapid. If I'd stayed down another second I'd have inhaled water. The water was too cold and I got out. The trip to Punta Abanda was becoming a bust!

We had a sandwich, took a short nap, and then tried the Northerly cove again. This time our diving spot was close to shore and the water was considerably warmer being protected by a barrier of thick kelp beds.

Launched and lying face down in the water, this experience sold me on the miraculous beauty of underwater diving. I was gently lifted as the bed of the kelp lifted when a swell came in and as gently lowered when the swell dispelled. I loved the smell of kelp and the living sea and the fresh breeze all the way from Hawaii. The water, like glass when shielded by the kelp and the protective curve of the distant Point made me feel I was in my element and particularly alive.

Looking down, I gazed to a rippled sandy bottom, 6 or 7-feet below, against which played the bluish shadows of kelp leaves. Eel grass, attached to protrusions of rock, coiled and released and occasionally whipped like loose, green hair in response to the swell and release of the waves breaking on shore. Through their miraculous domain, hundreds of tiny fish in a moving display of gray and silver flowed quietly and curiously around me. Streams of sunlight slanted through the kelp leaves and made rippled shadow patterns on the ocean floor below. Like magical lanterns, orange Garibaldi brightened their undersea dwelling. I swam under a shaded canopy of kelp shielding it's jeweled and treasured areas. I thought *we of the air haven't the faintest idea this exists.*

While I was thus taken, my experienced diver friends were beneath the black rocks and among the eelgrass grabbing lobster with their bare hands. The star diver got a 17-pounder and his friend got one that weighed 12-pounds. In that cove I got a lifetime of memories.

We rested and tried the cooler Southerly cove and hoped the shallower water would be warmer as well. It was freezing, but if we stayed close to the surface, we were able to be warmer for a reasonable time. Six feet below was unbearably cold

There was no kelp in the southerly cove. It was a large, gray, bowl-shaped oval descending gloomily into the sea. The cove contained a few immense boulders, like mysterious, powerful sculptures, that thrust and twisted from the bottom. The top and sides of the boulders were dotted with spiny sea urchins, some black, some purple, and between them, in curious patterns, were simply shaped brown sea cucumbers. Each was three to five feet long and six to seven inches in diameter, their size being magnified by the darkish salt-water. We had a dim view to the bottom from fifty feet above where we hovered like bright balloons over a brutal, unapologetic, rocky basin sloping darkly into the unknown.

On the sides of the bowl and close to the bottom were round caves partially obscured by rocks. It was from one of these caves I saw two six-foot blue sharks snap their tales and flash to sea, disappearing almost before I could become frightened. I felt the snap in my eardrums before the frightening depths swallowed them, leaving only an indelible impression. I was in the same element with something that big and fast. That something was dangerous and infinitely mobile. If it wanted, it could have snapped me in half like a fresh bean.

22 - Doug with sand shark and lobster.

About 3:00 PM we finished diving, packed our belongings, wrapped the lobster in a couple of wet towels, and headed back along the bumpy, dirt pathway to the paved, two-lane highway and San Diego. On the paved highway an hour into the drive I heard a muffled sound and began to lose steering. I pulled off to the shoulder and discovered we'd blown the right front tire. We changed it and

25-minutes afterward, about 5:00 PM, were off again, but twenty minutes later I heard another muffled pop and knew I'd blown the left rear. We were now fifty miles from Tijuana on a desolate two-lane highway with only three tires. We thought we'd hail a Mexican car but sign language was our problem, however it was unlikely anyone would have a tire for a '37 Chevy. None of us spoke Spanish.

No cars appeared in either direction for 45-minutes, then one came from the south and we waved frantically for it to stop, but it sailed by, the Doppler affect remaining in our ears until utter silence resumed. There were no gas stations. We were too far from the nearest Mexican city. We couldn't walk home. There were no cars coming by to stop. There were no houses anywhere, just dry desert and a rapidly setting sun. We had no water and were hungry. The gravity of the situation was becoming clear.

Suddenly there came another car from the south. It whined by like winning an Indy race. We waived at his dust even after he'd passed. Then, well off in the distance, as in a dream, it seemed the car had stopped. We yelled and waved our arms. He was backing up. It was a '46 Dodge. The owner was American and said he had a tire in the trunk. He got it out and it fit the '37 Chevy perfectly. We didn't question our good fortune. We were ecstatic, paid him five dollars and drove home.

Now, I'm questioning: *Why was he carrying a '37 Chevy spare tire and not one for a '46 Dodge? What was he doing in Mexico going by just when we needed him? What if I'd blown the tires earlier on the Mexican dirt road? What would we have done without this miracle? Was an angel watching over us? Was this really a coincidence? What are the chances of this happening again? Why did I blow 2 tires in a row in Mexico when I'd never blown one before?*

Truth is stranger than fiction.

DATES AND MISCELLANEOUS

One of Phil's diving friends fixed me up with a blind date. We doubled and though I wasn't smitten, I got through it. Later, feeling desperately alone, I gathered my courage and called for a date. We went to the show and parked afterward. I discovered she was airline stewardess, a devout Catholic, moderately attractive but underweight, two year's older than I, and only had a high school education. I was a little too forward and she called a halt. I didn't call her a third time because she was not interesting to me and I decided I'd rather be alone than be with her on Saturday night.

I remember driving one evening with two guys and a girl. We were on one of the San Diego six-lane freeways, the 805 I think, going south from Pacific Beach up the hill against a stream of lights into town. Our lane had heavy traffic and I was forced to maintain speed at 60 to 70-miles-per-hour. I perspired lightly as I realized the awesome responsibility I had as driver of the automobile. That my own life and the lives of my passengers were at stake moment-to-moment and that I was unfamiliar with the new city, or any city for that matter, and was inexperienced at driving, let alone in heavy traffic at night on a six-lane freeway. My passengers paid little attention to me, assuming I was as experienced as they.

I went to a party with some younger guys and their girls and was teamed with one of the girls, an attractive beach-bunny kind of girl. She was younger than I, perhaps 18, attractive, and looked sharp, but of course we didn't talk much, so how was I to know. When we returned to her apartment, the others left and we were alone. Presently she lounged on the couch and gave me a dreamy-eyed look and waited. I panicked and thought *what do I do now? I just met this girl, today, and already she's overly friendly!* I felt awkward and waited until, you might say, I missed the window of opportunity. After a short time she rather dejectedly dismissed me and that was the end of that date. Again I felt like a dork!

After saving my paychecks, I went looking and discovered a '41 Plymouth coupe. There were two seats in the front and a space behind which could convert into a couple of jump seats. It looked modern in comparison to the '37 Chevy. After all, it was a three years newer car. But then a year had gone by, so it was still a 10-year-old car, but not a 13-year-old car. *(I was upwardly mobile.)* The car was a kind of gutless wonder, but had reasonable compression and seemed to run well. I paid $400.00.

WORK

*A*t the Kistner, Curtis and Wright office, *Foreman* invited me into a contest for the design of the new high school for Lemon Grove, or National City, or Linda Vista or some other nearby community. I would be competing against my friend, the *Designer,* and one other firm member I don't recall.

I did quite a good design, but not better than *Designer's.* He won the contest and I presume they did the high school according to his plans. I was flattered by the design opportunity and felt more at home in creation than doing the working drawings from which it would be built.

Looking back I can see my time in San Diego was about finding out who I was. For some reason my job held little interest for me. *Foreman* invited *Army Student* and me to make a Saturday supervision trip to a school project presently under construction. My weekends were normally filled with ab diving, so the invitation to do what I considered more work was a disappointment. Invitation is the wrong word; *Foreman* had given me *an offer I couldn't refuse.* I gave up one day of ab diving to *Foreman* and his tedious supervision. I remember *Army Student* and I walking in and out of big dirt ruts and seeing wood, partially braced, standing against the sky and random pieces of steel jutting from concrete, but little else. I didn't know what our trip meant. I was not in a learning state of mind. Supervision for me was filled with regret that I was losing a day in the water.

The following Saturday, I ignored the *offer I couldn't refuse* and went to Pacific Beach.

PACIFIC BEACH TO LA JOLLA

*O*ne might ask what did I get out of living in San Diego for the most part of a year? I could hold the entire underwater scenery from Pacific Beach Cove to La Jolla in my memory! I dove exclusively alone and remember the salt air, climbing barefoot on the rocks, holding my faceplate and jumping into the surf, the hot days and hot sand. I loved the *to-kill-for* tan, the foggy summer overcast, and the full dimensions of the underwater coast. I reveled in the rocks, seaweed, underwater sand, deep crevices, protruding boulders and underwater canyons appearing suddenly and without warning.

I could always find abs in the underwater rocks where the surf broke in shallow water. A white foam swell would come in filling the nooks and crevices and underwater caves, and I'd dive. One time I went into a shallow water cave as deep as my body and about 3 or 4 feet in diameter. It's doubtful my fins were showing outside the cave. I had no scuba gear, but had to take a deep breath and hold it as long as I was under. Dim light shone in from cracks and openings in the cave and I saw a glistening green and silver ab at the end of the cave. I tried to slip my ab iron between its soft foot and the rock but missed and the ab closed down. I knew it was fruitless to try again. Their grip is too strong once they have a good hold on the rock. Perhaps, I'd nicked the abalone during my try.

I left for different adventures and in about half an hour found myself back at the same shallow cave. Wondering if the ab was again unaware and feeding, I dove into the cave again and was about to try with my ab iron. As I pushed it forward a huge moray eel thrust his ugly snout from the dark crack beyond, opened his mouth, showing razor sharp teeth, and placed them gently around my ab iron blade as if testing it's edibility. My hand, holding the ab iron, was 4-inches away from the eel's teeth. I did what Monte Python did when he was afraid in the *Search for the Holy Grail, Run Away! Run away! Run Away!*

LA JOLLA DIVING

One sunny Saturday I was skin diving just south of La Jolla Cove, in clear water about 40-feet deep. This was the place, by the way, as announced in the San Diego and Los Angeles papers, where two scuba divers were diving and one witnessed a great white shark coming out of the darkness, grabbing his underwater friend in his mouth and retreating lazily into the murky depths never to be seen again. What a frightening report! However, it came out *after* I dived on this sunny Saturday.

Forty feet was my limit for *hold breath* diving. I made a few attempts at the bottom but was not able to stay long enough because

I'd have to save air for the 40-foot return. One time I made a plunge and discovered an ab. What good fortune! It occurred to me that if I returned to the surface, the current and winds might move me sufficiently away from this lucky spot that I wouldn't be able to find it again. I decided I'd better get that ab now. I made a stab and it clamped tightly against its rock. Previously I'd been successful in making another attempt and had retrieved other abs on the second or third try. I tried this and got absorbed in my work. Soon my need for breath became urgent and I was forced to abandon my pleasure and begin swimming for the surface.

Normally, in deep water you can push off the bottom with your legs and gain a lot of initial speed. In addition, your full breath buoys you as you speed to the top.

I missed the push off from the bottom and began to swim the 40-feet, vertically. A racing swimmer will sometimes exhale air to gain time for a flip turn or to take another stroke before breathing and at about two thirds to the top, I did the racer's thing, blew out air to gain time. Unfortunately, having now lost my buoyancy ten feet below the surface, my upward motion stopped and air-starved and tired I began to sink. Panic seized me.

Fortunately my fins were still going for me and I kicked them with a desperate effort and completely exhausted myself to the surface where I gulped God-given air. I was lucky to have survived. With no one with whom to share my unpleasant experience, I abandoned deep diving for the day, and considered myself grateful to be alive.

PACIFIC COVE

Off Pacific Cove was another large semi-circular sandy cove. Phil and his diving buddies had shown me an underwater reef about a quarter mile from shore where calmer water became open ocean. From the shore, no reef was visible, but as you swam toward the sea you could watch the shore carefully and when you could align the ridge of a two-story house with a telephone pole several blocks behind and rotating 45 degrees around the cove, see the chimney of a blue house with a palm tree also a block or so back, all you had to do was look below and see the underwater reef with it's swirling eel grass and seaweed undulating mysteriously from the black rock outcropping 10 to 20-feet below.

It felt safe swimming out there with inner tubes and a couple of guys and the relatively close underwater rocks were reassuring. I rarely took an inner tube when I dived alone because it was too inhibiting. Inner tubes had netted bags attached as a place to put my catch but they had a tendency to be blown away by the wind. Then I'd have to chase them and lose my spot. Inner tubes interrupted my diving flow. I stored abalone in my trunks, soft side in, until I had four before swimming them to shore.

We went to the underwater reef three or four times, but one twilight I went alone. I swam easily out the quarter mile, and aligned myself with the markings and looked down for the reef. There it was! The swirling eel grass like watery hair covering the tops of black and brown rocks jutting steeply from the pebbly, sandy bottom, perhaps thirty feet below. The rock's sides were covered with a diversity of seaweed that responded in concert to the ocean's rhythm. I dove through a couple of hundred fish, each silvery and a foot long. I was on the side of them; I was in the middle of them while they circled, then behind them until they dissolved into deeper water. Near the bottom, a 2-foot long, red, black and white sheepshead nudged among the pale green seaweed and rocks and near him a larger white sea bass gave me a curious look before he lost interest and moseyed away. I saw numerous abs, but neglected to collect them because the diving trip was too exciting. I became involved examining the undersides of overhangs and kicking curiously along the projections and tops of the rocky bottoms, intrigued by the ceaselessly moving undersea life. I was investigating this new world and my concentration was so intent on what I was doing that certain facts no longer occurred to me. *"What was I doing a quarter mile from shore?"* I wore no watch and had lost sense of time. I looked up and could barely make out surfers, a half mile away, off Pacific Cove shooting the curl and skimming along the white crests of breakers that broke silently on the beach. It was darker. I could no longer see clearly. A brisk wind arrived from the west and a breezy chop engaged the waves. I shivered.

Then the whole sandy bottom lifted toward me. In disbelief and widened eyes, I watched this moving delusion until I saw a thin tail and something that resembled a head as it's side fins wiggled and it made it's way decidedly out to sea. The sand swept off its smooth black back revealing a relatively harmless angel shark, mildly annoyed and deciding to move. For a moment I actually considered grabbing it's tail, but then thought it would probably swim away with me into the enigmatic gray of the deeper ocean. I didn't want to go there. Before I made up my mind the shark was gone.

23 - Doug. Picture taken by Dona Rutkowski just before I left her house in December of 1951.

This experience brought me back to reality. The sun had been down 45-minutes. The atmosphere was overcast and night was setting in. It was twilight and feeding time for hungry members of the silent deep. I was alone and a quarter mile from shore and had just agitated something alive and bigger than me. Perhaps it was better I forget this underwater land, so intriguing in the daytime, but so foreboding in the coming night, especially so with a disturbed angel shark. If there could be an eight-foot long harmless shark out here, I wondered what other eight-foot long thing there might also be? I was over an underwater reef, which means there is deep water on all sides of me. I thought, what's *in* the deep water all around me? I got moving with my flippers, fast, toward shore. So fast, I didn't want to see what might be chasing me. I was glad to kick off my flippers and remove my mask safely on the sandy beach that evening.

GLIDERS

*O*ccasionally, Georgia or Phil, or one of my buddies would go with me to the bluffs at Del Mar. There on top of the bluffs, which dropped vertically 200-feet to the narrow beach, would be 5 or 6 gliders. A line would be attached from a winch on a truck to a glider about a hundred yards away and when given the signal, they'd flip the switch and the winch would pull the glider, smartly riding on it's one wheel down the dirt strip for take off. With nothing but a rush, it would lift into the air and at a hundred feet or so the winch line would fall away and the glider would go sailing off the bluff into the sky. After a short time it would bank, steeply, leveling off and become subject to the sometimes-whimsical thermals rising from the steep cliff. Empathizing with the pilot and his girlfriend taking off was a thrill. Would I like to try it? I'd have been afraid.

There would be two or three gliders already up, riding the vertical winds created by the prevailing westerly's striking the high bluffs. Depending on the wind, some glider pilots were able to achieve great heights and stay up the better part of a day. When they ran out of wind they circled over the ocean and those who'd lost too much altitude landed far below on the beach to be rescued by more difficult means.

OCEANSIDE MEET

*O*ne day someone said, *Oceanside Meet!* I said what's *Oceanside Meet?* It's a one-mile swimming marathon around the Oceanside pier. I said, *ALL RIGHT!* I decided to go for it! I was a former Illinois swimmer. I had been skin diving for many months. I knew the water. I was a winner. It's only around the pier. Why shouldn't I try the mile marathon?

Georgia and I got there early on a Saturday morning. I signed up, got my number, pinned it on the rump of my black Speedo's and loosened my arms and wiggled my hands and flip-flopped my calves in preparation for the big event. There weren't too many in the meet, perhaps a hundred, and the swimmers audience was mom or dad, sometimes with younger kids, wife or husband, or swimmer's friends. The contestants were of all ages from 13 to 70. I was 24. It was to be a fun-filled family meet with trophies for the first six places and medals for all contestants.

I was a little unsettled, because that morning while driving up, I'd noticed the surf coming in was slightly on the large side. *That meant when I rounded the pier the water was going to be choppy, it would be difficult to see, I would be prone to a mouthful - therefore not be able to breath and the water around the pier was deep and the nearest person was 30-feet above on the water. Were sharks a half mile out? I might drown!*

But I didn't have much time to let that bother me! The gun went off with a shout from the meager crowd and there was a scrambling of bare feet in the sand and grunts as the hundred men, women and children ran down the sandy slope to the water. A 13-year-old girl and me both in the middle of the pack arrived at the water's edge at the same time and plunged head first into the oncoming breaker. I was a little ahead of her and started swimming vigorously through the surf until I was dragged back toward shore by the power of the first breaker. Recovering my balance, I lurched forward again, pushing off the sandy bottom, pitching myself against the water, until the next surge tumbled me and I was buried in swirling silence and caught again in the breathless shoreward flow. It was like being in a washing machine with no OFF button.

I decided, for the next breaker, I would dive under water and let it flow over me and hang on to the bottom. My competitors, undaunted, struggled beyond the surf break into smoother water and stroked to sea. I dove under with mild success, even though there was nothing to hang on to. *You can't hang on to the bottom! You can't hang on to sand! Maybe if there was a rock down there, I might hang on to that. I couldn't even see the bottom!* My 13-year-old friend was having trouble too and then a big set came in - the type you have to swim *toward,* to prevent being caught inside and tumbled to death. I got caught inside anyway, behind one, two, three big ones, and as I rose to the top, just before tumbling backward over the falls, for a gasping moment at the peak of the breaker, I glimpsed the bulk of receding elbows of my competitors already halfway to the end of the pier.

I was exhausted from tumbling in the gurgle and splash of white water and I hadn't even started the race. My 13-year-old friend was feeling it too. I was tired of trying to make it through the breakers. If I did make it out I was already so exhausted there was no way I could have finished the race. If I made it through the surf, I'd drown. It was quit, or death!

My little friend went with me, too. She couldn't make it, either. We two almost drowned in the surf. I avoided everyone's glances as I walked the beach's slope. Spectators were unnervingly quiet. No one else had decided to give up on the race and come in. We were the only two. Thank heaven the little girl couldn't make it either. How would it have looked if I had come in alone?

I just had time to dry myself off, throw a towel around my neck, put on a baseball cap and walk to the other side of the pier when the winners reached the surf. Two were about tied and the winner's friends gave a cheer or two and a whistle. The first one caught a giant breaker and surfed in, the other missed the same wave and had to wait for the next one. The best swimmer's time was about a half hour. I took Georgia home and we didn't talk about it much.

TO CHICAGO AND BACK

Early in August 1951, I asked the *Foreman* and Mr. Curtis if I could have a month's leave of absence to visit my parents in Chicago. I hadn't been home since December of 1950 and felt I wanted to go. They reluctantly understood but agreed.

I drove to Chicago alone. It must have taken me four days and I don't recall the trip. I stayed with my parents who had moved to Le Claire Street by then. Dave was home from Tucson for the summer and I probably saw a few old friends like O'Hare, Mac and Scheck, and probably sunned myself and swam at the North Avenue Beach. Toward the latter part of August it was time for David to return to the University and I agreed to give him a ride in my '41 Plymouth along with one of his player friends called Wallendorf.

I drove to Chicago the Northern route through Arizona, New Mexico, Colorado, Kansas, Missouri, Iowa and Illinois, but we returned the Southern route, through, Missouri, Oklahoma, Texas, New Mexico and Arizona.

I remember only one thing from the trip. One mid-morning going through New Mexico with Wallendorf asleep in the back seat and me dozing in the passenger seat with Dave driving, we heard Dave yell, *OOOOOh!,* just before the car plunged off to the right and rattled down a steep slope. Dave frantically hit the breaks while Wallendorf was bouncing in the air, stomach hitting the ceiling, and me lurching side to side in the passenger seat. We pitched uncontrollably for what seemed to be forever before the old car jumped and rolled to it's dusty stopping place two feet from a six foot, 20-ton boulder.

Dave had dozed off and lost control of the car and it had drifted off the pavement to the right. We had gone steeply down a diagonal slope and come to rest in a cloud of dust at the boulder. If we'd hit the boulder with any speed God knows how we'd have survived.

By the time we climbed out of the car a number of people were standing on the road 20-feet above us asking if we were hurt. Dave shouted, *"NO!"* put the Plymouth in reverse and carefully backed out. We resumed our driving with no further mishap.

Dave says I was at the wheel but I beg to differ and this *is my book*.

PACIFIC BEACH

*R*eturning to San Diego, an opportunity arose for me to live with a friend, whom I'll call Tony since I've forgotten his name. We rented a small, breezy and somewhat dilapidated two-bedroom house with front porch in Pacific Beach. It was close to my favorite diving spot and would afford me independence from the Rutkowski's. Tony was a veteran and had some kind of job. I would describe him as a rough but sensitive guy and street wise, having known active service in the Army. He was willing to talk about meaningful things and take an art class with me.

Our Life Drawing classes met every Tuesday and Thursday evenings from 7:00 PM to 9:00 PM and we had fun. Yes, we had nude models of all types, young men, young women, and old women, old men. The instruction went well and we were learning, and there was even an attractive lady in the class about my age whom I wanted to know. She was pretty and interested in art. I was pleased we had at least this much in common. We would see how things would go.

One day Dave limped in from Tucson. He was disappointed to have been dropped during the second year of his scholarship because he'd injured his knee. He was upset and stayed in our house a couple of days while Tony and I tried to cheer him up. He called home and got the money from Mother and Dad and took the train home. He felt he was unjustly treated and the University was playing unfair. Dave would have to decide his next action at home.

At work, they had relocated my drafting area and I was in a different room and away from my friend, *Army Student*. Strangely, my lettering underwent a change. On my working drawings sheets, the height and size and spacing of my letters was in proportion to the space available around the letter rather than all letters being of uniform size. This looked disorganized and made my work seem like it was done by a crazy person. I could have looked for examples in previous work. Certainly there were enough of them there. There was no one in my isolated space to give me an objective view and correct me, but I attribute this mistake to lack of interest in the job. *Foreman,* who was studying for the architectural licensing exam was treating me cooly. Then, for diving purposes, I decided to get a butch haircut. Having short hair required little care but it made me look even younger than I already looked. Given my lack of social grace and naivete this was a poor job move. At work with those mature family draftsmen I looked like a kid.

One Friday, being familiar with my poor lettering and looking at me with my new butch haircut, *Foreman,* passed me in the hall and seeing me as a kid skin diver and a person uninterested in architecture, even unwilling to learn, since he'd tried to take me out on Saturdays and I'd ignored him, said to me in a calm voice, *"If you find another job, don't pass it up."*

This quiet sentence while passing me in the hall *steamed* me. I turned red in the face. His words told me, unmistakably, he would be happier without me. I decided I was basically fired unless I turned over a new leaf, came back with apologies, corrected my lettering, went on Saturday supervision trips, and really turned my act around. This, I was not going to do! I didn't know it then, but the most important thing for me to do was to grow up. The job was a means to that end, but because the job was unfulfilling, leaving was going to be easy. I didn't want to be a school architect anyway. My character was leading me to do something easier, like houses.

I went to the bathroom, gave it some brief thought, then walked straight to Mr. Curtis's office and told him I was quitting. There seemed to be no argument, nor could there have been any. His position was clear; he could get along without me. Mr. Curtis was unfamiliar with my or anyone's work and I presume he said to himself, *"OK."*

I gathered my few things and left the same day. I had made no other arrangements for this decision and had not even considered quitting. I did not even collect my paycheck. I had to think hard about what I was going to do. I decided to go to the Los Angeles area and get a job. This would leave Tony without a partner to share the rent but he'd been through worse things. Then, too, I'd made a first date with the lady in the art class for tonight, Friday. Regrettably, that would have to be called off. Like many men, I was too preoccupied to give her the courtesy of a call to explain. I was insecure and obsessed about leaving immediately. You might say I fled San Diego that very evening!

SAN DIEGO RECAP

I might ask myself, *"What was San Diego to me?"* I can tell you what it wasn't for me. It wasn't the place for me to learn to be a school architect. I needed a job quickly so I wouldn't be a flake in my own eyes or those of the Rutkowski's. If I were more mature, I might have investigated the San Diego area more carefully and been more particular about my job choice. But no! I just wanted to get any old architectural job to make money. As in Denver and Tucson, I wasn't ready to face a competent architectural job in a small office so I'd really learn *architecture*. Becoming an architect was *not* my cutting edge in San Diego, and though it furthered my architectural career, it was *not* what I was trying to do.

What I *was* trying to do in San Diego was to become a man by learning to relate to the opposite sex and become at ease with my peers. Less difficult, but still important, was maintaining my self-respect through sports activities, learning to skin dive. Being lost in San Diego made it difficult to learn about girls in spite of the fun-filled beach activity.

My trip to Chicago and back was nothing more than a slight vacation from architectural troubles already brewing, a tactic of delay. When I look back, *Foreman's* comment to me was entirely justified. He was forcing me to look at reality, which was: *I really didn't want to be accepted by the architectural profession, yet, if ever. Foreman* called my bluff.

Having heard my old grammar and high school buddy Art Schlakat had an apartment and pizza joint in Alhambra, a part of East Los Angeles, I gave him a call and told him my situation. He invited me to stay with him a couple of weeks until I found a job. Missing my Friday date, I packed my few belongings, including fins and faceplate, and took off up the coast in my '41 Plymouth for L. A.

ALTADENA

ALHAMBRA

*I*t was good to see Schlakat. I met him at his eat-in, take-out pizza place. I sat in a booth while he was working and he gave me a free pizza. We had a good visit and meal. When he closed we returned to his apartment and Art fixed me up on the couch.

Schlakat was 24-years-old and owning a pizza restaurant meant he was doing well for his age. He was unmarried but had a girl friend that I never met. His voice was a scratchy whisper. He told me he had vocal cord nodes and had been to the doctor and was watching them. I thought that was strange but it looked like he was taking care of himself.

I got out the phone book and started calling every architect in the Los Angeles area for a job. Occasionally I'd go and see about one. I was pressed for money.

One Saturday morning Art invited me to play sand lot flag football. I hadn't played *"touch ball"* since 1949 but still hadn't lost the football urge. I joined him. There were eleven guys on a side and I didn't get to play my normal position, quarter-back, but played right end or tackle. About half way through the game, I felt sick. Something was upsetting my stomach. By the end of the game we were both nauseous and he explained we were affected by deep-breathing the smog. Smog was a serious, chronic condition in Alhambra.

24 - Art Schlakat

Art introduced me to his landlady, a woman with an Italian accent. One time I was looking through the L. A. Times trying to find a job. She said, *"Fruehauf Trucks needs draftsman. Why didn't I try them?"*

I said nothing, but thought to myself, *I don't want to do truck drafting! I didn't go to school 4 years to do mechanical work! Doesn't she realize I am capable of more than just having an arbitrary truck job!* I don't want to be a truck architect. I was indignant and if I said what I was thinking it would not have been kind. Her thoughts about who I was were not my thoughts about who I was. Nevertheless, I forgave her because she was only being a kind lady.

PASADENA

*A*fter staying with Art a week and a half I heard of a job in Pasadena. A firm of about 20 had just acquired a big job for the Navy to be built in San Diego. Their contract called for completion of plans in 2 short months and they were hiring any draftsman they could find. I thought I'd rather have a job for 2 months rather than none at all. I took the job.

The firm of Morgan, Mitchell and Meyers, a fake name, since I don't remember the real one, was on the second floor of a modest office building in Pasadena. I worked under a young, handsome, dark-haired job captain who, by his dress and mannerisms, seemed a bit of a *sport*. His attitude was loose but competent and, since most of my work would be tracing and copying and the *sport* had no ax to grind, I got along well and had little trouble. Also, I'd corrected my lettering and my sheets once again looked neat and clean. The *Sport* turned out to have a sense of humor, accepted me for what I had to offer, and was uncritical and continually available to answer questions. I was able to do a slight bit of architectural learning under his influence.

J. R. Davidson, an employee who worked there, was considered by some to be an impractical dreamer type, however, I got the following information from Esther McCoy's, book, *Case Study Houses, 1945–1962,* which included three Davidson houses. A short description and pictures follows:

J. R. was born in 1888 in Berlin and studied in
Germany, France and England. He opened an office
in Germany in 1919 and came to the U. S. in 1923. He
opened an office in L. A. in 1925 and was an instructor   at
Art Center and Chouinard's.

In 1952 he would have been 64-years old. I saw him a few times. He was making a buck an hour more than I. We were never close. This was my earliest proximity to fame.

25 - J.R. Davidson

26 - Entry to a 1,100 square foot house by J.R. Davidson.

APARTMENT

I got myself a tiny apartment in a little row of four efficiency units off a private alleyway near Raymond Street in Altadena. It was one room with many niches and doors. One niche held an early version *Acme Kitchen* that was six feet wide with under counter refrigerator, oven, sink, and two-burner range. Above were shelves for food storage, plates and silverware.

Another niche held a fold down bed. I pulled down a vertical piece of painted plywood, *(color to match the wall)* a couple of legs folded down. *Voila! A* bed! Since the room was only 12-feet by 16-feet, when the bed was down there wasn't much room for anything else. Next to the bed were two doors opening to a 5-foot closet. Near the entry was another door to a small bathroom. My furnished room held a couch, easy chair, end table, and wooden eating table against a wall with two chairs. There were windows at the front and rear of the one-room apartment. I had no TV because they were costly and rare in 1952.

I acclimated myself to my new surroundings, scouted out Pasadena, Hollywood and Santa Monica. In the evening I wrote letters home or went to the show. On weekends I toured the coast or tried some murky skin diving in Malibu's Paradise Cove.

STATE EXAM (1)

*A*t work one day I learned that The State Board of Architectural Examiners was giving their January licensing test at USC. *(University of Southern California)* I was qualified because the rules were such that an applicant would be permitted to take half the exam if they had graduated from an accredited University, yet didn't have the required 2 years experience under a licensed architect.

I hadn't done an ounce of preparatory work for the test, however I decided to take the half-exam because I wanted to experience the mechanics required to take it. I wanted to see what it would be like at USC, how to get there, where I would park? What would USC looked like, how the test room looked and to see the instructor and understand the test procedure? I wanted to see how it felt to be in the exam and to have the experience of taking the real exam to be a California architect. It could only be a benefit. Nothing would be lost but time. So I paid the hundred-dollar fee and took the exam. It consisted of 4-hours of Architectural History, 4-hours of Structural Engineering, 2-hours of Site Planning and 2-hours of Mechanical Engineering over a two-day period, Friday and Saturday.

Between exams, I was surprised to find a former Illinois Architecture student, Herb Kaiser, also taking the test. At school, Herb had been a G. I. Bill veteran earning extra money selling candy and cigarettes to late working students. He was a medium sized, athletic looking guy with dark brown hair who chain smoked Lucky Strikes. At Illinois University he had been married to lovely southern woman who had a young daughter by a previous marriage.

Time had moved on for Herb, though, because in Pasadena he was divorced and living alone. In fact he was in the process of constructing a home of his own design for himself in Pasadena. Herb always had a ready smile, a good sense of humor and an aura of being street wise and mature.

A month or so later I received a letter saying though I had failed the important three quarters of the exam, I had at least passed Site Planning. I was pleased to have made some progress toward getting my license, particularly without studying.

THE CONAN'S

By return mail from Mother I learned she had a close friend named, Lois Conan, who lived at 1961 Skyview Drive, Altadena, *"and was I near there?"*

I told her Altadena was in my back yard. She said Lois was married to Duke Conan and they had a daughter, Karon, who was 19 and a son, Dick, who was 15. Thinking I might find another home away from home, she said I should introduce myself. It was likely Karon, who was four years younger, could show me around.

I had no phone and decided to drop in on them without calling. Since Mother had written Lois about me, they were delighted with my visit. Having come unexpectedly, Karon, wearing informal Saturday clothes, disappeared for 20 minutes and when she reappeared she was in a clean skirt, blouse, shoes, in full make-up and smoking a cigarette. This obvious display of being attractive for my benefit was flattering and, though still shy, I was anxious and desirous of making a good impression on her as well. We talked for about an hour until I became disillusioned when I discovered the reason she had dressed so attractively was that she planned to go out on a date that would be there momentarily. The date came and took Karon off. I stayed on for a few minutes before saying goodbye. Lois more formally invited me to dinner for the following week.

27 - Kneeling, Dick. Back row, Karon, Lois, and Duke Conan.

UNKNOWN JOB

My job at Morgan, Mitchell and Meyers came to an end as expected and I found another job in the area that lasted three or four months.

I don't remember much about it except we were *not* doing wonderful post-and-beam work. We were doing what I call *ugly houses for speculation.* There were about 4 guys in the office and I was working on a small house in my hot little corner with yellowish light and no window. The job's middle name, as I remember it, was *utter tedium.* The job was nothing into which you could pour your heart. Most of the draftsman felt the same way.

One time, about 2:00 PM when everyone had just returned from lunch we were nodding through the rest of another boring day. The boss was out. Everyone was silent because they were too sluggish to say anything when an older, good humored draftsman on his way to the cooler passed my desk and whispered, *"Keep moving."*

STATE EXAM (2)

*A*t the invitation of Herb Kaiser I had been attending the last half of an architect's Structural Engineering course, designed solely to enable future architect's to pass the state board exam. This course was a godsend to me and I owe it all to Herb. He encouraged me to continue with the Exam and offered to study with me on all the subjects. We were to motivate each other to study. I went to his apartment frequently and several times he came to mine. We worked hard on the course because Structural Engineering was the flunkout test.

While working, I had written to Groves, Kistner Curtis, and Wright, MMM and Unknown and had gotten written signatures affirming I had exactly the required two years experience under licensed Architects required to take the full exam.

Six weeks before the exam I received a letter from the State Board saying, *due to a typographical error, I had not passed the 2-hour course in Site Planning as originally reported.* Instead, *I had not passed any of the exams!* I was ground zero! Kaput! I would have to take the entire exam over! I was extremely disappointed, but since Herb and I had been studying so hard, I decided to take the State Board Exam anyway including Site Planning. For History we made notebooks and worked with the major text for all universities, Fletcher's *History of Architecture.*

We went to USC again. This time I worked steadily through all 4 days. Day 1, Architectural History in which I had to draw the floor plans and sections of the Byzantine Church, Hagia Sophia in Istanbul from memory and was tested in Mechanical Engineering. Day 2, Structural Engineering and Office Practice. Day 3, Site Planning and Electrical Engineering. Day 4 was a full day Design Project.

I was notified two months later that I had passed, Architectural History and Structural Engineering. I was elated because I'd passed the flunkout courses and knew these two tests were the main ones to pass.

CULVER HEATON

When the *Unknown* job ended a month or so later, I heard that a Pasadena architect, Culver Heaton, needed a new man. I applied and worked for him eight months, which was long enough to make some casual friends. Heaton had an office with three draftsmen and was doing primarily churches. His work was passable. If I were to grade him in a design class, I'd give him a good *"C."* His office was near downtown Pasadena and upstairs in what had been an old house. The stairwell came up into the center of the drafting room, which was large and breezy, having windows on every wall. It felt like home.

During this period of time and having had 2 years of professional drafting, I still knew nothing about how to construct a building. In Heaton's office, it became painfully obvious that I had to find out. On Saturday I drove to one of his jobs and made sketches of typical wall framing. I sketched typical corner framing, typical bottom and top plate, an intersection of interior wall framing, simple beam connections, typical soffit framing, and other details that I put in my own reference notebook. For the first time at the age of 23 I got an inkling on how buildings were actually *built*. This made a major difference in my drawings. This was an "*Aha!*" experience. I became dimly aware of what I was drawing.

One simple anecdote: The guys and I had come back from lunch and were talking loudly about Heaton's prissy idiosyncrasies when one draftsman put his finger to his lips and shhh'd us, softly. He motioned to the other part of the room with his eyes where Heaton was sleeping beneath a drafting table. Culver had constructed a sleeping platform under one of the tables and was resting six inches off the floor with his nose six inches below the bottom of one of his tables. He had arrived during lunch and crawled into this unique resting place. We didn't know if he'd heard us but this was a fine example of one of the idiosyncrasies we were talking about.

CONAN FAMILY

My dinner went well with the Conan's and since it became evident I was a sincere fellow with a respectable job, I was well accepted. I dated Karon until we were married in June of 1953.

Duke Conan had been well publicized in newspapers and the College Annual for his football fearlessness as a first string guard playing both offense and defense for Northwestern. While being a 60-minute dynamo, he obtained a Doctorate in Jurisprudence and after graduating, passed the Illinois bar to become a lawyer. He did all this in spite of the then standing Illinois Jewish quota for lawyers. Though born as Herman D. Cohen from Jewish parents, he had no religion but was a professed atheist. As an attorney he assisted his lawyer brother for a couple of years until his brother's early death from cancer.

Devastated, he joined the Navy and saw heart-shattering action in the South Pacific. The ship's job was collecting dead and wounded bodies from the war torn islands such as Guadal Canal, Saipan and Iwo Jima. The war took something out of the man. Afterward he seemed no longer as interested in law, particularly since his brother was dead. While trying to come to a decision on his future he got what he thought was to be a temporary job as road salesman for the Baby Ruth Candy Company. He was still working with Baby Ruth when I met him in Pasadena.

Lois Conan had been a teenage girlfriend of my mother, Evelyn. I have seen old photos of them being sassy and smart in the then disgraceful *bloomers*. My mother, four years older than Lois, was still a close friend. Not only were they *Bloomer Girls,* they were also *Girls Who Wore Men's Pants.*

28 - Evelyn Costello (my mother) and Lois Johnson (Karon's mother) .

According to Mother, Lois had been in love with someone else when she was 18 years old and being crushed when the relationship fell through, married Duke on the rebound. What the real truth is, I don't know. While Duke was in the Navy, Lois became a registered nurse, apparently a good one, since it was rumored patients loved her.

With the married name of Cohen, Karon and Dick were being

annoyed and teased at school because they were thought to be Jewish. Duke, an atheist and Lois, a non-church-going Presbyterian whose maiden name was Johnson, felt the children were being prejudiced against for no reason. Lois had the families name legally changed to Conan. What her husband, Duke, had to say about this was never discussed. Lois was an extravert and given to saying anything on her mind often without any thought whatever. As a young woman she enjoyed singing, loved laughter, gaiety and parties, and basked in the glory of celebrities.

Dick Conan was a good looking, intelligent and extremely photogenic young man of 15 going to high school. In Chicago he'd played the part of Rush, a 10-year-old son on the radio program called, *Vic and Sade,* and remained in that part until it was made into a daytime television program. He also performed a supporting roll in a motion picture as a young boxing enthusiast attempting to be like his older ideal. At the age of 13 he retired from show business and returned to being a student and son. Dick had a wonderful sense of humor and he could tell a joke in a strong and confident voice. One of his specialties was one by Lenny Bruce.

A candy storeowner in a Jewish neighborhood finds an old lamp and rubs it and out comes a huge Genie that grants the shopkeeper's wish for him to watch the candy store while he does an errand. The Genie agrees and a Jewish customer enters and not having seen the Genie before, asks if he's from this neighborhood?

The Genie replies, "I'm the GENIE!"
Customer asks: "You can take care of a candy store?"
Genie angrily shouts: "I'M THE GENIE, I CAN DO ANYTHING!"
Customer: "Make me a malted."
Genie waves his arms: "YOU'RE A MALTED!"

Lenny Bruce was making a hit in stand up comedy at this time and his 33-1/3 records had just come out.

In 1952 Karon Conan was a good-looking 125 pound, five foot, three inch brunette with an acceptable figure. A bit overweight at 19-years of age, she was on an academic scholarship to Pomona College studying Theater Arts.

29 - Karon and Doug on the lawn at the Pasadena House.

She was a superlative senior in the Theater Arts department and particularly loved art. She basked in the Art History instructor's personal attention along with each of his 15 students. A long-standing and experienced soprano soloist, she volunteered to sing for the pleasure of the elderly in homes for the aged and for the ill in hospitals. She was conversant in philosophy and the literary classics and loved the ocean and water. She had an excellent swimming stroke, so much so that at Evanston High School north of Chicago, she considered trying out for the Olympics. She wore the best clothes, looked intelligent and smoked cigarettes. Though I didn't like cigarettes, nevertheless, for me at that time, it gave her a sophisticated air.

DATING KARON

*M*y dates with Karon were many and varied. On weekends, I'd drive 30 miles to Pomona College and we'd attend plays or musical concerts, or I'd go to a *Home for the Elderly* and listen to her while she sang *Sigoiner* and other German songs. She was an energetic, impressive person. Sometimes we'd go to the beach all day, ride the waves and get sunburned. One time we went to the Salton Sea and water-skied with friends who had a 40 HP outboard motor boat. We made trips to Disneyland and Knotts Berry Farm and were together so often her friends at school began thinking of us as a couple.

Karon seemed to like me and wanted to be my steady girl friend. I was flattered I had a girl friend at all. She said she'd just broken up with someone, but that I was *not* the one on the rebound. She was the first date I had that I could talk to and get to know, someone with whom I felt a kinship in art, architecture, ideas, philosophy and water sports. She wasn't just a date; she was an attractive young woman, my perfect size and possibly someone with whom I could share my life. And share it we did. We *looked* a good couple and almost *were* a good couple.

I was trying to make it as a draftsman and architect and slowly taking my exams while trying to have youthful fun by going to art shows, movies, plays, and the beach. I was comfortable with these things, but there was a residue from my past that hadn't been addressed. I was uncomfortable and jealous of her school friends. While being too young for me, they had experienced things, which I had not. She shared classes, activities, jokes and a social life that was foreign to me. I hadn't been through the kind of life she was living. My school experience was work at school and work at the job and when it came to a social life, there wasn't any.

My close friends had been the six year older, Don Patton, who had his leg blown off by a tank shell and gathered his wits for a year in Canada before returning to school. Or I had a four year older, cigarette smoking veteran, Herb Kaiser, married with child, now divorced and studying for the architect's exam, or Charlie Davis, a nine year older veteran and married person, now in North Carolina, having kids and being a new architect. Four years earlier than Karon, I had gone to college in a large University with returning veterans. In each class I was with 60 others, mostly males, taught without coddling. Illinois might have been a socializing experience for someone, but certainly not for me.

30 - Doug

31 - Karon

In contrast Pomona was a school for the rich. Classes were small and extremely co-ed. Fraternization between the sexes was intimate and rumors circulated swiftly. Who got drunk, who went to the party, who slept with who, who was disciplined, and so on. Where I'd known only a few girls at Illinois, I'd have known them all in Pomona.

As a Pomona guest, I felt the older *inexperienced* man. I felt I didn't fit in. I was the outsider. I didn't form friendships easily with those in her life. I was jealous of her and there was nothing within me that could relate to her experiences. Nevertheless, the rewards were greater than the struggle and I continued the relationship.

One evening, on returning from a beach party and with more passion than sense, we made love. Karon cried, not because of our act, but I suppose from an unexplained sense of guilt. I was confused by her reaction and was left to figure it out for myself - which I couldn't do. I finally had done what was expected and thought she should have been pleased. I thought our act was a cause for celebration but it was tinged with guilt and hiding. Even so, our relationship escalated.

MARIA

*S*imultaneously, Mary my landlady, introduced me to a beautiful young art student named Maria, who was slightly younger than Karon and gorgeous. She looked like a younger Sophia Loren. At eighteen she was more my speed. I, *socially delayed,* she *socially appropriate.* I could have grown with Maria. My horizons were widening and I caught a glimpse of a possible future life, one of comfort and sociability, a life in which I had dates with desirable females. A time when my life could have come together, with first loves, lessons to be learned, regrets, and all the adolescent information apparently so necessary to a lasting marriage. That's what I wanted, but everything for me was too soon and too early. I hadn't made my mistakes yet. I was unprepared.

In 1952 I didn't know what I wanted or where I was going, but I was unconsciously moving along in architecture, dating and having recreation, and doing the best with what I had. I always wanted to love someone and to be loved by that someone. I hadn't intended to rush myself, but remain in the learning process.

I had three or four dates with Maria and found the pressures less. Not so much drama. No feelings of inadequacy. No jealousy. I didn't have to perform. I was right the way I was. I was liked because I was *me!* Things were easy and seemed correct. I'm not saying she was *the one,* but certainly a serious maybe.

GIRL NEXT DOOR

Strangely, there was a young married woman who lived in a house behind our row apartments. She was mildly attractive and her husband was in the Armed Services. I learned this from Mary, my landlady, and from one previous conversation I had with the young lady out the back window.

From time to time I would notice her house lights on or her back door slam or the sound of her radio. But in no way did I know her nor was I remotely interested in knowing her. One evening while reading a tap on the rear window startled me. I lifted the shade, slid the window up, and looked outside to see this next-door person dressed in a kimono. She invited me over to watch TV and eat popcorn. This was very nice, but I politely refused. She looked distraught and asked if I'd like some popcorn, anyway. I said, yes, so she went back in the house and brought out a bowl of popcorn. I raised the window screen and took it in and thanked her. *I was being asked in for an evening while the married lady's husband was away in the service.* This was too much.

MOTHER

Mother decided she missed her son, that a trip to Pasadena would be fun and that she could once again see her former friend, Lois. She arrived by plane from Chicago and I put her in my fold-down bed while I stayed on the floor. We visited the Conan's.

Karon, probably suspecting I was dating, decided she was going to date, too. To explain for a moment; I was not serious about Maria, had not had serious dates with her, and thought she was too young for me anyway. It surprised me Karon was miffed. She said things were not progressing between us, that evidently I did not want to be engaged, that from her position our relationship was not on her time schedule and I was apparently not interested in commitment. This, of course, was true.

I had briefly gained my sexuality after years of repression and didn't want to let that go. Karon was an extremely unusual and interesting person. She had quite the flair for the dramatic, but in marriage one must cultivate a sense of forgiveness. I was not interested in commitment.

We argued most of the week about her decision, but seeing she was determined, I would have to make the best of it. I worried about this all night, then at 5:00 AM on Friday I awoke and told Mother I was too disturbed to sleep and was going to the Conan's to see Karon.

Mother sensed what was up and said something that stuck in my brain, *"So, this is the one?"*

I said nothing, but got dressed and left, and climbing through Karon's bedroom window, had an impassioned conversation with her for two hours. We agreed that we would be engaged, the marital date to be set at a later time.

I was desperately trying to become a man and unconsciously knew marriage would validate that manhood. Karon had all the necessary requirements necessary for a love match; unusualness, integrity; beauty, health, age, an artistic temperament, music, drama, sculpture, literature, philosophy, sports, and our mothers were friends. She had all that could be expected. On paper our relationship looked solid. If I wasn't ready, it was obvious she wasn't going to sit around and wait for me. She was going to date! I felt jealous of her dating because I had nobody I could think of to date except the virginal Maria, while she had a whole school full. If I were to become ready for a permanent commitment, then I would have to see other people, have more experiences and become more socially secure. Dating someone as good or better was not an option for me. I was new in the area, 2,000 miles from home and knew no one. Picking up girls in a bar was not my style. I had the best thing available in dating Karon and was afraid to lose it.

It entered my head that an agreement to be *engaged* did not mean that we were *married. I could always change my mind.* If the marriage were set far enough in the future, perhaps I would find the maturity to actually desire matrimony. Mother went home at the end of the week. Groucho Marx said when he was growing up; most marriages were made to satisfy repressed sexual needs than from real love. Some of this might have been true for me. I yielded to Karon's, perhaps justified, ultimatum.

32 - Karon Conan and Doug Rucker in front of the Conan's Pasadena house.

PAINTING

*A*fter our agreement to become engaged, Karon started knitting me unique and highly artistic socks of her own design in blocky shapes of blacks, reds, and whites. She'd work on them during art history class in Pomona while they showed slides or while sitting in the evening in her dorm room listening to classical music. She'd write me letters expressing her undying love, which I dutifully returned. We had dinner at her folks. I came to her plays. We went to the shows and to the beach. From her standpoint, things were getting more serious. Our sexuality continued.

Having a girlfriend interested in art, I started oil painting in between studying for my exam and dating.

Later in my life, I gave myself a theoretical question, *"Would I rather be a neurotic painter, or a well adjusted non-painter?"*

I answered, *"A well adjusted non-painter!"* The assumption of the question is that most painters are neurotic and they paint to fill a need. Many would frequently disagree, but I still think some painters require a neurosis. It can also be seen as a crutch to help the entire person function.

Shall we say that my paintings were those of a *neurotic attempting to fill a void*? I didn't know what the void was. I was just trying to fill it. When at a modern art show, I've seen paintings, which were clearly derived from the *painter's neurosis.* An artist had *painted his neurosis for me.*

At my landlady's suggestion, I decided to paint a 13-foot wide by 5-foot high mural on my apartment wall. She assumed I was an artist since I was working in architecture and thought I would produce a little cottage with smoking chimney and a little path under the trees with a daughter and her dog playfully rushing to meet Mother on the porch. You get the picture, with fluffy clouds on a darkening sky.

I bought $25.00 worth of oils and brushes and one early Saturday morning before breakfast, filled with more passion than inspiration, laid out the design in broad strokes with a piece of charcoal.

It was eventually to be a large, white, amorphous figure charging upward diagonally from lower left to upper right, stretching across the whole thirteen feet of wall. The white figure valiantly thrusting against the annihilating power of orange flames, tinged in red, the symbol of total and complete destruction. In the burned, mottled, yellow and green background, charred stick figures, their limbs awry, sailed as pathetic victims through the accursed space, while in the lower right corner an ominous and hateful looking black head stared, unflinchingly, at the viewer.

I continued through the day. While examining my emerging creation at 2:00 PM, I grabbed a peanut butter sandwich, a can of pineapple and a glass of milk and worried it down. About 5:00 PM it was evident what the painting was going to be and I broke into a nervous sweat thinking I had revealed more of my inner self than intended. A little voice whispered to me *"Perhaps the mural thing was not such a good idea after all."*

By 9:00 PM at night the deed was done. It was not meticulously detailed or well-finished but more of a passionately colored sketch. The artwork seemed an unwelcome intrusion, immensely permanent, and beautifully expressed. I hated it! It was *me!*

Reactions were indefinite. My landlady was pleasantly non-committal, shaking her head *"no"* while giving me approval. Karon's reaction was positive. Others who saw it thought it took a lot of courage to do a mural. I was admired because I was an unusual enough person to do something others feared or hadn't the ability to do - a mural on the apartment wall. It was permanent and had a spirit all it's own. It was cursed and blessed. In a small room it had a presence. Sometimes I'd awake in the middle of the night and the moon would hit it and I'd be reminded it was there and look at it and start the familiar cold sweat. I'd be reminded of my engagement predicament. The mural wouldn't come off. I wasn't going to take it off. I was going to live with it whether it was good or bad. I had expressed my neurotic fate.

STATE EXAM (3)

*A*mid rumors that the Heaton job would end, I continued studying for the State Board Exam. I had passed a good portion the last time and would try to pass the rest this time. It consisted of Mechanical Engineering, Electrical Engineering, Office Practice, Site Planning, and the 12-hour Design test. Herb and I went again to Southern California University and labored through it.

In about two months I was notified I had passed the Mechanical Engineering, Office Practice, and the 12-hour Design examination, a railroad station for a mid-western city of 300,000. What remained was Electrical Engineering and Site Design. Slow, but making progress.

DECISION

Karon and I had picked out the engagement ring. It was ready on a certain day and we were to meet at Pomona College. I was to give it to her as an expression of my choice.

On the way I found my mind wouldn't come to grips. I was anxious and pulled off the highway to a side street, made a U turn, and parked to think the whole thing over. If I were to give her the ring, it meant we were officially engaged - one step closer to marriage. The ring would be a symbol that I was on track, that we were on track, that we had not changed our minds but more sure of our decision than ever. But was I?

Time was fleeting. I had said I would pick her up at eight o'clock and the longer I sat to make up my mind, the later I would be. If I were late, I'd have to explain. If I were not to go at all, her disappointment would be severe and an indication of my doubt about the whole marriage idea. She would leave forever. I was in an agony of indecision. My actions said yes, but inside I did not want to solidify my relationship. I was not mature! I wanted things to go on and on until I became mature, whenever that might be. Was this right or fair to her? Certainly I couldn't be so much of a cad as to back out now? Could I? Such was my turmoil and indecision.

I decided to leave it to fate. Leave it to the great unknown. I wouldn't decide. Something else would decide for me. I'd approach the intersection and see whether I turned *right to the engagement or left to end it forever.* I knew the underlying ultimatum. I would drive toward the intersection and observe which way the organism turned.

I turned right - toward engagement.

Karon was happy with the ring. Now she could show it to her school friends and they would envy her. We decided our marriage would be on June twenty-first, 1953, the longest day of the year. We would get married on the date of the summer solstice.

CAR

Sometime after the Heaton job, when I probably had the money, I bought a car. More correctly, Karon and I bought a car. Karon had a former roommate, rose-queen-pretty, who had married a tall, slim, handsome, used car salesman with a slick, black pompadour. They invited us over for dinner, but before we ate we had to see what was in his garage. Lighted with thirty or forty strategically placed bare bulbs in the open garage ceiling, was a glistening black, 2-door Ford convertible with red leather seats and the top down. She was sleek and black and shone like a polished apple. One look and Karon was drooling with anticipation. The interior was spotless. Not a detail out of place. The black Ford Convertible was immaculate.

Of course the amount of the sale came out, but he said, to his friends he might be able to reduce it somewhat. Of course we were his friends. When we heard the discounted price, $900.00, our hearts leaped. Now I had to look at the deal more seriously. I walked around it. Kicked the tires. Saw my face in the hood. Sat in the red leather seats and wiggled the steering wheel. Tried the clutch and brake. Tried to find a spec on the carpet. Nope! It looked OK to me. *"Can I look under the hood?" This was a brilliant thought!*

"Sure, no problem." He opened the hood.

33 - Doug and Karon and the Ford Convertible, Black Beauty.

The space under the hood was jammed with engine, water cooler, hoses, wires, spark plugs, battery, cylinders, valves, knobs, gauges and so on, to the hilt. But it was dirty and black. He hadn't steam cleaned the engine. That prompted me to ask, *"How many miles on this sucker?"*

"Eighty one thousand, Pal, but you can see the exterior of the car has had beautiful care." He gently closed the hood and continued, *"You can always change the engine and mechanical parts, but you can never replace a good body."*

The mileage appalled me but in looking at the outside body and upholstery I had to agree the car had been beautifully cared for. Karon was excited about buying it from her girlfriend's husband and it gleefully occurred to her she could use my '41 Plymouth for her car.

I gave him a couple of hundred dollars down as an initial payment and Karon driving the Plymouth, drove off in the *"Black Beauty."*

ZOOK

Christmas, my 24th birthday and the end of a very busy 1952 closed to a month's more work with Culver Heaton and job looking. I found one with a somewhat special architect named Harold Zook. He was doing acceptable work in the Pasadena area and I was proud to be associated with him even though I practically never saw him. I was put to work on a mundane little house, far less than what I would have expected from a coming architect like Zook.

During this time I had developed five large, ugly warts on my hands. One on my ring finger and two on my palm in a row, one on the left hand forefinger and one at the base of my right thumb. Impulsively, I decided to have them taken off and dropped in to a doctor's office at lunch time, showed the secretary my problem, and within the hour I was under a local anesthetic and watching the doctor burn them off with an electrical blow-torch. The smell was sickening as he made deep little circular cuts around each wart. I paid the man and within 45-minutes, hands wrapped in bandages, I was dismissed into the too sunny street.

For a week or so I tried working with heavily bandaged hands. From Zook's standpoint, he must have wondered how it was possible for me to draft at all. The job folded after about 6 weeks when I'd completed about half the working drawings. Whether I was let go because the client quit, or because I hadn't had sufficient experience, or was without full use of my hands, I'll never know.

LITTLE FOXES

At Pomona College, Karon was cast to play the part of Birdie in the Tennessee Williams play, *The Little Foxes*. I frequently attended rehearsals and was polite and aloof with her friends at the cafe. I participated in the experience of being a part of the couple we were. Karon was outstanding in her portrayal and was highly complimented by her director. She received excellent reviews in the Pomona newspapers. I was disturbed that it was necessary she play the part of an old lady under the influence of liquor. Of course on stage she drank lukewarm tea but my prudery followeth me. A number of her college friends were in the play and David Rhiel became a lasting one after our marriage.

CAR STOLEN

One evening Karon and I went to a late movie in an unfamiliar area near Covina. We parked the Ford convertible in the large adjacent lot and enjoyed the performance. When we returned to the parking lot we noticed most of the movie-goers had taken their cars home and ours should have been easily in view. We checked the broad expanse and our car was gone. We called the police who arrived shortly and took us to the station where they collected our address, phone number, license plate number, make and color of car, and other necessary information they'd need to recognize the car if it turned up. The police took us home and we used the Plymouth. Two weeks later the police called and reported the car had shown up in an orange grove, stripped of radio, tires, and engine parts. We had it towed to the shop and with our insurance, $200.00 bucks, and about two months of lost time, were able to have it restored.

NISHIMOTO

After Zook, I was again on the loose. I put flesh-colored Band-Aids on my hands and turned up another job in Pasadena at the firm of Taylor and Nishimoto. I worked there only a month and found Kenneth Nishimoto to be a wonderful American architect of Japanese descent. He was the firm's designer and had been a graduate of the University of Southern California. I think I did well in his office, but again within a month, they ran out of work, or so they said, and I was out looking again.

34 - Ken Nishimoto at home in his traditional kimona. (1973)

It was now so close to our wedding date that I decided not to look for a job, but to concentrate on studying for what I hoped would be my final architectural exam and get ready for the wedding. The Site Design segment was to be given on the exact date as our wedding, the 21rst of June, The Electrical Engineering, Monday.

During non-working hours, Karon and I found a basement

apartment under a garage overlooking a shallow barranca. It was at the top of Raymond Street in Altadena, about two blocks from the mountains, and available for occupancy immediately after the marriage

MARRIAGE

MARRIAGE - STATE EXAM (4)

Karon and Lois decided we should be married in the *Chapel of Roses* in Altadena. A close friend of Karon's named David Dyer was to sing for us. Brother Dave was to be my best man and Dick Conan, Karon's younger brother, also stood up for me. Herb Kaiser was to be my one and only friend and local guest. Mother and Dad drove in from Chicago The remainder of guests were friends and relatives of Karon and the Conan's.

On the day before the wedding, Herb gave me a big, fat, pill and said, *"Take it with a glass of water on the morning of the exam and marriage."*

I said, *"What is it?"*

He said, *"Don't worry about it, it will calm your nerves."*

I took the pill on Saturday morning, made my way to USC, took the Site Planning Exam and was back by 1:00 PM. I got into my tux and helped brother Dave, Dad and future brother-in-law, Dick, get dressed. They seemed more nervous than I. Karon had chosen an attractive, contemporary looking, ankle length, bridal dress, and cautioned me I wasn't to see her in it before the wedding.

Ina Nuell was Karon's bridesmaid and the other in her party was the former Barbara Crawford, a roommate of Karon's and wife of James Brown who had sold us the Ford convertible. I thought Karon, Ina, and Barbara stunningly beautiful in their wedding attire.

35 - Duke, Lois, and Dick Conan

36 - Dad, Mother, Doug, Karon and Dave.

37 - Karon, Barbara Brown and Ina Nuell.

Mother looked beautiful too and complimented me on how well I was doing. She didn't know about the nerve pill and said I seemed especially calm for the wedding. I agreed.

The elderly Doctor Benjamin Scott marrying us was one of Karon's friends and a retired pastor from Pomona College. Light haired and balding, with an easy smile, he was charming and we took his words seriously to heart. We were married in front of about 50 people.

The wedding celebration must have taken place at the church recreation room. I remember trading cake slices with Karon. In the pictures Mother kept in her scrapbook, I see we were a young and beautiful couple and appeared to all and especially to us, full of hope and promise. We thought we would have a joyous future because of our mutuality of interests and to a large degree we did. When we married we believed we would grow together and our marriage would be a happy one.

38 - Doug and Karon cutting wedding cake.

One happening, which was to haunt me for the remainder of our married lives, because Karon brought it up so repeatedly when we disagreed, was this:

People at the wedding had been assembling just outside the church doors to throw rice at the departing married couple. My mother, Evelyn, and dad, Phil, decided they had to leave at the exact time as the rice throwing ceremony. I don't know why. Couldn't they have thrown rice at us, too? Perhaps they were trying to catch a plane, or train, or check out of their hotel, or I can't imagine. Once they were gone, I would have no time to thank them for coming from Illinois and bringing presents and telling them how much I appreciated their being my parents. I would not have the proper time to say good-bye. Bad timing seemed to be one of Mother's life long habits. They would be leaving for Chicago. I hadn't seen them for a year and wouldn't see them for several more years. I wanted to say good-bye. I was sorry they had to leave right then, but *I didn't control the timing.*

I ran out across the grass in my tuxedo to the curb to show my appreciation and try to salvage a proper good-bye. Our friends at the church were assembled, their hands and pockets filled with rice. My bride, dressed like Cinderella at the Ball, was aching to have rice thrown at her while running to the car with her new husband. The time was ripe! The dramatic moment was there!

I ran back to the church as soon as I gave Mother a peck on the cheek, shook Dad's hand, and thanked them for their presents and for coming so far to the wedding. This took 5 minutes.

But 5 minutes can seem a lifetime, particularly if you are the bride and your friends are waiting impatiently to throw rice. I ran back, grabbed Karon's elbow, and we both ran toward the waiting car, her friends throwing rice. We got in the car and drove off five minutes later than the prescribed time.

In later years I discovered this event was permanently engraved in Karon's memory along with two or three other incidents and was used as a reminder over and over again, ad nauseam, as evidence of a major vacancy in my brain. Perhaps it was, or perhaps not.

Repetitive questions:
Why did my parents have to leave right then?
Why did I have to say good-bye, just then?
Was this a conspiracy to prevent the newly married
Son from the rice throwing experience?
Was this a direct attack on the new bride?
Didn't I know how embarrassing it was for the new
husband to be five minutes late for the rice throwing?

Repetitive answers:
I don't know!
They'd miss their bus?
Because I hadn't seen them for years and wouldn't see
them for years and they were my PARENTS!
I don't think so.
Don't be ridiculous.
It must have been embarrassing. I'm sorry. Please
forgive me. What can I do now to help? Can I

apologize to your friends?
Want to go to dinner?
Sign a paper saying it's all my fault?

I hate to belabor what went wrong at my wedding. Other than my being late for the rice throwing, everything else went superbly. I must also explain that I regret taking Herb's nerve pill. It prevented me from having a clear mind and body for my first, and hopefully my only, experience of marriage.

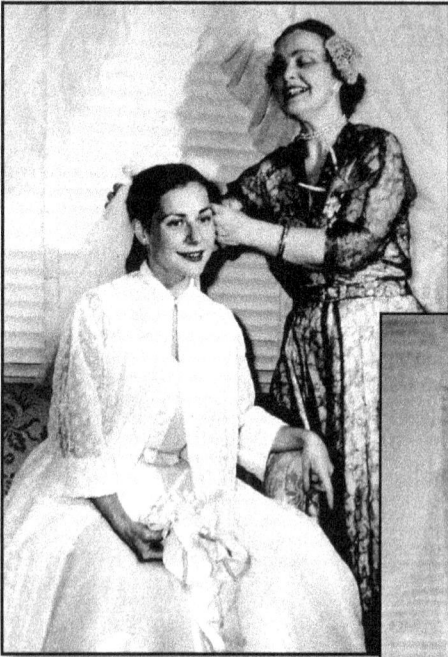

39 - Karon and Lois

40 - Karon

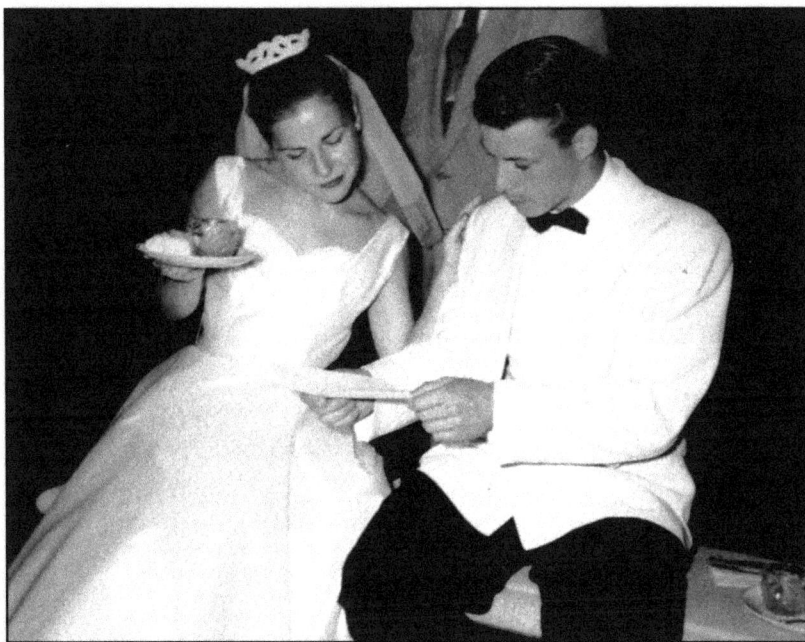

41 - Karon and Doug

42 - Karon

APARTMENT

*M*y mother's scrapbook reminds me that we went for 4 days to Lake Arrowhead. We stayed in one of the separate little cabins in the woods near the lake and probably went for a boat ride and walked the dappling trails and visited the Arrowhead grocery store. As I remember, it was pleasant and good to have a break before life's onslaught.

We returned into the driveway at 3113 Raymond Street, Altadena and past a large middle class house on the property into a motor court serving a three-car garage, separate from the house. Our basement apartment was built under a garage on a slope facing a narrow wash. We approached by walking down concrete stairs separating us from the weedy incline and the garage wall.

Once in the apartment the three large picture windows opened to a shaded view of a barranca, with tall, green weeds and little willow trees that descended from the San Gabriel Mountains. The apartment's one room was about 20-feet deep and 30-feet wide with wardrobe, bath, and galley kitchen at one end. At the other end I elected to put my drafting table with 4-feet behind for my stool and passage space. We positioned our queen-sized mattress on the floor in one corner, partially obscured by my drafting board, which became our bedroom. A cheap furnished table with wooden Salvation Army chairs next to the windows provided a place to eat. We constructed bookshelves from pine boards and concrete blocks. A couple of bean bag chairs and an orange canvas Hardoy chair kept us off the floor.

We stayed here for a year and, though we were comfortable in our basement apartment, did little if no entertaining for a number of reasons. *(1) Job, (2) Neurosis, (3) The Gondoliers.*

JOB

I located a job in a 3-man office in Glendale with an architect named Ray Jones who had just been commissioned to do the Los Angeles City, Kenter Avenue High School in Brentwood, California. It was L. A. City's 1953 policy not to have individual architect's do school buildings from scratch, but to have them adapt to the cities standard plans. L. A. City had stock plans for the Cafeteria, Administration, Auditorium, Gymnasium, Library, Classrooms, ¼-mile Track and Football Field, Practice Fields and Baseball Diamonds, Swimming Pool, if any, etc. It was the selected architects job to take all these components, assemble them, complete with parking requirements, into a well-organized Site Design and produce the working drawings in a finished, cohesive package for cost estimates and construction. Ray Jones had completed a competent Site Plan and now it was his job to produce working drawings.

Since most of the work was copying and tracing, it was appropriate that a person who could legibly copy and trace was what was most needed. Ray would then only have to worry about the connections one building to another, which were the connective links, different in each new Los Angeles school. When Ray was out of the office, his chief draftsman was next in charge. We were his right-hand men. Or better, my friend was his right hand man and I was his left hand assistant.

I worked compatibly without special incident until it was completed about a year later when I left to take a job with Hap Gilman in Brentwood Village.

NEUROSIS

The job didn't bother me. What bothered me was a neurosis I developed, or at least noticed, since the first day of our marriage. I took this terrible thing to the office every day and though I confided in nobody, it was part and parcel of my every waking and working moment.

I was obsessed about Karon's smoking. I couldn't stand it! I suspected she was not being honest with me about whether she was a virgin before we met. I had a thing about that. I didn't know it at the time, but it was because I lacked security as a man, which stemmed from my former sexual innocence and social ineptitude. When I asked her she had answered she was a virgin. My mother and father had been virgins when they married. I thought my life was supposed to follow my parent's rules. I was overly concerned. One day I found a picture of her old boy friend in her wallet. This provoked an argument about what I was doing rummaging through her personal affects. I thought since I'd been going with her a year and a half and had now gained her hand in marriage, carrying a picture of her old boy friend in her wallet was a thing of the past. I descended into a fit of inadequacy and jealousy about her former life.

I begged her to quit smoking. She said she would try, but I was hypersensitive to the aroma of cigarette smoke and could always detect it, usually in the bathroom. Though I hoped in vain, I could no longer believe she was trying sufficiently to stop.

I read all there was to read about the health hazards and recited stories of my uncle's deaths from smoking and emphysema, my aunt and uncle's death from tuberculosis exacerbated by smoking, about the doctor's newest warning against smoking and it's involvement with the circulatory system and it's addictive qualities. I begged her to go to a psychologist, hoping he would dissuade her, but she refused to go. Finally, after a particularly bitter argument, she said, since I was so obsessed, why didn't *I* go to the therapist?

I slept on this and thought about it hard. My obsession with Karon and smoking wouldn't leave me alone for five minutes running. My mind kept popping back to Karon smoking. I couldn't stand it! I had no peace with either the smoking or the lying about former affairs. I decided I'd be strong and take her advice. I'd get a psychologist for myself. After all, it was not *her* problem. It was *my* problem. I'd go!

PSYCHOLOGIST

I found him in Pasadena, a man of about 40 who would take my case. I went to him weekly for about 9-months. In the beginning I had to recap my life, tell him about my parents and brother and relatives, about my sports activity and my shyness and lack of opportunity and fear of becoming social. I told him of my feelings of inadequacy in boy-girl situations and how I abruptly came to marriage. We talked about cigarettes and how they were so bad, and that my new wife, Karon, was doing something to harm herself. I told him it was hard to watch someone injure herself. I sensed his agreement, though he never committed himself about the subject of smoking.

One time during session he got out a cigarette and smoked it while we were talking and afterward asked if it bothered me while he smoked. He asked if I was bothered if *anybody else* smoked. I wasn't. We deduced my obsession was related only to the person I'd married and to the personal problems the state of marriage provoked. I resolved to look at that situation more closely.

I learned the cigarette could be seen as a phallic symbol and that when she put it in her mouth it would suggest her sophistication and experience with other men. This, in light of my sophisticated *inexperience* with other women, told me there was nothing I could do about her having had an outside affair or two before she knew me. I learned I had married her to *avoid* shyness with other women. Unconsciously I had thought having a reasonable and comfortable relationship with girls led to promiscuity. I had too much dignity and forthrightness, I thought, to be promiscuous; therefore, being married and having a permanent sensual outlet would keep me from being promiscuous. Her smoking expressed what I took to be her comfort with males, therefore her comfort with promiscuity and my discomfort with females and discomfort with her promiscuity; her sophistication, my naiveté; her adequacy, my inadequacy. It was difficult to admit, but I was jealous of her former libidinous life and relationships with former men.

Within a few months Karon, having done the best she knew to avoid this touchy subject, gave in and told me she'd had a longer affair with the person with whom she was in love and with whom she'd expected marriage. Hurt and disillusioned after their break-up, she'd had relations with others a few times. My suspicions were correct. In my prudish and neurotic way I found out I had indeed married what I thought was a promiscuous woman. What was my neurosis going to do with that?

I'd gone to the psychologist and learned, yes, I was naive, and yes, she was sophisticated, and yes, I was trapped in a situation unlikely to change without divorce, and yes, my mate was interesting, attractive and unusual, and yes, so was I, and yes we did have many good things in our relationship. But what was I going to do?

This sounds weird but I decided to take up smoking myself. My reasoning? *Everyone sophisticated smoked, therefore smoking made one sophisticated.* If I smoked, I would no longer be conscious of her smoking and I would no longer be conscious of the foul smell and couldn't blame her because I didn't smell so good myself. The perfect solution! *"If you can't lick 'em, join 'em."*

It was idiot thinking, but at that time I was an idiot! I would stay in the marriage and try to salvage the good parts and overcome the obsession against what Karon and others trivialized as *only a bad habit.* Hopefully, this would be a start in losing my sense of inadequacy. The Gondoliers also helped me along with this.

THE GONDOLIER'S

Karon announced she was going to try out for the musical production of Gilbert and Sullivan's, *The Gondoliers,* to be performed at the Pasadena Playhouse in six weeks. She invited me to try out too with encouragement like, *"You'll get in. Musicals are always short of men."*

Visualizing myself alone in our dim little basement apartment with nothing to do while Karon was out three or four nights a week rehearsing and for 4 performances a week for a full month at the Playhouse was unpleasant. Considering my jealousy for irreversible deeds that I'd, perhaps, wrongly accused her, and worrying she might meet some attractive fellow during her extended theatrical work, thereby heightening my already active jealousy, I decided it was in my best interests to try out too. At least I could keep my eyes on things.

We tried out and I got in. Yes, the company needed all the men they could get. About 30 men and women rehearsed in a large room in downtown Pasadena. Principal parts were chosen quickly and the chorus rehearsed separately from the principals. We had an outstanding piano player who'd run off the selections with enthusiasm and good humor. She played with ease and loudness, if not grace, as our director took us through all the songs.

At times we'd have to practice diction. How does a stage performer say P? The class would all pronounce our P's. Then L's, and M's, and G's, and if we were to sing a word like, *great,* we'd have to roll the R's, G-*R-R-R-R-R*-EAT!

43 - The Gondolier's program advertisement.

The songs were funny and a joy to sing. They were complicated enough to be interesting, but not too complicated to learn. When away from the rehearsals, we'd talk in an English accent and pronounce our P's and roll our R's and sing our chorus parts. Eventually we learned the principal's parts as well and would sing those, too, sometimes as a duet in the car or shower.

The Duke of Plaza Toro *(Portion of a solo.)*

In enterprise of a martial kind,
If there was any fighting,
He led his regiment from behind,
He found it less exciting.
But when away his regiment ran,
His place was in the fore -o!
That celebrated, cultivated,
Underrated nobleman,
The Duke of Plaza Toro!

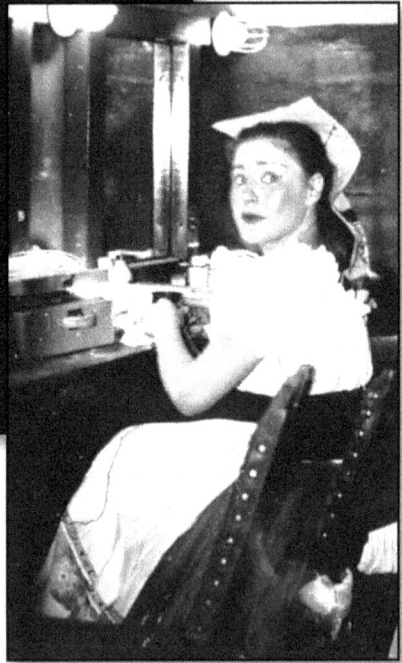

44 & 45 - Doug and Karon made up and ready for a performance.

We sang, *There Was a Time, I Stole the Prince, When a Merry Maiden Marries, Oh, My Darling, Oh, My Pet, Rising Early in the Morning, Take a Pair of Sparkling Eyes, There Lived a King, I am a Courtier, Grave and Serious,* and other songs, just for the fun of it.

Yes, I was handling it all right with my architectural job at Ray Jones, but stage experience in *The Gondoliers* was also happening.

As time progressed we became friendly with others in the cast. In fact the cast became like a family. We cared for one another. There was teamwork and spirit and everyone enjoyed themselves. When rehearsal was over, many of us would go to our special all night cafe for coffee, laughter and discussion.

In about 6-weeks the director and cast had put the musical play all together. Full costumes were made, tights, 17th century coats, wigs, vests, ruffles, shoes, hats, and so on. A full stage set had been constructed including a boat that moved forward, backward and rocked and seemed to float on stage. We learned about applying make-up, powder, rouge, lipstick, eyeliner, and to comb our hair in an odd, 17th century, way. Without my wig, I parted mine down the middle and flatly forward to each side. The dress rehearsal on the main stage was appalling on the night before the opening but we resolved to make it come together next time. *"Oh my God! Tomorrow night!"*

Karon and I were in the chorus and were understudies for other principals. On opening night, which I see by the program in my deceased mother's scrapbook, was January 7, 1954. I can remember standing in the front row, stage left, with members to the side and behind me all in make-up and costume. The orchestra was tuning up while a noisy full house was on the other side of the curtain. It was an event at the *Pasadena Playhouse!*

The audience noise receded as the musical director entered the stage, and then became deathly quiet until the full orchestra, perhaps 20 musicians, played the first measures of *The Gondolier's Overture.* Soon the curtain would open and once our first chorus song, *Roses White and Roses Red,* was started we were lock-stepped onto a systematic track, note by note, measure by measure, singing, acting, dancing, until that multitude of beats, measures and bars methodically reached it's end.

Each performance was filled with gaiety, bright lights, colorful costumes, riotously loud music, funny and sad songs, entrances and exits, dancing and overall laughter and light-heartedness.

On the Saturday Matinees, when I had to sing the solo opening lines of the show, my knees were wobbling. The curtain opened and in a voice trembling with fear, I sang the tenor lines, *"Good Morrow, pretty maids, for whom prepare, ye? The Royal Gon-do-liers, extra—o-or--di--nary?"*

46 - Karon and Doug before the Gondolier's performance.

I remember the orchestra racing to stay with my too fast singing of this one short line. I never got it right. I was always too fast and instantly developed an appreciation for one of the difficulties of regular soloists; timing.

47 - Karon and Doug before the performance.

When the performances were over, the cast would retire to the Green Room and the principals would gracefully accept compliments. After that, still in the excited state or being *psyched up*, we'd go to our favorite cafe, for post mortems, laughter, jokes, smoking, and conversation.

HOW I FELT

*H*ow did I feel in the front row, left, on stage? Doug Rucker, famous as a workaholic in college to such and extent that he couldn't find time to make a date. School jock so shy in class he had to sit in the back of the room for fear of being called upon. A shy one who frequently *"tied-*

up" in class. One who was completely ignorant of ballroom dancing and who, at twenty-five, was finally able to kiss one girl without feeling a perfect ass. How did a person with a life-long aversion to the limelight feel about dressing himself in a frilly costume, putting on a white wig, face powder, eyeliner and lipstick? One who got on a bright stage danced and sang in front of an audience before a brilliant set, accompanied by the full Pasadena Civic Orchestra? Why would I do that? What would the guys on the team think? Was this all right? Was this what I was meant to do? Was this fun?

I'd say yes for the following reasons:

One: Karon forced me to open up by giving me a broadening experience, which were within my capabilities.

Two: My parents met during a stage performance and I'd seen pictures of them in makeup under lights, singing, dancing and making jokes. To them, this was all right.

Three: Dad played and sang over two hundred songs to us and I knew about a hundred myself. In the TKE kitchen I used to sing harmony to *Wait Til the Sun Shines, Nelly, Oh Tell Me Why? Goodbye My Coney-Island Baby*, and other barber shop quartet numbers. Brother Dave was studying music. Music and singing was within my sphere.

Four: Mother was a dancer and had been a teacher and leader of a dance group for a short time on stage. Dad was a fine ballroom dancer who was frequently compared to Fred Astaire. My own athletic abilities provided me with the necessary coordination to be a dancer. Dancing, too, came easily to me.

These latent qualities would never have been brought forth if Karon had not taken a firm stand. She forced me to make my decision. I joined the Gondolier's and was able to experience myself in a new and unusual way.

We did 16 performances, Thursday night, Friday night, Saturday matinee and Saturday night to full houses. I had a good time singing and dancing. It was nothing I'd ever expected to see myself doing. Football player, architecture student, swimmer from Illinois, now with make-up and costumes singing funny songs under lights on stage in front of everybody. I was too inhibited for this but I did it and though at times it took courage, I enjoyed myself.

STATE EXAM (5)

Somewhere during the time that I was battling my neurosis and being in the Gondoliers, I took my final State Board Exam to become a licensed California Architect. I had been notified that I had passed the Electrical portion of my examination, but not Site Planning. Herb Kaiser had already received his license, so I went alone to S. C. to take my remaining 4-hour Site Planning test.

I sat at the familiar table with about 30 others and the instructor handed out programs which were to remain face down on our drawing tables until the stroke of 9:00 AM. At that time we'd flop them over, study them, and begin work.

Our project: *A Tuberculosis Sanitarium, including, Administration Building, Convalescent Rooms, Cafeteria, Hospital, Receiving Area, Parking for both staff and guests, and Burning Area for waste products and soiled hospital goods, all to be set close to town in a rural area at a freeway-highway intersection. They gave us a prevailing wind direction, and points of the compass.*

There wasn't a sound in the S.C. drafting room, except the clicking of triangles against the T squares, erasures, the sound of sharpening pencils, a muffled curse now and then, and the atmosphere of urgency to accomplish a monumental task in so short a time.

Four hours later we were told to put down our pencils and turn in our work. I was exhausted as I'm sure others were, too. There was little discussion, afterward. Everyone seemed strangers. It was the general feeling that those who had put the convalescent rooms down-wind from the burning area, failed the test. Thank God, I put mine upwind.

A couple of months later, some time in early 1954, I was notified that I had passed the Site Planning exam. It was ironic that on my initial test, I was erroneously notified that I had passed Site Planning and now, five tries later; Site Planning was my final test. Such is life. What remained was the State Board's Oral Examination. I would have to bring written approvals, examples of my recent work, and meet four State Board Architects on the staff to answer critical questions about architecture.

WRITTEN APPROVAL REQUIRED

As a requirement for licensing in the State of California, the Board required confidential letters from two licensed architects and one adult person who knew the applicant well and could attest to his character and ability to fulfill his duties in an intelligent, legal and straight forward manner.

I asked architect Ray Jones to give me a letter and he sent one immediately with a copy to me. I thought it a good recommendation. Duke Conan, my new father-in-law, at my request, sent in a letter with a copy to me describing his son-in-law in glowing terms. What else could he do? I was newly married to his daughter. His letter made me ecstatic. My third choice was architect, Kenneth M. Nishimoto. Even though I'd worked under him a year ago and only for month, I couldn't think of another architect boss in my profession who had been as real and as encouraging to me as a young, would-be architect. I sensed Ken as a fine human being. In contrast, I felt treated as a commodity at the firms of Kistner, Curtis and Wright, Harold Zook and Culver Heaton. Their concern was what I could do for them and nothing more. When and what I did seemed the total of their concern. E.G. Groves was out of the question since I had left him and he was located out of State. That left my fate in Ken's hands.

I was unfamiliar with Ken's background at the time but later I learned he was born in Japan and married to a delightful person named Kay and had a young, adorable daughter named Diane. He'd just finished building a fine contemporary home for his family in Pasadena, was a dedicated member of the American Institute of Architects, and had just begun leading the annual three week A.I.A. sponsored Architect's Tour to Japan. As a choice for a letter writer, it was fatefully one of my best. Later Ken, Kay, and Diane became personal friends of ours and though I only spent one month under his supervision I have counted him all my life as my mentor.

Ken helped me form a philosophy of architecture. A graduate of USC, he loved all forms of contemporary work, particularly that of Frank Lloyd Wright, Oscar Niemeyer and Gordon Drake. He thought, as I did, that Drake was the architect he thought most exemplified his own architectural philosophy. Gordon Drake, after doing architectural work in the C-B's and Japan, came to California where he developed *a style of architecture completely compatible with its climate and life-style. A post-and-beam style where the structure of the perfectly designed indoor-outdoor plan is also the principle substance that makes it beautiful.* It was in a, *"what you see is what you get,"* style with nothing added purely for decoration or to *"fix"* something already wrong. Ken taught me the words *proportion* and *scale.* I have always hoped that I had *scale* and *proportion* in my work.

Ken wrote a letter of recommendation for me to the State Board of Architectural Examiners. I never knew what he said, but I did get my license and so it mustn't have been too bad. He didn't send me a copy of the letter and I didn't ask him for one. I did notice, however, that after I received my license, he called me often to make sure I was doing well. Perhaps he wanted to make sure his positive statements about me were justified. At that time we knew very little about each other. I have always valued that he was able to read my character as positive and that, hopefully, I proved him right.

48 - Kay and Ken Nishimoto. (1973)

ORAL EXAM AND LICENSE

In April of 1954, about two months after I had passed the written portion of my State Board Exam and had turned in my written approvals, I was still working for Ray Jones. His right hand man and I were moving right along on the Kenter Avenue School with a minimum of problems. I remember little about my work there except the completion of numerous sheets of standard drawings made under the heavy duress of my personal neurosis.

Ray Jones was a respected architect in Glendale. He was 55-years old, slim, about 5-feet-10-inches tall, with balding hair, the sides and rear of which were combed straight down. When Ray worked over his board he'd raise his head to see through the bottom half of his bifocals and snuffle now and then with chronic postnasal drip. He was a quiet man and drove an old car because, as he told us, *his clients by contrast would appear richer and more worthy and he would appear a clearer servant of the rich.* A curious philosophy!

While we were doing Kenter Avenue School, Ray would work on small additions in Glendale. He had an apologetic grin and seemed pleased to see those that called on him and would gently smile, getting up from his stool offering his hand. I liked old Ray, though I never knew much about him, nor he of me.

Then came the day of the Orals. I asked Ray if I could take some prints of the School with me. He agreed, so I showed up with my current work, having studied the answers to general questions I thought might be asked.

My appointment time was for exactly 10:30 A.M. Others were in the waiting room, too, but shortly thereafter I was ushered into an enclosed room in the center of which was a dark mahogany table with four middle aged architects sitting relaxed around. Some wore suits and ties and others were in coats and open collared shirts. A chair in the center of the table was conspicuously vacant. I assumed it for me and put my fat roll of Kenter School drawings on the table and sat down.

I was dressed casually and had the look of a childish, well conditioned, bright young man. I was 26. I must have looked much too young to be qualified as an architect. Few, if any, in California, had been licensed at the age of 26. The architects must have been appalled at what had just come through the door. I was a definite indication that Architecture in California was slipping away.

Nevertheless, they were polite and treated me with respect. I showed them my current work, which they admired and asked me questions about school contracts. I was in the examination office for about 20 minutes and felt, with minor exceptions; I had answered most questions correctly. Then I was politely dismissed and told I would be notified later about passage or failure. It was common knowledge no one actually failed his or her Orals. You might be required to write a research paper but the rumor was if you passed the written, you'd get your license.

In about two weeks I received a notice that I would not only have to write one research paper, but two. I think one of the questions I had to answer was, *How does an Architect close out a School Contract.* The other, I forget.

I completed my research in about a month and mailed it in. Within two months I received my California License, dated, July 21, 1954. My number was C-1721 and I was now an authentic California Architect. No one could take it away from me. So much for my general rule – *continue with the next step.*

RECAP

*E*isenhower is President and Nixon is Vice President. The U. S. Senate for abuse of certain Senators and celebrities using sensational tactics and insupportable evidence censures Senator Joseph McCarthy. Popularity of TV causes radio to adopt a musical format. William Golding publishes *Lord of the Flies.* Joseph Salk develops a vaccine for polio. *American Cancer Society reports higher death rates among cigarette smokers, while Tobacco Industry cites 36 specialists who deny that lung cancer is caused by cigarette smoking.* Supreme Court rules that segregation violates the 14th amendment and blacks are now admitted to *all* public schools. Roger Bannister is the first to run the mile under 4 minutes. *(3.59.4 seconds)* and Elia Kazan directs the motion picture, *On The Waterfront,* starring Marlon Brando and Eve Marie Saint.

What was I doing? During the past two years I worked at a number of jobs in Pasadena, met the Conan family, dated Karon, made an emotionally charged mural, continued taking the State Board, bought a new car, got married, went into a neurotic fit, took up smoking, did a chorus part in _The Gondolier's_, worked for Ray Jones which gave me a total architectural experience of 4-years, and finally got my architect's license. My little notebook of architectural details was now pretty thick and I knew infinitely more than I did at Kistner, Curtis and Wright.

About September the Jones job was coming to a halt. Ray had an architect friend named, Art, working in Brentwood Village who knew another architect named Hap Gilman who was looking for a draftsman. I called Hap, went to Brentwood and applied for the job. Since I'd been recommended by Art, a friend of Hap's who apparently knew of my work through his friendship with Ray, I got the job.

I had been living with my neurosis for over a year. I was smoking, trying to deal with my issues, trying to see myself through a rough spot. I had to come to terms with not being perfect. The psychologist, seeing I had stabilized to some degree and was at least functioning, dismissed me. My philosophy was, _I was dropping the subject!_

Because of my therapy and _dropping the subject,_ Karon and I were getting along better. With the Brentwood job we'd have to move closer to work but this was a happy thought. We took Black Beauty, our Ford convertible, and wandered through the streets of Santa Monica. We toured Santa Monica Canyon and the full length of Amalfi Drive, checked out Pacific Palisades and inquired of rent prices on San Vicente Boulevard. Both Karon and I were _water babies_ so we loved the idea of being near the ocean and decided to rent a lower apartment in Santa Monica near 4th Street on San Vicente.

The one bedroom apartment was a two story, green and white with 20 units in a U-shape on the west side of San Vicente, south of 7th Street. It had a standard kitchen and bath with windows facing the front courtyard and rear walkway. The manager lived upstairs and across the courtyard and seemed a reasonable person. We felt lucky. The rent was an affordable $80.00 per month.

TO CHICAGO AND INDIANA

Before starting my new job, Karon and I decided to take a two-week vacation to Chicago and Fish Lake. I wanted to introduce Karon to my relatives and visit my parents who had moved from the Kedzie Avenue basement to the rented Le Claire Avenue house. We drove to Indiana to see Bud, Soph, Mom, Aunt Marge, and sleep in the fish lake cottage once more. We had fun, and then drove back to the new San Vicente apartment and new adventures.

49 - Karon and Doug in front of their Santa Monica Apartment.

50 - Doug with Aunt Marge and Karon.

51 - Karon, Sophy, Mom, Bud and Doug.

BRENTWOOD

HAP GILMAN

I showed up bright and early one Monday morning at Hap's office. It was a charming, partially sunken one-story railroad tie building off Barrington Avenue a block east of Sunset and on the edge of a commercial center called Brentwood Village. A client would enter from the sunnier commercial district through a gate-sized opening in the railroad ties and find himself in a trellis-covered courtyard from which hung a powerful vine, a Copa de Ora that cast rich, dark shadows over a blue concrete floor that continued inside the office through a heavy plank door with burl handle to a hallway displaying architectural photos. Between the photos were doors leading to a powder room and Hap's small, somewhat messy office. In the office was a worn, walnut desk under north-facing windows and three well-used leather chairs for him and two clients. The office had the look of *studied carelessness,* perhaps more careless than studied, and made no concessions to his wealthy clients, though some lived close by in the affluent areas of Rustic Canyon and Brentwood.

Beyond Hap's office was the main drafting room lit by high windows on the north beneath which were three drafting tables with small layout tables. To the right were file cabinets, larger layout tables and an overhead wooden rack supporting tubes used as storage for rolled drawings. From the tube ends hung round tags on short strings with client's names.

The large north light over the drafting tables and the row of high, openable, windows on the south allowed the fresh ocean breezes to cool the air and slip deliciously past our nose and face. The ceiling of 2x6 tongue-in-groove planks had a few strategically placed skylights which lent optimism to the interior and were partially obscured by a fig leaf plant growing with great enthusiasm down the hall, across the ceiling, and curving back over the drafting tables. The entire office, built of such a unique material as railroad ties, was bold, well proportioned and a satisfying space that evoked freedom, naturalness and creativity.

Hap had two architects working with him, Bill *(Willie)* Moore, 34, and chief designer of the modern projects, and Frank Young, 40, senior partner, draftsman, job captain and office manager. I was the third draftsman and architect, (27), raised in salary from $2.25 per hour to $2.50 per hour and given a table in a row under the windows between Frank and Bill.

Frank gave me a preliminary drawing of what was to be The Malibu Sand's apartment building and hotel on Pacific Coast Highway in Malibu. Hap was in partnership with a close friend and businessman named, Bill Baines, and I was to do working drawings on their project.

I began in the typical way for every job, laying out the floor plan, then tracing over it for the foundation plan and drawing sections from those. Then the exterior elevations, plot and roof plans, interior elevations, structural, mechanical and electrical, drawings, door, window and cabinet details would have to be drawn. It was Hap and Frank's job to do the specifications. When drawings and specifications were finished the package made a complete set of working drawings and specifications suitable for submission to the Building Department and obtaining contractor's bids.

Occasionally Hap's partner, Bill Baines, a trimly dressed middle-aged business man whose socks and tie always matched, *(sometimes both were yellow and tan striped)* clicked heels down the cement floor to my table and we'd talk about my progress. He was delighted with the project and happy to share it with me, especially if I were under such expert guidance as Hap and Frank.

I soon found Bill Moore and Frank Young loved to talk. My

worktable being between them, I heard every conversation, a lot of which was so meaningful to me I incorporated it into my later life. They were both philosophers and avid practitioners of Yananda Yoga. Turning into the entrance patio I was sometimes startled to see almost hidden in the dim shadows of the Copa de Ora, a vertical body, and upside down, against the wall. It was Frank. It was his practice every noon to stand silently on his head and elbows against a wall for five minutes to meditate. I often wondered what clients thought about this.

I was still smoking cigarettes and soon discovered Bill and Frank disapproved of my bad habit and resented it. It was hard for them to watch me injure myself and they didn't like the smell or untidiness. I was messing up their atmosphere. After a short time, I took my smoking outside.

FRANK

Frank had recently been through a major growth period in his life to achieve a more relaxed, natural way of being. According to Frank, he had been a rigidly dressed, coffee drinking, cigarette smoking, and up-tight, anxious kind of guy. Then Willie came to work with a different set of habits. Practicing Yoga as a way of life, Bill was a natural philosopher, waterman, surfer and beach boy. At work he wore go-aheads, shorts and an open Hawaiian shirt through which was bared a strong, hairy, sun-tanned chest.

Through Willie's example, Frank decided his way of life was not the best and began to change. He cut out coffee and cigarettes and began dressing in open collars, loose pants and gym shoes, frequently without socks. He became a vegetarian, took up the study of Yoga, and in a year was doing admirably under Bill's influence. He felt relaxed and liked himself more and his wife and two children liked him better, as well, so much so, that his wife took up Yoga, too.

Growing from anxious to relaxed, Frank had made a positive change for the whole family. He was reformed. His family was reformed. There was no way he'd go back. He'd been there, done that! He loved his new self.

52 - Frank before the change.

53 - Frank after the change, with Doug, Rocky and Evelyn.

Frank was a great reader of meaningful books, usually about the meaning of life and how to live it the best. It was his practice after reading such a book to jot down four or five especially significant quotations and read them or give them to his family and special friends. Examples

(1) *Anger, depression, insanity and physical sickness are four permanent substitutes for failure to perceive self worth.*

(2) *The human body is a marvelously intricate machine that is not replaceable, and you have only one.*

(3) *The alternative to self-examination is to be led by the unconscious.*

I am honored to tell you Frank called me every year on my birthday, New Years Eve, since 1956 until his death in 1999 at the age of 82.

One time I got to see Frank's house off Tigertail Road in Brentwood above the Kenter Avenue School. It was a lovely, open, natural wood and plaster house on a hillside with a loft overlooking the living room, decks and landscaping below. It was one of the finest contemporary houses I had seen in Southern California. I could never understand why Hap had chosen Bill or me to do his contemporary work, since he already had a contemporary architect as a partner.

BILL

Bill would come to his desk each morning, say a few pleasant things, then turn his surfer's back on us and become lost in his drawings. He was newly married to an attractive middle-aged person he called his *bride*. I suspect she was older than he and seemed jealous and possessive. This suited Bill's personality because he liked being possessed and loved her for her out-of-the-ordinary ways. He relished public kissing and the genuine affection she lavished on him and returned every display of affection.

Bill and wife with wigs and fake beard.

They were a love-match. He eventually built a romantic house for each of them in Laguna Beach, replete with potted flowers and hanging plants with an outdoor swimming pool that curved inside the house into their private sleeping quarters. Bill explained, *"So he could roll out of bed into the pool."* His spouse, who had one child from a former marriage, had Bill's child shortly after Bill left Hap's office. The two had a close personal relationship and enjoyed their privacy. Frank and I enjoyed their loving connection.

Bill's latest design in Hap's office was a house on the beach in Malibu for John and Charlotte La Ronde and their two children. Karon and I drove to Malibu and found the Ronde house to be a natural wood, two-story, post-and-beam with Hawaiian overtones. Its distinguishing feature was a long, powerful, horizontal, orange beam, dashing unashamedly across the whole front. A *Willie-ism,* Frank called it. The house was different than anything in Malibu at that time. It couldn't be missed, not only because of it's orange beam, but because it was of a much better quality than the adjoining houses.

During his discussions, it became evident that he loved architecture second only to his *bride* and the beach. One of the best things about Bill was his point of view and philosophies. He was always opinionated, but it was also obvious he had thought about his opinions. Talking about architecture, he was convinced the entry to a house should be a long, narrow exterior hallway, ever more confining to those that would enter, until all that remained was a small good quality entry door. When the door was swung open, anyone could experience the overwhelming beauty of the interior, perhaps with it's feeling of indoor-outdoor living, or interior garden with waterfall, or unusual fireplace illuminated by a skylight. *His philosophy was to lead people to believe less than that which he delivered.* It was his personal psychological ploy, but also a meaningful touchstone to a young architect

Bill was questioned into lengthily explanations of his views or feelings about almost everything, which he joyfully answered. I loved his views and agreed with most of them and took them to heart. I didn't seem to have any comparable ideas of my own and remained in the listening mode.

HAP

*H*ap was of medium height, about 55-years old with graying hair, black mustache and heavy eyebrows with a few white hairs curling whimsically into the wind. He considered himself important but never took advantage of those that worked for him for that reason. There are some who are meant to be leaders in architecture. Hap was one. Hap loved his attractive wife and the boys. The Gilman's had two bright sons, Stewart and Nicky, both of whom were to become architects. I was not privileged to know them well, but to me, the Gilman's appeared the perfect family.

Hap had made his reputation doing period style homes. He had gone to Europe and sketched a portfolio of French and English Provincial, Colonial, Tudor and other classic styles from the original buildings. He was an expert on all historic styles and his clients loved him for it. Bill Moore's education was in the modern, post-and-beam style and Hap allowed Bill to do work under Hap's name when he got a request for modern work. Bill always did the working drawings on his own designs and Frank would do the working drawings on the period designs done by Hap.

At odd times Hap cruised in and out of the office. When he was in, he made phone calls or confided in Frank about time schedules, or commented on the work, or discussed prospective clients, or on-going supervision.

I enjoyed working for Hap. He was honest and treated his associates and clients fairly. He was serious about his work. Once I was able to see Hap's house in Sullivan Canyon. It was a 3,000-square-foot house adjacent to designer, Cliff May's own 7,000-square-foot house. The Gilman house was definitely *not* a period piece and showed great creativity and individuality of thought. The walls were made of vertical wood siding with large sliding glass with wood framed doors to a garden.

It had a heavy, low sloping, open natural plank ceiling, over which was placed roofing, a six inch layer of topsoil, sprinkler system and rye grass. Hap had one of the few sod-roofed houses in Southern California. His stables were of railroad ties and large glass areas and were its essence in character. It is strange that one who'd made his reputation by doing period designs took such a dramatically different approach designing his own home.

Painting of Hap Gilman. (Photo: Courtesy of Hap's architect son, Stewart Gilman.)

BILL REID

During weekends and in the evenings, while working for Hap, Karon and I went to the beach and scouted the new territory of Santa Monica, particularly Santa Monica Canyon. On lower Amalfi Drive, we admired an unusual house built in the post-and-beam style and situated at the end of a row of more normally designed houses. One Saturday morning we knocked on the door to tell the owners how much we liked their house and how much we'd appreciate seeing the interior. An abnormally tall and slim, but powerfully built young man answered the door and introduced himself as Bill Reid. Bill was pleased that an architect had admired his work and introduced us to his proportionally tall wife, Paula. He was pleased to show us around.

The house had beautiful views over the Santa Monica Canyon Creek with pitched open beam ceilings left in their natural state and a small imaginatively landscaped outdoor rear patio. The prominent display of piano, guitars, and drums indicated they were a musical family. We learned they had two children, a girl and a boy. The girl was twelve years old, pretty and bright. The younger boy was handsome, but sadly autistic. Later we discovered Bill was the son of former silent screen actor, William Wallace Reid, who'd died at the age of 35 as the result of an excessive private life and difficulties in narcotics and handling early success in Hollywood. His son, Bill Reid, Junior, was a general contractor with personal integrity, and who loved to do modern work. He had designed their unusual contemporary home.

Later we came to know him as a neighbor and found he could be very interesting. We eventually learned he had designed and built his own thirty-foot powerboat with a single hull hollowed front to back in a catamaran-like shape. The hulls and hollowed bottom were for increased stability and to eliminate friction for faster cruising.

He had worked at Hughes Aircraft during the early years of his career and knew and had flown with Howard Hughes. As a free spirit, he had much in common with Howard Hughes and the two, I suspect, were of a kind.

Bill married again after his first divorce and the two belonged to the Unitarian Church in Santa Monica for many years. Toward the end of 1980, Bill was flying alone over the Los Angeles Bay in a plane designed and built by himself, one in which he had been flying for many years. Evidently he lost orientation in the low clouds and fog that day and plummeted into the water and was killed. Perhaps his instruments were non-existent or mal-functioning. There were rumors that Bill may have committed suicide in this way. It was said,

"This is the way he would have chosen." I don't think so, but we'll never know.

REQUIEM MASS AND STORY OF CHRISTMAS

Karon lost little time in locating a singing group. She found one in The Pacific Palisades Civic Chorus with Lillian G. Englar, Founder and Director. The Chorus was funded by the City of Los Angeles, Department of Municipal Art, Bureau of Music, and was giving *The Requiem Mass in C minor*, by Maria Luigi Cherubini, at the Pacific Palisades elementary school.

The 35 volunteer singers rehearsed two months before the performance, which was to be on November 13, 1954. I had sung in the *Gondoliers* and hadn't anything else to do on rehearsal nights anyway, so agreed to go. Lillian put me in the bass section and I looked at the music and tried to follow along. The performance went well and it was fun for me to be with the group following along mostly by ear. We were becoming acquainted with the local musical community.

As a follow-up to the *Requiem,* Lillian Englar began rehearsing *The Story of Christmas,* by H. Alexander Mathew's. It was to be performed on the beautiful grounds of Saint Mathew's Episcopal Church on Bienvenida Street in Pacific Palisades.

It was to be an outdoor Christmas Cantata-Pageant and we acquired more members. Karon was the soprano in the quartet and had a solo part.

This is a quote from the program:

With the picturesque panorama of the mountains as a backdrop, The Story of Christmas - in pantomime by a cast of over 30, directed by Ray Verity - and a chorus of 80 voices - brings to the thousands that come out, dress warmly, an inspiring beginning of the Holiday Season.

```
                "R E Q U I E M    M A S S "

                      in C minor

                       ─────

                 Maria Luigi Cherubini
                       ─────

                   presented by the

             PACIFIC PALISADES CIVIC CHORUS

                  City of Los Angeles
               Department of Municipal Art
                    Bureau of Music


                       ─────


                 LILLIAN G. ENGLAR
                      Director

                    LES NORDGREN
                    Accompanist

                       ─────


           AUDITORIUM ELEMENTARY SCHOOL
           PACIFIC PALISADES,  CALIFORNIA
```

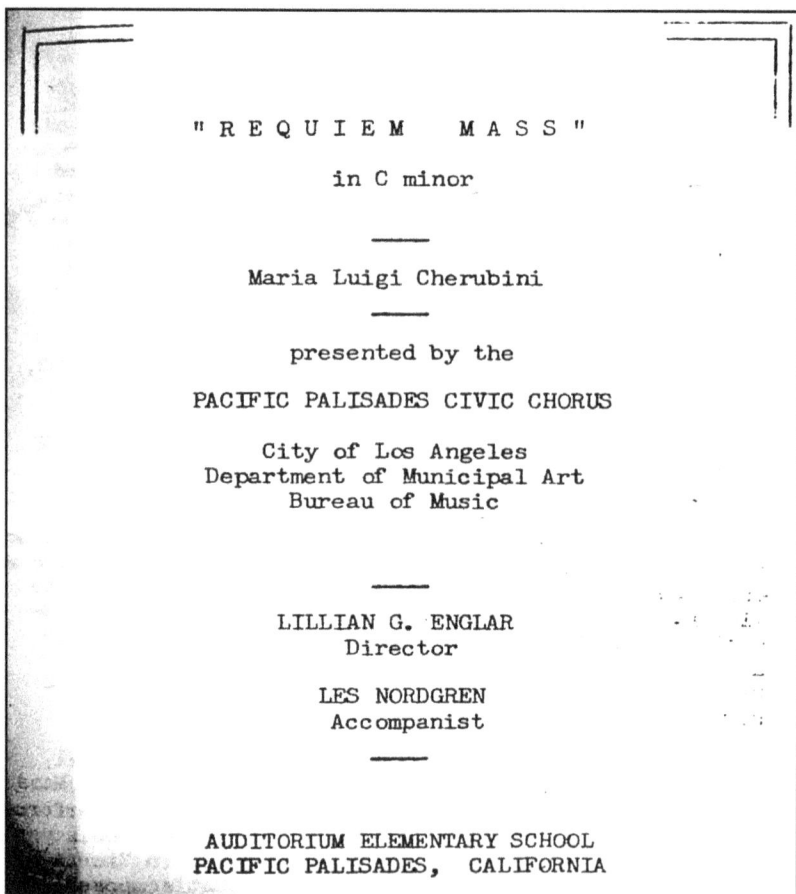

56 - Cherubini's Requiem Mass Program, November 13, 1954

In this way Karon led us into a ten-year singing career.

Christmas card - 1954
Merry Christmas to our mother and dad.
We miss you and wish we could all be together - the whole family.
It would be nice if we could arrange it, sometime.
I, too, am now in the rat race.
BUT, Merry Christmas.
                    Doug and Karon

You . Your Family and Friends
are invited to enjoy the

THE SIXTH ANNUAL

PACIFIC PALISADES OUTDOOR

CHRISTMAS CANTATA-PAGEANT

*"The Story
of Christmas"*

An inspiring Holiday Musical Spectacle

SUNDAY, DECEMBER 19th, 1954
5:30 P.M.

LILLIAN G. ENGLAR
Founder and Director   On the Beautiful Grounds of St. Matthew's Episcopal Church
Bienvenida Street—two blocks north of Sunset Blvd.

*57 - Program for The Story of Christmas, Lillian Englar director.
December 19, 1954*

LAND AND FIRST HOUSE

On our trips around Santa Monica Canyon we came upon a vacant strip of gently sloping land, 200 feet wide *(4 - 50 ft. lots)*, by 150-feet deep, overlooking West Channel Road and the creek with a small ocean view off to the right. The land in 1954 was covered with weeds, had once been rich river bottom with dark, pebbly deposits in horizontal layers. This meant the land was extremely stabile.

We dreamed of owning a house there. The owner lived on the Northerly edge of the property in a classic Mediterranean Hillside Villa cut into the hillside about 1920. Mr. Grant *(not his real name)* was elderly *(85)* and had been wondering what to do with the property. He felt fatherly to the young couple before him, yet compelled to dispose of his possessions before dying. Doing what we asked seemed to be a kindly thing to do and would also rid him of property for which at his age he had no use.

I told him we wanted to build houses for sale. If he would give us the lots with no money down and agree to subordinate his interest in the land to a 2nd Trust Deed, I would be delighted to get a loan and build on the property, lot by lot, if necessary, and pay him back at the time of our sales. We hoped to keep one of the lots for our own. Mr. Grant agreed to think about it.

A few weeks later he was willing to give us the two southern lots closest to the ocean. Each was 50-feet wide by 150-feet deep with an easement, and included an agreement to subordinate what was owed on the property to a first trust deed necessary for the bank to hold the first trust deeds.

He'd agreed to give our neighborly contractor, Bill Reid, the northerly two lots. Bill had tried to get all four lots to develop as houses for speculation. Seeing him as a greedy guy, I was rankled then and I remain rankled today because he sold both lots and each was developed poorly. Were the lots given to Karon and me, the property would have been developed properly. Later he redeemed himself by doing a decent addition to one of them. An architecturally insensitive couple bought the other lot, destroyed their property with a bad house and diminished the neighborhood with what serious architects called, *"a dingbat."*

Nevertheless, we were overjoyed at having found ourselves in possession of at least two lots and particularly pleased we'd spent no money. The subordination clause allowed us to get construction loans.

I told my story to the guys at work and asked them what I should do. They mentioned general contractor partners, Jack Laughtenslager and Bob Butte, who might be willing to go into business with me. We'd build the houses and each share a third of the profits. I contacted them, they agreed, and I made a house design for the end lot closest to the ocean. We split the cost of permit fees and within a couple of months the first house of my own design at 242 South Amalfi Drive, was under construction. A post-and-beam! A style I'd always loved! It was framed and roofed without windows in June 1955.

In August, we received an offer of $24,500.00 for the unfinished house. Butte, Laughtenslager and I agreed to accept it. We took $5,000.00 and paid off Mr. Grant, kept $1,000.00 profit for each of us and I began work on House 2, the one we intended to be Karon's and my home.

FIRST HOUSE EXPERIENCE

Building my first house was very exciting. I drew the plans, got the permits, bid it out through Butte and Laughtenslager, and watched my idea transformed into three dimensions. This was fun. I derived the first satisfied feeling as an architect designing and building.

58 - Building our first spec house on Amalfi Drive.
(A year later it was to become our own.)

However I must put this experience in perspective. I had good contractors for excellent help and a proper deal from the elderly person who lived in the Mediterranean House. In addition I had a new marriage, was trying to grow up, had a challenging new job with persons with whom I could relate. I was attending Karon's rehearsals and performances for two plays, *Gigi* and *Blind Alley,* and during construction we were both in rehearsal for *Girl Crazy* and taking tap dance lessons one night a week. Looking back, the excitement of doing my first house had to be shared with all the other exciting things I was doing with my life.

I felt reserved about the early sale of the first house, because it was incomplete. The owner was going to paint the walls and do his individualistic touches after we were gone. I was reluctant to sell because I couldn't see my work to completion. It was like I wouldn't get to finish my artwork. I agreed to sell it because I was only 1/3 of a partnership and Jack and Bob thought it a good idea because they would get their money out, plus a small profit. They said a quick sale was *safer*.

I justified the early sale was a way to get in my own house sooner and leaped into designing the second house on the next lot. It would be a two-bedroom, two-bath house with one large bedroom that could be divided down the center with a Pella wood folding door, should we want one, to provide the third bedroom. While I was designing, doing the working drawings, getting the permit, bids and construction loan, I continued working at Hap Gilman's.

PLAYS

During the construction of house 1 for speculation, Karon got a small part in the musical, *Gigi*, at a non-profit playhouse in Pacific Palisades called the Ebsen Theater. The generous actor, Buddy Ebsen, created the Ebsen Theater. The musical was to be performed 6 times between April 21 and 30th, 1955. She sang in the chorus and had one good solo on Thursday, Friday and Saturday for length of the show.

When *Gigi* was over, Karon immediately began rehearsals for next months play called, *Blind Alley*. It was to be performed seven times between May 19th and 29th, 1955 and was about a psychiatrist, his wife and child held hostage in their home by a killer, his gun moll and henchman. The play shows how the psychiatrist, with superior knowledge of the human mind, eventually wears the killer down, frees his family and brings the killer to justice. Though totally unlike her character in real life, Karon was sensational playing the gun moll.

One of her lines was, *"Every time he pipes up, he jumps all over me!"* was delivered as, *"Every time he jumps up, he pipes all over me!"*

Karon, as Sidonie, in Gigi with butler at Ebsen Theater, Pacific Palisades, April 1955.

I was a *Stage Door Johnny* for most of the performances. The killer, a method actor, got into his character too deeply and lost the fact that he was in a play. He assumed the character of a real killer. During a scene when he was to fire blank shots at the moll he pointed the gun directly at Karon and fired the cardboard pellets into her body, which left deep bruises. Karon and the director had a serious talk with him. In subsequent performances he was more careful, but he'd lost the trust of his fellow actors. In one scene he was to shoot a henchman and did. In the next scene the real body had been replaced with a dummy under a sheet. In a fit of passion and hate he knelt down and beat the sheet with both fists for such a long time the audience lost the carefully built sense of belief. Not good for the show. Not good for the actors. Not good for the audience. Not good for the method actor!

60 - Karon as the gun moll Mazie Stoner in Blind Alley at the Ebsen Theater. Harvey Korman playing Dr. Anthony Shelby.

The show had good attendance and got excellent reviews despite the idiosyncrasies of the killer. Harvey Korman, the psychiatrist, did a wonderful job of acting. He knew his part and knew all the other's parts. He had focus and concentration. He was dependable, had passion, was smart, and if necessary, could ad-lib and continue a scene even if the rest of the players were lost in the script. His fellow players, Karon in particular, worked well with him and held him in high esteem. Later, he starred as a comedian in The Carol Burnette Show with Tim Conway and Vicki Lawrence.

61 - Henchman and Mazie.

62 - Scene with Korman and others.

MOTHER AND DAD VISIT

Mother and Dad visited us in California in July of 1955, in time to take a picture of Karon and me in the construction of our first Amalfi Drive spec house.

They were able to visit the Conan's and our apartment on San Vicente Boulevard and make a trip to Portuguese Bend on the Palos Verdes Peninsula to see the location of a future house for the Vawter's. While there we visited the oceanarium on the peninsula and the Wayfarer's Chapel, constructed of glass planes separated by wood posts and beams. It was designed by one of Frank Lloyd Wright's sons, Lloyd Wright.

63 - Wayfarer's Chapel designed by Lloyd Wright.

GIRL CRAZY

About the time of completion of House 1, Karon and I were in rehearsals for the musical, *Girl Crazy*.

It was to run from August 26 to September 24, 1955, at a small community playhouse in Santa Monica called the Morgan Theater. Karon said again, "*They always need men in musicals.*" so for the same reasons, but a little wiser since I'd been in the Gondoliers, I went to rehearsals.

64 - Jerry Razor and Karon Rucker in Girl Crazy August 26th to September 24th 1955.

While plays were given in the evening on Thursday through Saturday, the theater was dark for the rest of the week. This allowed time for new rehearsals.

Karon got the lead part singing, Molly Gray, opposite the male lead, Danny Churchill, played by Jerry Razor. She had plenty of work to do, but I was busy, too. They needed dancers, chorus work, and someone to sing bass in the quartet. I was able to do all three and spent more time on stage than Karon.

There were solo parts in the quartet. I'm not a soloist, but in those days it was difficult to find a quartet of any kind for a small community musical. The original bass man was unavailable, so the director asked me if I'd like to try bass. I was afraid but complemented and said I'd try. As it turned out it was a piece of cake. Music had rubbed off on me from Dad having played the piano by ear and from listening to my brother practicing to be a professional trumpet player. The main quartet song was *I'm Bidin' My Time.*

> *I'm bidin' my time,*
> *'Cause that's the kinda guy I am.*
> *No need complaining*
> *When it's raining,*
> *Bidin' my time.*

There were 4 verses to *I'm Biding My Time* with four one-line solos to be sung for each verse by each quartet member. One evening, while we were singing verse 3, baritone, James B. Sikking, made a mistake. He sang the lead-in for verse four instead of the one I was rehearsed to complete, verse 3. I quickly thought *if I sing verse 3 it won't make sense. I'd better sing line 4 of verse 4.* Finally remembering it, I started to sing, however in the confusion the orchestra played through my bars and finished and in that tiny silence before they started verse 4, I clearly heard myself saying *"Oh Shit!"* which unfortunately the audience also heard.

65 - Doug and friend in "Girl Crazy" stage fight.

66 - Sikking, Rucker and Ernest.

The main chorus dance program was *I Got Rhythm.*

> *I got rhythm!*
> *I got music!*
> *I got my gal!*
> *Who could ask for anything more.*

The choreographer, Carole Sherman, was an attractive 19-year-old dance teacher. Karon and I decided to study tap dancing with her and attended her weekly lessons during the rehearsal period, but we never did our practice at home. She dropped us! Anyone need tap shoes?

67 - Doug and Karon

Later in his career James B. Sikking made his name and I presume became wealthy in television playing a detective on Hill Street Blues. Karon played her roll admirably singing, *Could You Use Me? Embraceable You,* and *But Not For Me.* I had fun and chalked it up to another weird stage experience of the poor boy from Chicago.

STILL AT HAP'S - MURDOCK

After doing the working drawings for Hap and Bill Baines on the Malibu Sands Motel and Apartment, I helped finish working drawings on a house in Mandeville Canyon whose plan was in the shape of an arch, the radius point being the center of a two hundred year old oak tree. The specimen oak had strong, black limbs driving vigorously into a shock of powerful leaves that moved in maturity and dignity with the ocean breeze. Every panel of the house, sliding glass doors, fixed glass panels, planks in the semi-circular deck, and projecting roof beams, derived their position being centered on the radius point from the oak.

At the beginning of construction, ominously, here and there among the green oak leaves, growing in quantities more than would be desired, appeared *brown leaves*. By the time the owners were ready to move in nine months later the tree was dead! The purpose for the semi-circular house had departed. Poor Murdock's!

CLYDE

At the office I'd noticed an agreeable youth, apparently an architectural freshman at USC. His name was Clyde Augustson, a slim young man with a perpetual grin and a shock of wavy brown hair behind bespectacled eyes. He seemed like family to Hap, Frank and Willie Moore and he'd obviously been following the firm's practice for years. Everyone treated him as one of their own and exchanged views and answered his challenging questions during his bi-monthly visits. After our brief but interesting conversations, he'd quietly lose himself with newly arrived architectural magazines, or if none, then pick up back issues and leaf through those and read them. Hap would relinquish most of his older magazines to the well-thumbed files of this fine young protégé. Clyde must have had quite a file.

I accepted him as a youthful friend and enthusiastic student; one thoroughly devoted to the field of Architecture. He challenged me in a mild way, forcing me to imagine myself as a young person as dedicated to architecture as he at such an early age. I assumed he would be brilliant as a young architect and I questioned myself. *"Where was*

I?" He made me wonder how much farther and how much better an architect I could have been with his kind of dedication and enthusiasm at so young an age. We were to meet later on.

FIRED OR RAISE?

*B*ill Moore had decided to leave Hap and Frank to build a house in Laguna for he and his bride. Shortly before he left, Hap called me into his office.

68 - Hap Gilman – 1955. Courtesy of Stewart Gilman.

My heart raced and my breathing was shallow. I'd been called into the boss's office before, every time to be told my services would no longer be needed. My life flashed before me, my heart raised from

72 to 82 beats per minute and a flush of perspiration formed on my temples.

I sat down and Hap said, *"You've been here for a year and a half and I'm going to raise your salary from $2.50 per hour to $3.00 per hour."*

I couldn't believe my ears. I thought he was joking. I waited a long moment for Hap to say more, but there was nothing. *"Is that all you wanted to talk to me about?"*

He said, *"Yes?"*

"Well, thank you very much!" I was astounded and said, *"I really appreciate it!* And returned, stunned, to my drafting table to complete the day. I was offered a raise! I was not being fired! Frank was pleased for me as well.

HALLIBURTON

*W*hen Bill left, Hap gave me the Halliburton job to design. Dave Halliburton was the son of the family who owned Texas Halliburton Oil. Dave and his wife, Sue, and two children had bought an acre lot in the Serra Retreat in Malibu below the Franciscan Monastery. I was overjoyed, attended meetings to write the program, did the preliminary studies, and presented them to the Halliburton's with Hap.

It was a 2-bedroom, den, family room with kitchen, dining and living in a single area, with master bedroom and large wardrobe space and bath. In the post-and-beam style with open beams and wood plank ceiling, it had floor to ceiling glass and was classic in design. *Classic means what was necessary was in full view, and what was in full view was also beautiful.*

The plan included a fifty by twenty-five foot pool and landscaping as well. After our presentation I made the appropriate changes, did the working drawings, Hap and Frank did the specifications, and we were lucky enough to draw low bidders in Butte and Laughtenslager as contractors.

Supervision of the work was exclusively Hap's job, but Karon and I drove out on weekends to monitor the progress. The Halliburton's appreciated what appeared to be double supervision and were pleased they'd hired competent, caring people. The house was an unqualified success.

BLOW

*F*ollowing Halliburton I was given the job of doing a guesthouse cantilevering over Mandeville Canyon. It was to be a unique house, designed to work as a companion to the client's large traditional house on 10 acres. The owner's name was Fred Blow and he had decided that though his main house was traditional, he would live it up a little and go for modern.

Freddie came in the office many times, right to my table to enjoy the process and stay in touch with his new guesthouse. Fred was of medium height, rather chubby and balding, dressed in comfortable, but relaxing clothes. More than a few times I smelled alcohol on his breath. A man of about 50, he was unmarried, and whether he was gay or not, I'll never know, but he had the air of the rich about him and the location of his property was proof positive.

I did a 1,200-square-foot post-and-beam guesthouse, this time with a plan in the trapezoidal form. It had a long deck that extended in a strong horizontal line that contrasted with the verticality of the slim, ancient trees. The house was supported by five, two-foot diameter caissons 30-feet deep, over which extended tapered reinforced concrete grade beams cantilevering ten feet evenly and dramatically over the steep canyon slope.

When the job was completed, I stood in the house under the clerestory windows and looked across Mandeville Canyon. In the foreground rose the 100-foot long trunks of Eucalyptus Citriodora, the tops of which waived in the westerly wind that blew down the canyon. The trunks moved left and to right a few feet, blown by the breeze, all the while appearing perfectly plumb.

One thing Fred Blow insisted on was a pigskin floor. I didn't know a pigskin floor existed, but Hap found one, I specified it and the contractors installed it. I thought it a mistreatment of intelligent animals.

We surreptitiously called Fred's house, *The Blow Job*.
I once asked him, *"Joe, what business are you in?"*

Glancing to the left, he coughed, looked to his feet and in a deep voice lost in his throat mumbled, *"I own hotels."*

I said, *"Oh!"* and left it at that.

Later I asked Frank and found he owned a few hotels in France and Italy and they were plenty to keep him financially solvent for a lifetime of building and booze.

BECK

*I*t had been crossing my mind to quit Hap's and begin in an office of my own with Dwight Pollock as partner. Hap was traveling to Europe with his family for three months and gave me what was to be my last design job in the Gilman-Young office, a house in Sweetwater Canyon, Malibu, for a radio sports caster and his wife, Mr. and Mrs. Fred Beck.

Hap said his goodbyes and I took over designing another post-and-beam, this time on a bluff overlooking the Pacific. Frank consulted with me and while Hap was gone, we tried to keep Fred and his wife smiling. *We were doing a house without Daddy!* I presented the Beck's a house, which to my thought had a valid, if strange, floor plan. It was another post-and-beam, with open beam wood ceiling and a *"V-plan"* shape. Fred and his wife were not ecstatic, but leaving the professional work and responsibility where it belongs, to the professionals. The bids came in double what was expected and the owner's were shattered. Frank and I, having little to do with the cost side of architecture, were following the written program and hadn't paid attention to the owner's available money.

When Hap got back, he and Fred got into an unpleasant sharing of feelings and the job did *not* go ahead. Several years later another firm designed and built a different house on the same lot for the Beck's children. I counted our job a failure because *we hadn't the awareness to watch the client's budget!* A powerful lesson!

ANOTHER PLAY AND OUR NEW HOUSE

Karon performed again for the Palisades Players in a musical review called, *Off the Record.* She was in 12 performances between June 21 and July 14, 1956, and sang in two choruses. I attended a couple of shows but don't remember the reviews. Instead, I was furthering our new house, which was completed about September 1956.

SECOND HOUSE

69 - The second house, intended for the Rucker's.

Sadly, prices had gone up. There was too much money spent on the new house and without additional cash it was too expensive for us. However the owners of our original spec house were having trouble making mortgage payments and planned to put it on the market. We bought it quick, in whatever state, about a year after our original sale, then sold the second house for speculation to Milt and Mania Black and their three children. We used that small profit to help in buying back our first house.

The selling owners were loose living people with gay, straight, and hippie friends and used to many boisterous parties. The first thing they did to the house after purchase was paint all the interior walls different colors, pink, chartreuse, purple, and yellow. They thought they'd bought a modern house and wanted to paint it in the modern way. Thank the good Lord they didn't paint the natural wood ceiling. The carpeting was worn jute, complete with fleas. The windows were cloudy, having never been washed, the walls were scratched with big nail holes, and there was no landscaping. The house was a mess!

The friendly 50-year-old owner, whom I'll call Al, was pudgy and unshaven with watery red eyes and a pale skin. A friendly drunk, I'd call him. With laughter, music and bright lights, his parties continued their wild, semi-orgiastic celebrations until early the following morning. About 2:00 AM after one particularly raucous time, Al rolled side over side down the front bank until the weeds stopped him and feeling exhausted and warm enough and drunk enough, he slept there all night.

We bought the house and began repairing.

FIRST HOUSE

*W*e began by cleaning all the plaster walls in the house with towels and a pail of solution, then covering the variously colored walls with white primer and finishing with an off-white called Mushroom. All walls were now the same color and the dignity of the house, with a sigh of relief, returned. We scrubbed the windows inside and out, and polished the kitchen, and raked the land around the house, and made a stair down the front bank to the sidewalk with a gate at the top for safety. Then we called Eric Armstrong, landscape architect, and requested planting advice. Eric was to become a strong business associate and friend in later life.

We wanted something to grow rapidly at the rear of our property near the carport to obscure the neighbors deteriorating wooden fence and their unattractive roofs. Eric took us literally and said the fastest growing plant he could think of was *Wigandia Caracasana,* available only from Venezuela.

However, it had the unfortunate side affect of giving a burning itch when touched. We said, *OK! Mr. Landscape Architect! Do with us what you will! We are your slaves! Our mind is putty awaiting your great sculpture!* And were stupid enough to have the plant installed. It grew at an alarming rate, threw out leaves a foot across, spawned flowers, roots shot up through the soil and even through the cracks in the paving. Seeds from the plant quickly turned in to fast growing miniature Wigandia. We tried to cut it back, but with great difficulty from not being able to touch it. Like brushing against poison oak, our arms or hands or ankles became itchy and inflamed with what looked like multiple bee stings.

70 - Wigandia Caracasana.

Evidently, once established, *there was no getting rid of Wigandia Caracasana.* The best we could do with it over the years was to protect ourselves with gloves and heavy clothing and hack it back. It grew in a hedge about 16-feet high and was still dangerous by the time we sold the house 6-years later. It is probably still there.

Another unplanned plant took root in the first six months of our occupancy. A strange, six-foot shrub emerged from the weeds on our front bank with strong dark leaves covered with needles. It looked like a thick-stemmed thistle, but grew with more authority, daring and permanence. In three months it crowned itself with an ominous gray and white flower, huge, odd, weird and menacing. Eric looked it up and told us it was a *Dieffenbachia Rhudolf-Roehrs,* member of the Bitter Nightshade Family, rare for these parts. We didn't know what that meant. It was a dark green, thick-stemmed, super thistle with thorns and a powerful, don't mess with me, attitude. It dared us to cut it down.

71 - Amalfi house with plant called, Dieffenbachia Rudolph-Roehrs, a member of the Bitter Nightshade Family.

If we did so, we'd reap the consequences. It was a symbol of something dark and sinister, perhaps a sign of all I'd done wrong. It was there to warn me! I'd pay for what I did! I had never seen a plant like this before and I have never seen one since.

We took a wait-and-see attitude and ignored it's threatening potential. It was a messenger of fate. *Twilight Zone theme, Da Da Da Da - Da Da Da Da.*

KARON

My relationship with Karon progressed as I'd expected it to - positively. I never mentioned the word *smoking,* I was smoking myself, so who was I to talk? *(The subject was closed!)* My curiosity about her past affairs was satisfied. I decided to live with my pique. I was working hard in my architectural practice and Karon, until now, was busy with musicals and plays. I was singing in the Pacific Palisades Chorus and things were going as expected. We went out to dinner occasionally and particularly loved movies.

72 - Karon watering.

73 - Doug, Lois and Karon.

She never told me so, but my feeling was she liked what I was doing architecturally and always had new and good ideas for my improvement. I had adjusted as well as I was able and had validated myself as a man because by being married, I no longer had to prove to myself. I could get a woman! I'd already got one. Still, my social insecurities occasionally arose.

One time we went to a party with more of her friends, which always made me uncomfortable, and the hostess insisted we play charades. I felt like an ass even before the game started, but it was agreed I alone would stay out of the game. Karon, being trained as an actress, played charades beautifully and the other guests were more than adequate. As time wore on, and because I was not participating, I became anxious and wanted to go home. Karon was having such a good time it was unfair for me to ask her to leave early. I felt alone. I didn't know the people well. We weren't getting to know each other as much as I would have liked because they were playing a game. I decided to leave the party. Actually, I walked out on the party to sit in the car fuming and waiting. Karon eventually came out and we argued and I sulked all the way home.

I carried unresolved problems with me during the marriage, but other than a few experiences like the charade party, one would have to say our relationship was flourishing.

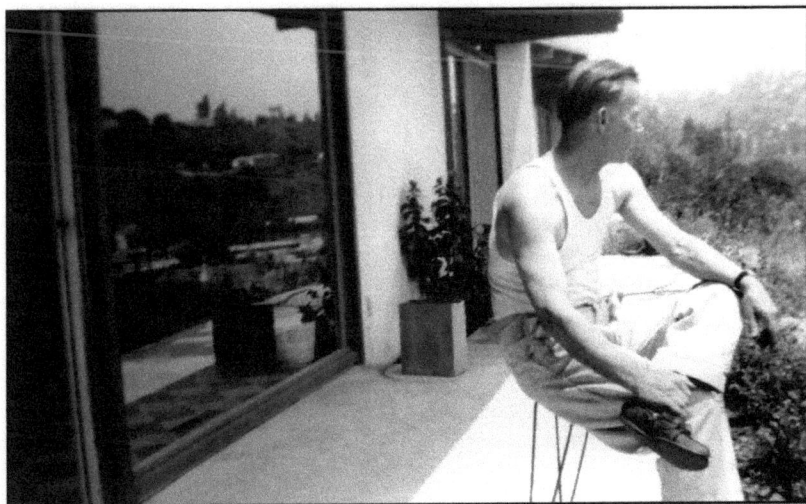

74 - Dad on front patio.

Karon was certainly dedicated when it came to painting walls and fixing things and she always added the artistic touch that I liked, but she always had a lot for me to do and wasn't hesitant about asking. Besides her intelligence and many talents, she brought passion, dignity and a strong moral sense to our lives.

With our new mortgage, property insurance and taxes, and other bills, we needed more money. Karon felt the need for a job, so we turned in the 41 Plymouth and purchased another used convertible Plymouth for Karon to look for work. She went to UCLA and got one in a responsible position as secretary to Doctor Freund, head of the Theater Arts Department. Not wishing to waste any time, she began taking graduate classes in Theater Arts on her lunch hour.

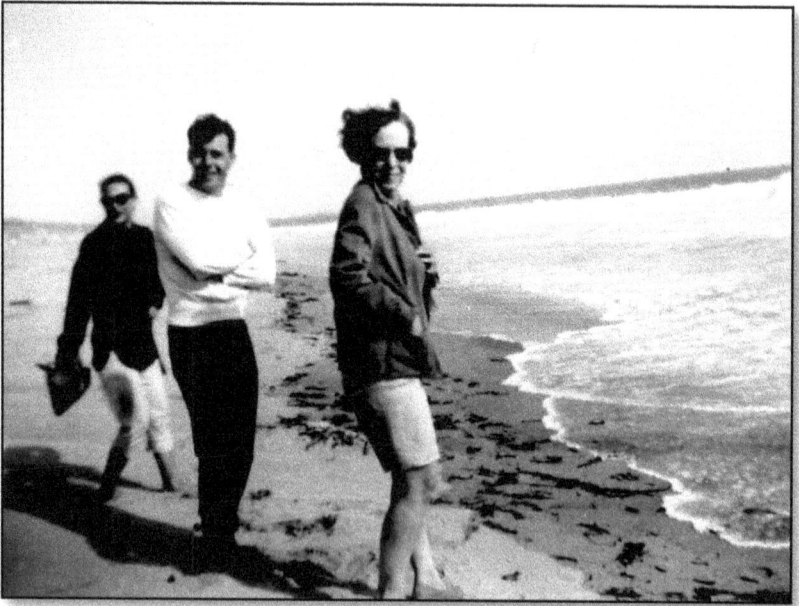

75 - Karon, Doug and Mother.

HOME JOBS

I picked up more work at home. A carpenter working for Butte and Laughtenschlager had decided to move to Palmdale, a city about 50 miles north of L. A. and wanted plans for a house for his wife and three kids. He would build it himself. He had three hundred dollars to spend for plans and asked me if I'd do them.

I made myself a drawing board out of a hollow core door and 2 x 4 supports and got a new Mayline Parallel and sitting on a wooden stool under the window in one of our extra bedrooms, created a serviceable home office. Soon I had the plans drawn and delivered. He invited me to come and see the job some time. A year or so later we drove to Palmdale and I saw the third house I'd designed. It was crafted acceptably considering the weak architectural effort.

76 - Doug drafting in converted bedroom in Amalfi house.

Then Harry Heckendorf, a carpenter-contractor who'd heard of me through my work with Hap Gilman, called me to do a house for Mr. and Mrs. Zenn who wanted a house on a bluff on the north side of Pacific Coast Highway overlooking the ocean and Malibu Cove Colony. He would pay me $400.00. I took it!

Then a divorced Yugoslavian carpenter-contractor asked me to do a house in the Malibu Sweetwater area. I charged him $500.00 and when I completed the plans and got him the permit, he attacked the job in a furious, almost desperate manner, working late into the night after his day job. The house was L-shaped, an all wood post-and-beam with large glass areas overlooking the ocean and a flat roof with a four-foot eave overhang. I was sick at heart when he cut the eave to three feet from the four feet I had designed. He reduced the desirable horizontal shadow lines and made the building look shorter and fatter and out of proportion. He did it for financial reasons, but it made me angry. When the original owners sold after thirty-seven years the new owner's painted the all-wood clear-heart redwood siding and paneling, inside and out, and natural Douglas Fir beams and plank ceiling, *white!* Thank heaven the house was put out of its misery in the treacherous 1993 Malibu brush fire. It burned to the ground!

I was beginning to realize without a tighter relationship with my clients and supervision of the work I couldn't control the end product. It was becoming important to control what I was doing. Why do I have to control things? I answered myself, perhaps because of my parental upbringing. Perhaps leaders feel they *have* to control their work. I reasoned if I didn't control my product, what was I doing? Was life worthwhile just doing plans with no involvement with the result? *Am I drawing plans to make money, or am I creating a house?* Was my involvement to be just for cash or should I be doing something more? *If I don't control the end product, somebody else controls the end product; therefore I need to control my work until it is done.*

And then I had to ask, was my work me? Was I my work? Was I involved in my work? I reasoned if I was not involved in my work that took such great amounts of time, I would not be involved with my life. Would life be worth living then?

POLLOCK AND FIRST OFFICE

*A*t Gilman's I'd heard of one of their former excellent draftsman named Richard Irwin. A few times he dropped in to see Bill and talk to Frank. I saw his old drawings and they were the most beautiful working drawings I'd ever seen. His hand lettering was perfect, his variety of line weights should have been in a text book, his sheet composition was artistic and carefully thought out. He seemed like a great guy. He was married, had one child, and though he had little money, he drove an Italian sports car and wore expensive Italian sweaters. His philosophy seemed to have been, *don't buy more, buy quality, but less.* He had one expensive sweater, he had one expensive car, and he had one small, but expensive house.

Another person I met and respected during my time with Hap

was a fellow 12 years my senior named Dwight Pollock. Pollock, according to stories, was a contemporary designer, doing work of the quality of Cal Straub, Craig Ellwood, Thornton Abell and Quincy Jones, all strong post-and-beam architects. Frank showed me a publication of one of Dwight's houses on Upper Amalfi Drive in a richer section of town that revealed an unusual structure of natural wood and glass. Karon and I drove to see it and agreed it was, indeed, contemporary in spirit.

77 - House designed by Dwight Pollock in the Uplifter's Ranch.
Photo – September 2000.

Dwight stopped by the office one day and told us he had a new commercial job and was going to move his office out of his home and into a permanent, commercial office in Pacific Palisades. I had been thinking of having my own business, myself, and asked about his other work. We drove to Rustic Canyon Park where he showed me a beautiful, natural wood house in the Uplifter's Ranch, off West Channel Road, near Santa Monica Canyon. He had used roof beams that appeared too small for the span but they hadn't sagged because he'd engineered the upper joints as rigid frame connections. The house overlooked Rustic Creek and was obviously a sincere effort.

I immediately liked Dwight because of his love for contemporary design, his inspiring conversation, his sense of humor, his brilliant engineering ability, his apparent architectural experience and his inability to do something less than that which he was capable.

I had been working at Hap's for about 2-1/2 years and was readying my mind for a change. I'd been the chief designer of contemporary jobs for Hap and Frank that lent me self-esteem. I'd designed and built two spec houses and was living in one. I was capable of doing additional houses and getting them built, though I hadn't been controlling them properly because I couldn't command payment. Karon had a good job as secretary to the head of the Theater Arts Department at UCLA. We had enough money if, in a partnership with Dwight, I could earn at least as much as I was making.

I discussed this with Dwight and he was excited about me being part of his firm. Dwight hadn't earned his California architectural license and was forced by law to call himself a designer. A designer could not legally do work over 3-stories high, but if he were in partnership with a licensed architect, he could legally do any kind of work he was able to get as long as the architect signed the plans. Dwight had a new commercial job over 3 stories and had hopes of doing larger contemporary designs through his client, Captain Wilson, who owned a shopping center in the Palisades.

Our firm would be called *Pollock and Rucker* and our new office would be in Pacific Palisades on the Northeast corner of Bienvenida and Sunset Boulevard behind the gas station in the location of the present Gelson's Market. We'd be in an office freely donated by the now demolished shopping center owner, Captain Wilson. Of course, I was excited about this because I wouldn't have to come up with *rent* money.

VAWTER HOUSE

While the new office was pending, a young couple, Mr. and Mrs. Vawter, contacted me. I don't remember their first names or the names of their two children since it's been a long time and my files, which would have had that information, were burned in a brush fire in 1970. I do remember this was the first house to which I felt I could give my complete heart. The owners had selected me to do their house and it had to be especially suited to their needs.

78 - Exterior of Vawter house.

79 - Interior. Mother and Karon

This was a lot more fun. I wasn't drawing something in the dark. I had actual clients with whom to work things out. The Vawter house wouldn't be the hollow experience of spending valuable time and effort doing a house for some big question mark. The Vawter house was a definite commission.

They had a modern temperament, needed a house to suit their needs, and would pay me a reasonable compensation to provide that service. Since the house was to be in Portuguese Bend, I would not be getting the permit or having bids submitted or be supervising construction. Nevertheless we trusted each other and I'm proud to say they built the house exactly according to plans.

I had the Rucker and Black houses in Santa Monica Canyon, the Carpenter house in Palmdale, the Yugoslavian Man's spec house and the Zenn house in Malibu and now the Vawter house in Portuguese Bend. I had collected about $2,200.00 from my four paying clients to date. Six amateurish houses to my dubious credit, four competed without supervision and all finished prior to having my own first office. This felt like a beginning.

PACIFIC PALISADES

FIRST OFFICE

The half block square Wilson Building was a ranch style, frame and plaster, two-story structure, enclosing a courtyard with a specimen tree in the center. The courtyard was an architectural relief that everyone enjoyed. Lessors could sit on benches under the tree and have lunch, or shoppers from the neighborhood could meet and sit in relative seclusion and talk and use the free space as we now use the mall. The courtyard was served by three or four openings from commercial sidewalks and parking areas while the surrounding upper floor decks had a delightful look into the tree, or around the tree into the activities below, or to the sky, above.

On the lower floor were a shoe store, cosmetic store, haircut shop, gift shop, and small market, and the second floor held a real estate office, law offices, commercial sales office, and so forth. On the second floor was that hallowed space soon to become our office, a bare room with windows at each end and a door to the deck overlooking the courtyard, and the architectural offices of *Pollock and Rucker.*

For drawing boards we purchased four standard hollow core doors and supported them against the wall on diagonal 2x4's. The boards were covered with white linoleum and equipped with four black parallels, architectural swing lamps, and electric erasers. Dwight brought a standard desk from home and three chairs for our client meeting room just off the front entry. Outside, and along the courtyard deck was a public bathroom available with tenant's key.

We were deciding on stationary. I assumed it would be *Dwight Pollock and Douglas W. Rucker, Architect,* with our Pacific Palisades address and new telephone number, but that wasn't going to be.

HESS

*B*ob Hess appeared out of nowhere! Suddenly he was a fact with whom I had to deal. Bob looked undernourished physically and emotionally. He wore baggy trousers that slumped over worn shoes and a nylon shirt struggling to remain inside a poorly latched and dangling belt. A boyish 30, he wore glasses that slipped low on his nose that he continually had to shove up, probably due to a sweaty nose from chronic anxiety. He was not particularly attractive to women and I might call him the *perfect loser* for he seemed to have no imagination and little drafting ability. I don't think he was qualified to get a real job in the outside world; therefore he wanted to work for *us*. He would do anything to work with us! Give him a project and he'd work overtime! In fact, as part of a partnership, he'd work for us *free!* Aha! Dwight's magic word - *free!*

Bob was pathetic in many ways but a gentle young man. I liked him from a personal standpoint. He was honest to a fault and not in the least given to deception. To me, he was a mama's boy who'd studied piano for seven years and could read the pages of a score, but sadly only played noise. He had clean habits and was a teetotaler and a quiet and respectful lover of cute girls from afar. He had no friends and rarely left his apartment. For a while he slept on the office floor. Even though he was a sweet guy, I couldn't stand to have lunch with him. There was something about his lips fluttering in opposite directions while the spoon and fluid shakily entered his mouth that made me not want to know and not want to watch. I was always polite and careful never to offend him. Though I respected him as an associate and was flattered that I was highly regarded as a peer, it was never my intention to have him as a partner. I was never asked and had to question whether my own partnership with Dwight was ever really a valid one. Was I selected just to help Dwight accomplish his personal goals because I was naive enough to do so as a licensed architect?

Dwight got one of his lawyer friends to draw up an official looking document stating the three of us as legal architectural partners. Fate decreed the stationary read, *Pollock, Rucker and Hess, Architects.* I was the *"Architects."*

Our principal work consisted of doing free preliminaries for a multistoried apartment complex to be located on the Northeast corner of Pacific Coast Highway and Sunset Boulevard. We would be using the concrete lift slab method. Our client was Captain Wilson, the one who owned the Wilson Building and the one to whom we were indebted for rent. According to Dwight, he was the one who would *pay us later. Pollock, Rucker and Hess,* off to an inauspicious start!

DWIGHT

When he dressed casually, it was in tailored tan pants, an off white shirt with open collar, and dark leather shoes. Most of the time he wore a newly pressed suit that hung neatly from his lean body. With a clean shirt, starched collar with cuffs showing one half inch below his jacket, hair combed except for an uncontrollable colic, he gave the appearance of a boyish professional whose act was together. Dwight's voice was high and quiet and when he spoke I felt a personal connection with him. Sometimes he'd pose at a doorway or drafting table or walk confidently into the drafting room, appearing as a brash young architectural genius just in from the job.

There are classic tales of well-dressed architects that come to mind, Eugene G. Groves and Frank Lloyd Wright, being two. The theory is that if your person is attractive and well designed, well then so must be your buildings. Call it an idiosyncrasy, but somewhere in the past there is *the rule of the immaculate architect.* Dwight was an example of that rule.

My time at the Palisades office seems like a blur. It isn't as clear and graphic as I'd wish it to be. I remember coming to our rent-free office to work on the Wilson project and putting in a hard day making presentations of Dwight's plans, usually while he wasn't there. I did the preliminaries in ink and they looked rendered by a sincere amateur, which they were. Dwight would breeze in and Bob Hess and I, unable to wait would put down our pencils and feel privileged to delight in his stories that were told us with the flair and humor of an outlandish adventurer. We were as lost in our listening, as he was lost in his humorous telling. Dwight should have been a writer. He loved to meet people, build castles in the air, imagine highly engineered Pollock structures, and see himself as the wondrous source of their creation.

Numbers, formulas and geometric shapes fascinated Dwight and discussions of hyperbolic parabaloids, tent structures or catenary arches, captivated him. Sometimes in an engineering dream, pencil in hand, he'd draw diagrams before our eyes and prove them mathematically with equations and theories. Dwight, the instructor! Bob and I, the bumpkins! We were incapable of checking his work and were astounded at his engineering capabilities.

One time Captain Wilson came up with about $1,600.00 as a portion of a preliminary fee that should have been $20,000.00. We split it $700.00, $500.00, $400.00, Dwight getting the most and myself second most. To give the compensation perspective, consider that the rent in 1957 would have cost us about $200.00 a month or $2,400.00 a year. Our preliminary drawings were worth infinitely more. What was the problem?

Dwight loved engineering and good contemporary design and more than anything wanted to be the source of something brilliantly designed and lasting. He looked good, talked good, was an excellent salesman, a fine people person and easily capable of bringing clients to the proper enthusiasm to construct their building. The problem was, he couldn't get them to sign a contract and collect a retainer fee. He never presented them with a contract to legitimize the work. It seemed prospective clients would ask him to give them a contract and begged him to take a retainer fee and get their project going. But it seemed Dwight never had the contract ready and never made the appointment for signature. There was always something more important to do. Despite his great ability and the means in his two partners to deliver, he seemed to have an unconscious need to fail.

Bob and I sloshed around in an unorganized office, putzing around for five months doing free preliminary drawings, unable to control anything. I was not brought into any project as a principal because I didn't have the experience. I was not well enough informed. I had the license, but lacked the knowledge. Having done only six small houses - four of which I hadn't even supervised - was not enough to qualify me as an experienced architect, particularly one doing large commercial buildings. I would have been severely challenged doing commercial working drawings and Bob was learning from *me!* All we had was *the big guy* and due to some strange human failure he couldn't get the contract signed.

HOME LIFE

While I was trying to establish my first office in the Palisades with Bob and Dwight, home life was struggling. Our Amalfi house was acquired late in 1956, while the establishment of the Palisades office was about the beginning of 1957. At home I worked in my drafting room-bedroom while Karon used another as a sewing and art room. In the third, the master bedroom, we slept on a mattress on the floor. The rest of the house, the kitchen, dining and living room, had floor to ceiling glass doors overlooking Santa Monica Canyon. Our post-and-beam contemporary house was a joyful and exhilarating place to live, entertain, and be.

80 - Karon and new, used Plymouth convertible.

Karon's job at the UCLA Theater Arts Department was an absolute must. Her earnings were necessary to pick up the Pollock-Rucker-Hess firm's extra costs for printing bills, lunches and gasoline.

The used old Plymouth convertible was fun and cheap for Karon to run between Santa Monica Canyon and UCLA.

It wasn't long before Karon, as part of her curriculum, landed the part of Laura, the shy crippled girl in Tennessee William's, _The Glass Menagerie_. I worked at my board many long nights while she remained at UCLA for rehearsals late after class. Eventually she did the play and it was reviewed on March 12, 1957 by the Daily Bruin under the title, _"Bruin Reviewer Terms Play Solid Performance."_

---Karon Rucker as Laura excels in the same respect – that of building a unified personality for her character. She combines her throaty voice, nervous mannerisms, and face contortions, in pulling together the picture of a morbidly shy girl, holding herself inward, yet also possessing a hidden wealth of kindness, love and warmth.

   Miss Rucker must walk through the entire play with her foot twisted outward – the reason for her self-consciousness. This critic could almost feel her suffering with each painful step she took.

81 - Karon at the UCLA Kap and Bells Awards Banquet in
January 1957

And two days later under the title, _Stellar Performance,_ "Acting _honors for the production belong to Karon Rucker for her consistent and moving portrayal of the crippled daughter. For a young actress, Miss Rucker possesses admirable voice and body control, as well as obvious intelligence._"

I was proud of my young wife's abilities and admired her intellect, and that she could do so many different things so well.

On weekends we'd go to the beach and both being _water dogs_ take delight in the water. We loved to body surf at State Beach and walked down often to ride the waves. As in the old days, I soon became familiar with and could ride all the best breaks. I was usually seen the farthest out. I'd play in any kind of weather including heavy storm surf in which I'd frolic alone and carefree beyond the surf line in the muddy water like a visiting porpoise, occasionally riding a foamy breaker. Sometimes a strong current toward Venice that had scoured a channel ten feet deep just off shore carried me. When I finally caught a wave and was pounded shoreward a mile or so down the coast, I'd jog back along the beach and walk home. I was physically strong, had a great tan and with special fins, enjoyed myself to the fullest.

Karon seemed happy with her life, too. We were committed to each other, inseparable and alike as two peas in a pod. I worked around the house, put grass in the back yard and landscaped the front bank with landscape architect Eric Armstrong's advice, started trees in special places and designed a fence to separate the motor court from the private yard.

We got to know our neighbors better, too. Milt Black worked with Infinity Products, a firm that handled high-end electronic listening equipment. His wife, Mania, was a superb housewife who'd been a professional radio actress. She would frequently change into her squeaky voice, then into a low voice in comic conversation saying something completely ridiculous and getting a lively reaction from her kids. She was raising three children and had a fourth on the way. The oldest was a girl and the younger two were boys. An attractive couple, they were good neighbors, there when you needed them and not there when you preferred to be alone.

One day I got rid of Black Beauty and bought myself a two-year-old MG.

82 - Doug with MG.

I loved it with the top down and the pavement flashing inches away. Or wasn't it great, toodling the hills of Malibu checking out property or setting the brake before lunch in the parking lot at the Sea Lion Restaurant or getting out and hearing the door click as it was gently closed. Wasn't it nice listening to the rain on the light canvas rooftop? Didn't my clients love it? Wasn't I the hot-cat architect of Santa Monica Canyon and Malibu?

Surprisingly, our neighbors toward the ocean were an elderly couple whose children had grown. They were the *White's*.   Mr. White had been appointed by the Governor to be head of California Customs Service in San Pedro. His job was to police smuggling and illegal entry of banned goods into the United States. It was curious to say we lived on Amalfi Drive between the *Blacks* and the *Whites*. Were we gray?

I think that sometime in 1957 I began to build a little office extension to our separate carport at the rear of our lot. I dug the foundations, mixed concrete in a wheel barrow, poured the footings and a thin slab, left bolts sticking out for attaching the bottom plates, bought some two-by-fours and built the walls, posts, beams, 2x6 t & g roofing, left openings for windows, electrical for plugs and lights, etc., and slowly, over the period of a year, constructed a studio about eight feet wide by twenty feet long, separate from the house.

83 - Doug and Karon in my first constructed design.
Clay sculptures: Kneeling Woman and Black Goose by
Karon Rucker.

84 - Karon and Doug standing outside home studio and carport.

This place was a home architectural studio, a place separate from *our* Palisades office. I say *our* rather than *my* because I never felt the Palisade's office was mine. I worked on plans for a new home for Karon's parents, Duke and Lois Conan, on Poppy Peak Drive in Altadena. I had other projects of which I was dreaming and the home studio was built with enthusiasm, love and joyful sweat. I enjoyed having my own special place to think my own special thoughts and dream my own special dreams.

PALISADES OFFICE

Dwight, Bob and I limped along trying to get the Wilson Project to fly. It wouldn't, partially because the land at the corner of Sunset Boulevard and Pacific Coast Highway was not geologically stable. The land, though of the usually stable alluvial fill, was near Sunset Creek and underlain by a high water table. After geological studies, it was decided the footings would be required to go through the water table, perhaps sixty feet or more into the ground. This would mean that our two and three story buildings would not be economically feasible. An entirely new approach would be necessary. These projects take a lot of time to materialize because so many agencies and professionals must assess them and thoughtfully considered by architects and structural engineers. The architect's advice would be taken or discounted and the owner, with his usually limited funding, must take all that information and put it together and decide on an action. The Wilson Project hit the *slows*.

RUSSIAN HILL APARTMENT

Fortunately, Dwight dressed in his power clothes and trying to get the Wilson Project built, had met a few large contractors. One of them, C. L. Peck, offered him, and thereby offered Hess and me, a job in San Francisco. It was to be a thirteen-story building, high on the slope of Russian Hill. I knew nothing about the history behind Russian Hill, but I knew it *had* a history and that made the project seem romantic. There was a client also somewhere in the picture but I never knew who it was. Dwight made numerous trips to San Francisco and I got the feeling the client was more than one person. Perhaps it was committee. Dwight seemed to be dealing with the empowered spokesperson. It probably went something like this; Dwight would have to show the client what his office could do before the contract was signed. Since we didn't have an actual program, Dwight made one up. It would be a thirteen-story apartment complex with parking below and minor commercial on the first floor with apartment plans above. The preliminary would be a simple parking plan repeating plans of the apartments, and a luxurious penthouse.

Dwight made sketches. I made sketches. Bob diddled around with them until Dwight decided Dwight's were the best. Then I was to do a perspective drawing to show what the *Pollock, Rucker and Hess* firm could do.

Bob and I worked days, went home to eat, then returned to work until 10 PM at night, went home again to fall in bed for a few hours of sleep, then back to work the following morning. In about a month we had our free preliminary fairly well worked out. C. L. Peck's estimating contractor was in the office a good portion of the time following the progress of the preliminaries and talking to Dwight about the economy and his chosen lift-slab method of construction. Bob and I basked in glory of Dwight's making an important friend.

At one time Dwight was invited to a lavish party in Palm Springs where they did *I don't know what*, but the stories that Dwight told when he came back were entertaining, slightly prurient, and humorous. The immense cost of the party was far beyond our familiarity. It seemed to indicate Dwight was somehow accepted into the wealthier group and *that acceptance* we interpreted as a good sign. Perhaps we'd get the job, make a lot of money, become known for our good work, get hired again, then again, then again, until we had the money and it would be nothing for us to have a costly, prurient party, too.

I selected ink as my method of delineation. I did the plans and elevations and what I thought was a beautiful isometric view of the Russian Hill Apartment Complex. I finished early one Tuesday and went home for supper. Bob however was staying late almost every night and frequently sleeping there. I don't know what he did at night. I didn't ask. That night however he decided to *help me!*

When I came in the following morning excited to see my recently completed rendering, I was appalled to see Bob had made an infinite number of little ink dots all over the drawing. In doing working drawings, a few randomly placed dots are typically used to indicate the surface of concrete or exterior stucco. But on a rendering there was no need for an infinite number of little ink dots!

I turned white, then pink at the imposition, as my blood pressure went through the roof! How could Bob work on *my* rendering? I asked Bob. He said his intention was to *improve it,* but agreed it didn't look so good. Dwight saw it, agreed with me, and we spent the rest of the day with our electric erasers trying to remove the dots without destroying the surface of the paper.

Looking back, Bob was just trying to put himself into the project. If the dots on the major work had been accepted, it would show we all had had a part in the work. Bob would be one of the principal creators.

Dwight presented the drawings in San Francisco, to much success as he related it. He then called in a lawyer friend to have a contract drawn between the Owner and the Architect. The lawyer made up the contract and Dwight presented it, but changes were needed and weeks passed. Meetings were held between C. L. Peck's estimator and Dwight, and trips to San Francisco were repeated, and so on. Things took so long, or the owner was not convinced, or not motivated, or our design was not cost effective, or the job was the contractor's idea anyway and we were the vehicles to deliver cheaper plans. God only knows why they didn't proceed with the work, but the Russian Hill project hit the *slows.*

JOHNSON JOB

In the meantime, I had a job referred to me. It was to be a new house in Sweetwater Mesa for a couple with two children I'll call Mr. and Mrs. Johnson. I was delighted when I visited the owners and they seemed real. I told Dwight I wanted to do the job myself because I'd found the job. Dwight had to agree.

If I sound like I was together at this time, I can remind you I wasn't. I was extremely shy. I was smoking to find my manhood. I was new to coffee and caffeine and still hadn't taken a drink of alcohol because I was a bit of a prude and my purer habit patterns were still in place. I continued to be socially inadequate and had no real architectural experience, hence the reason I teamed up with an older, take charge partner, Dwight. He would be a kind of *big daddy* to run to if things went wrong.

I met with the Johnson's who gave me a $500.00 preliminary retainer with contract to come later and I made an attempt at their program. They had an incomplete survey that forced me to assume certain facts that may or may not have been true. I made designs in the post-and-beam style. The property was about an acre, the most of which was down a steep hill toward Pacific Coast Highway and unbuildable. The buildable pad was a semi-flat area about a hundred feet above sea level, looking south and west over Sweetwater Canyon, Malibu Pier, Surf Rider Beach, Catalina Island and Palos Verdes. A pretty heady site! My designs were in a U-shape, garage, two bedrooms and baths along the easterly side *(remember, the ocean is south in Malibu)* kitchen, dining and living along the south, and master bedroom and bath along the west with a landscaped atrium inside the *"U."*

The budget was low for the job, or the job was too big for the budget!

Lesson 1. An Owner can write a program too big for his budget!

Being *immature* and being *amateur,* I was anxious and spent too much time on the design. I struggled and fought and worried to get the square footage low enough to meet the expected cost. This resulted in a long, skinny, U-shaped house, too costly because of its extended perimeter, despite the sufficiently low square footage.

Lesson 2. Square footage is not the only determinate of the cost. The shape counts, too.

I took the design back to the Johnson's whom I thought were a nice rational couple and explained the problems. They seemed optimistic about the design, but worried about the cost. We left it that I would go back to the drawing boards and see if I couldn't design something to meet their requirements and stay within their budget. In other words, design a big house for a small budget. I said I'd try. I didn't know I was about to attempt the impossible. I went back to the office and struggled and worried and had fits and huffed and puffed and arranged and calculated square footages and could *still* not get the plans and budget to work. I had made a few insignificant changes and in a spirit of frustration invited senior partner, Dwight, to attend the next meeting with me.

PANIC ATTACK

*W*e met in the Johnson's Malibu apartment overlooking the ocean and Pacific Coast Highway. Dwight dressed in suit and tie, looked his immaculate best and I made an attempt at power dressing. I wore an open collared shirt and tan blazer. We walked up the stairs. *I was an Architect with a capital A.* I assumed the personality of one supposed to be an expert in the matter. We sat down in their living room and talked. Dwight had the most to say. I don't know what he talked about. I was too self-conscious. They and I smoked cigarettes and I consumed coffee. Soon I became so high on drugs and began to have a panic attack. I didn't know what a panic attack was in 1957, but I thought I was going to die! Panic attacks were not as known by the public in 1957. My face flushed, my hands were cold, my heart beat out of control, and my head felt like it belonged to somebody else. I tried to get hold of myself and the more I tried the worse it got. I don't know how I appeared, but uppermost was that I must get out of this place, now! I didn't care about the job, or Dwight, or being polite, or being debonair, it was time to *leave!*

The meeting dragged on while I thought I was going to die and an eternity later, to my immense relief, we walked out the door into the fresh night, into a light breeze with the friendly, gentle stars overhead. I drove home not knowing how to feel. Glad to be out of their house, glad not to be fighting with my designs, glad to avoid impossible cost problems, embarrassed that I didn't know what advice to give, unhappy I was unable to draw from experience.

I fell fitfully to sleep late that night. I don't know what Karon thought. Karon was tired of donating her hard-earned cash to the architecture business, tired of me contributing little or no income, unenthusiastic about Dwight or his practices, disenchanted with Bob Hess, and tired of the whole architectural try for independence. Anyway, I didn't care, and put it behind me for the night.

DWIGHT'S PLANS

The following day I was at the board, frustrated and going around in circles with designs I'd made endlessly before and thoroughly disgusted with myself. I couldn't make the elements come together. Dwight then grabbed my site plan and said, *"Here! Give me those drawings! I'll see what I can do!"*

I allowed him to take the drawings feeling a lost sense of hope. My friend had stolen my baby. Discouraged that it had come to this, I let him take the drawings with unmanageable jealousy sitting in my craw. With knowledge that his greater experience would produce the better design, rage rose up inside me. He had stolen my heart. Yet I let him sit there and work on *my* job.

I diddled around with bad memories of my own designs and fumed while Dwight's pencil moved swiftly across the sketch paper. His focus was clear. His touch was sure. His ideas were dominant. After three interminable afternoon hours he called me to his board to see his design.

It was stunning!

Instead of a rectangular house with an atrium, he'd chosen a semi-circular plan. It had a radius point! Instead of a U-shape, he'd invented a house in a series of harmonious curves swirling dramatically across the land. I was reminded of Frank Lloyd Wright, and was blown away by the beauty of conception. It hurt me that he'd done a better job in a few hours than that which had taken me weeks resulting in a lesser work. With a modest effort, he proved he was the more talented designer. I *was disillusioned. I gained maturity.*

However he had neglected to solve the cost problem. The budget evidently hadn't entered his mind either. Certainly, to build his curves was more costly than to build straight lines. I took heart that his design didn't work either. In any case it all turned out academic. The Johnson's called and told us their plans were changed indefinitely and they would *not* be proceeding with the job.

MAJOR DECISION

We lost the job, but I was faced with a philosophic question: *Should I create a building of lesser design,* which would be mine, *or should I give my job to a better designer, thus creating a better building for the world that would be his?*

I would always be able to find a better designer, one with more experience, one who was smarter, one who had more talent than I. Shouldn't I seek out that person and give him my job so ultimately the world would enjoy a better design?

Taking the chance I was not overly self-centered or ego-involved, and deciding I had something to offer the world, even if not equal to the award winners, I decided that hereafter I would design my work myself. Designers in drafting services were not as talented as I. If better designers were available, certainly worse ones were, too.

Lesson 3: It is better to create my own designs, though of possible poorer quality, than give them to a better designer and possibly create better quality. I opted for possibly *worse* designs, but *mine!*

LEAVING DWIGHT AND BOB

While this strangeness was going on, I had to decide whether it was ultimately to my advantage, and ultimately to Karon's advantage, to stay with the partnership. Considering breaking up meant I had to legally dissolve our partnership, make no claims on any of the future work that always seemed hanging around the edges, and to get myself removed from claims the partnership would have on me. These claims would be for past blueprint bills, telephone bills, supply bills and miscellaneous bills made out to the firm.

Karon made it very clear she was tired of her hard-earned money going to pay bills incurred by what appeared to be a group of architectural slackers. She begged me to get out, and though I wanted to leave, I did not want to be traveling the drafting circuit again looking for drafting work with another architect. I'd had my license for four years, had done a few houses on my own, including my own house, and had worked for a year in a partnership that had depended on me as a licensed person. In my mind, it was unthinkable for me to go to work for anyone else. I'd had a taste of freedom. I liked working for myself, seeing the results of my own labors, tasting my personal rewards for whatever they were.

One day, while drafting, I heard the telephone ring and went in the front office to answer it. The person asked for Dwight. Dwight rushed in making desperate hand-signals at the door and whispering, *"Tell whoever it is, I'm not in!"* Now considering my puritanical background, and considering I had never to this day spoken a swear word, had never tasted a glass of anything with alcohol in it, had never lied, *(cheating on the final math test in 1946 had stopped any mild latent desire to take the easy way)* and considering I had not shaken off my seemingly innate naiveté, anger surged from my stomach to my eyeballs.

In an instant I thought, *"Who was Dwight to think I would lie for him? If I'm going to lie, I will lie for a million dollars, or for something worthwhile. What's the advantage in lying for Dwight? I'd be assisting an irresponsible person to remain so. I would be selling myself down the river so another would not have to face the difficult situation his actions had caused. Not only would I not be getting a million dollars, but I'd be lying for someone to whom I'd been developing a year long disrespect and one who'd made me mortally jealous by surpassing me in a design on my own job?"* Then the instant was over.

I told the person, *"Hold on, he's right here!"* and thrust the phone into Dwight's advancing form. I was brave!

This incident was the turning point. Thereafter, I was convinced the partnership was not working and I was forced to acknowledge that continuing it would be like beating the proverbial dead horse with a stick. The love affair was over.

I sent out my legal documents and wrote my legal letters to our creditors saying that after a certain date I would no longer be responsible for payment. I then retired to my home and to my well designed, 8-foot x 20-foot, unheated studio off the carport to delve into new thoughts.

MONTENIDO

THE WORLD TURNS

Since our June 1953 marriage the world continued to evolve without us. In 1955 Rosa Parks refused to relinquish her bus seat to a white man. Marian Anderson became the first black to sing at the Metropolitan Opera house. The labor unions AFL and CIO merged. Rock and Roll exploded around the clock. Jack Kerouac and Allen Ginsberg became leaders of the beat generation. Albert Einstein and James Dean died at 76 and 24. McDonald's fast food leaped into existence. Jonas K. Salk introduced his polio vaccine to the public to save millions and Disneyland wowed the kids by opening in Anaheim. There were of course other world-shaking events.

In 1956 Dwight D. Eisenhower was elected president. Nikita Khrushchev publicly condemned Joseph Stalin. Prince Rainier of Monaco married Grace Kelly and the unsinkable ship, the Andrea Doria, sank in 12-hours. The scandalous book, Peyton Place, sold 60,000 copies in 10 days. My Fair Lady was first staged while Charleton Heston starred in *The Ten Commandments*. H.L. Mencken, A.A. Milne, Fred Allen, Bertold Brecht and Tommy Dorsey died.

In 1957 I was partially shocked to learn the Russians beat us into space by launching Sputnik and was only somewhat aware that actor Humphrey Bogart, Louis B. Mayer, and Oliver Hardy had died. *Baby Boomers* reached 4.3 million, the most in thirty years. I remained unconcerned. It dimly reached my consciousness that cartoonist Dr. Suess published *The Cat in the Hat,* but one thing I did know was that Ayn Rand had published _Atlas Shrugged,_ because I'd read it. We had no television, but apparently the _Perry Mason_ show and _Leave it to Beaver_ were newly popular. Most important to me was the availability of the water-cooled, high-speed dental drill.

FIRE

The Santana began a day before the Malibu Fire. A Santana is a contraction of the words _Santa_ and _Ana,_ so called because of the strong offshore winds blowing from the northeast direction of Santa Ana. The air gets dry, the ocean turns purple, the winds bend the trees and rattle the bushes, and garbage cans blow over, paper and trash scurries across the road and down the sidewalks. During a Santana wind I can't manage my hair, find myself on edge, cranky and unable to sleep because of the wind and abundance of positive ions in the air. Though our house was usually in no danger, the Santana is relentless, and I experience the atmospheric conditions as a crisis. During Santana time the radio newscasters were reporting an out-of-control brush fire burning what we understood to be all of Malibu. _Malibu was burning down!_

At a fiery red sundown, Karon and I joined other curious persons and visited Santa Monica Bluff Park overlooking Santa Monica Bay with a good view of the Malibu Mountains. In the whispered silence we leaned on the protective railing and in the distance, perhaps ten to fifteen miles away, tan and black smoke, thousands of feet high blowing out to sea filled the entire western sky. The sun, about to set, forced an eerie glow through the clouds that tinted the whole landscape red. As night fell, yellow flames, in contrast to the velvet-black mountains, burned along the slopes devouring and usurping all living things, brush, wildlife, people, and homes. The ugly-beautiful fire could be seen dancing along the ridges, and creeping down the mountainsides flaring frequently a hundred feet high. We went home to bed and the following day continued our business. In perhaps a week the fire burned itself out. The Fire Department and residents did what they could. There was loss of homes, despair, crying, tragedy, and later, terrible mudslides and new beginnings. This was our first introduction to Malibu fires.

KARON'S ACTIVITIES

Karon was finishing her work for her Master's degree in Theater Arts at UCLA. Among other courses, she had a one-semester course covering the subjects of lighting, sound, costume design; stage set design, and props. These courses were brought to life for the students in the form of many one-act plays written by students and given often during the year. Students majoring in acting courses did all acting. Karon was studying behind-the-scene work, though at times she appeared on stage for her fellow student's plays.

One lesson that has stayed with me over the years and that I have tried to apply in my own architectural business goes like this: In attending student's original one-act plays at UCLA, the audience was usually given a little slip of paper asking five or more questions about what they had observed. *Was the lighting effective? Could sound affects be easily heard? What criticism would we have of the set design? Did the costumes add or detract from the action?* But the particular question that has stayed with me is, *"Was the story line clear to you?"*

I have often asked others and myself about a motion picture, or play, *"Was the story line clear?"* When looking at a complicated building and trying to reason it out I would often ask myself, *"Is the architect's story line clear?"* If I were reading a book or story, I could ask myself the same question. I have been able to ask that question about most things I think are difficult, or complex, or complicated, or problematic for anyone to figure out. If the story line is not clear, whether in architecture, plays, books, stories, compositions, movies, landscaping, philosophy, psychology, dreams, family life, existence of the universe, I can always ask myself, *"Is the story line clear?"* Of course if it is not clear the fault usually lies with the creator. Since in my working life I'm the creator, I always try to keep my own story clear. When I am practicing architecture, then, I ask myself *"Is my architectural story line clear?"*

But more about Karon's work. Her set designs were ingenious. Sets, each side of which depicted a different scene, swung on pin-hinges located at the bottom-center of the walls. Low, raised, circular platforms housed three scenes as they were manually rotated for each set change. Sets descended out of the fly space and became trees or ladders or the side of a house. During Karon's 3-act play there was trouble with the curtain. It would not close and the audience observed sets swung around, flipped over, scooted to the center, and dropping from the sky, another disappearing and the other appearing like a mechanical clock. In five seconds the new look was brilliantly in place! The excitement was in how it all came together and applause for this magical set-change came spontaneously from a delighted audience. Unfortunately, showing this achievement was so intriguing it broke the play's continuity, a Cardinal sin. Though it was never done, a working curtain should have been drawn to conceal the magnificent set change. Other students were rarely able to repeat Karon's ingenuity.

Karon

I was at home and watched her design these sets. She used my drafting table. I too, was amazed and admired Karon's intellectual and creative ability to think through such difficult problems. Her spunk to try them out worked superbly.

One time she was given a small part as a foreign princess in a sumptuous children's show given in Royce Hall called, *The Adventures of Marco Polo*. Her Japanese friend whose name I've momentarily forgotten played Sulu in the original series called *Star Trek*. The Royce Hall show with its beautiful sets, lights and costumes created entirely by students, looked professionally mounted and made a stunning production.

Karon made one special friend who was studying stage lighting in the Theater Arts Department at UCLA named Tom Pincu. Tom and Linda, his wife, became good friends of ours and have remained good friends of mine until this very day.

1957

During 1957 I was working hard on my business and Karon was working full time at UCLA and taking graduate courses in Theater Arts on her lunch hour. We hadn't time for much else. On weekends we went to plays at UCLA, to art exhibits at UCLA, or the County Art Museum. Occasionally we went on an excursion down the picturesque one-way-street, Pacific Avenue, in Venice with Ricky Volkman, or attended our favorite movie theater, the Aero, on Montana Avenue in Santa Monica. The Aero had double features for a dollar fifty. Sometimes we had dinner with Karon's friend, David Rhiel, or Tom Pincu would come over for dinner, or we entertained or were entertained by Karon's close girlfriend Ina Nuell.

We loved the sun and beach and simple pleasures, but we were in the career-building phase of our lives and we also loved to work.

86 - Ina Nuell, Lois Conan (Karon's mother) Evelyn Rucker
(my mother)

WHAT TO DO NEXT

I heard from Frank Young at Gilman's office that the well-known designer, Cliff May, frequently farmed out work to various needy architects. I went to see Cliff who was elsewhere, but I was able to talk to his next in command who informed me that Dick Irwin, the draftsman who used to work for the Gilman firm, was in charge of drawing a large residential job. The job was for one of Cliff's clients named Brown and the house was to be near New Orleans, Louisiana. I said I knew Dick and would talk to him.

I contacted Dick by phone and he was indeed beginning the working drawings on a 10,000 square foot Cliff May style ranch house outside New Orleans. It was probable he would need help.

IRWIN

Dick Irwin had a wife and son about eight or nine. They lived in a small, partly finished house of Dick's design close to a blue-line creek in Monte Nido. Monte Nido is a small wooded community about 4-miles inland from the Ocean over Malibu Canyon Road. A blue line-creek is a watercourse designated by the Los Angeles County Flood Control Department as a creek that runs intermittently and handles storm-water run-off from larger watersheds. This one appeared to be a permanently running creek for most of the year requiring special setbacks.

In the carport was a small expensive Italian sports car, although the expense of the car was *not* an indication of the Irwin couple's wealth. The Irwin family lived on the financial edge. *Dick owned only one sweater, Italian and expensive, and seemed to own only one of the essentials of his life, but that one thing was artistic, expensive and impressive.* This was one of the keystones of his life's philosophy.

The small 2-bedroom house was in the post-and-beam style and had a refinement of detail. It was an outstanding concept. A glass living room, with a flat, natural wood ceiling, cantilevered between massive boulders and willow trees, out and partially over the rippling waters of the creek. Through one of the glass walls projected a five or six foot sandstone boulder to the side of which was attached a contemporary metal fireplace with a flat-black metal flue piercing a square skylight above. Low seating was comfortably arranged around the fireplace and sitting there I could see up, down or across the shaded creek. The sunken living room, that faced north, was nevertheless, cheery and delightful by reflected light from broad Sycamore leaves. On the upper level was a kitchen and across the wide hall an eating area next to a window overlooking the stream. Two sleeping areas and a bath were at the hall's end. Dick had set up drafting tables facing each other in the wide hall eating space with a fine northerly view of the wooded creek.

I have spoken of Dick's excellent drafting ability. I was to sit facing him while we both drafted on the Brown job. Dick called it, *The Big Brown Job*, a funny and crude connotation that he humorously intended.

I thought each sheet of his drafting was a frameable work of art and this house, this environment for living, was inspiring and delightful in it's simplicity. It was, as I would have expected it to be once having seen the beauty of his design and drafting. If a house looks simple, it usually isn't simple to build. *To produce a work worthy of being called architecture, takes more thought, is harder to build, and costs more.* I always hoped this was not so.

On the Brown job it was agreed the drafting should look the same and as if completed by a single mind, a single architect, a single draftsman, and a single bright person in charge. It was to be graphic and legible to make it easier for contractors to read. I would have to learn to copy Dick's style of drafting. How fortunate for me. When he was out, which was frequent, I would get to pour over his drawings. When he was there, I could watch him draw in his personal style.

In light of his drafting, two things surprised me. (1) When *he lettered notes on the drawings, he eyeballed two perfectly straight, fine, dark, printable lines, one above the other, as lettering guides, and when he lettered, he did so very slowly and deliberately so that each line carried the same dark, fine weight and each letter stopped precisely at the top or bottom of the guide lines. He proportioned his notes so they were well scaled to the drawings and left enough room around them so they wouldn't be confused with the graphics. (2) When he drew long lines to indicate dimensions or floor plan lines, he went over them at least twice in the same direction. If the lines were still not suitable, he'd go over them again and again, loving them and caring for them until they were to his liking, then brushing away the excess graphite. When his work was perfect, he'd sit back on his stool relaxing and examining his work and inhale his cigarette, (He was a chain smoker.) focusing attention on the drawings, before he'd start the next line.* I've made drawings so dirty I could hardly see the lines. The lettering was lost in the smudges. It printed a big blob!

Dick was not in to changing pencils after each line and he used no mechanical pencil but a plain *"F"* pencil for everything. I would have thought going over each line and being so patient with his lettering and sheet composition would have slowed his speed. Perhaps it did, but probably not much and certainly not over ten percent. I learned *time is lost because the draftsman doesn't know what he's doing, not because he uses time to make his drawing pretty. The fastest draftsmen are the knowledgeable draftsmen.*

At any rate, working with Dick was a chance to improve my drafting. I made a sincere effort and by the end of the job the whole work looked remarkably like one person had completed it.

SINCERE EFFORT

*W*orking with Dick on Cliff May's farm-out work I was earning four dollars an hour and I must have spent two months working in the inspiring, calm and intimate atmosphere of Irwin's house. During this time I was very regular. I got there sharply at eight and left at four-thirty with a half hour for lunch. Dick, however, was not so prompt or so meticulous about his work schedule. He frequently slept too long in the morning and had places to go in the afternoon. He seemed to have an arbitrary philosophy about work, particularly since I could assure the Brown Job would be completed. I have no idea what he put down for his hourly time on the drawings and it was none of my business. Let's just say I found myself doing, perhaps, significantly more than half the working drawings. This was good because it allowed me to put in more time and earn more money and delay the unpleasantness of my next step, finding my own work.

Within two months the job came to an end. Dick seemed to have minor work cropping up in the wings. He was doing one of his special designs for a rich person in Redondo Beach. I saw some of the designs and they looked terrific. Of course his draftsmanship was so good, he could have made bad designs look terrific. I don't think that was the case. The designs looked good, too, and I think the new client knew the fine quality of work he was getting.

Dick's special relationship with this client seemed more of a friendship in that his client would take him *(and perhaps his wife, too)* to Las Vegas for the weekend, or take them sailing to Ensenada, or spend time with him after a presentation at a bar in some fancy hotel to stay overnight. Let's face it. Dick and I led different lives. As I understood it then, he seemed to play while broke, while I was desperate and broke. We had one thing in common. We were both broke.

DREAMS OF MALIBU

Prior to our deciding to make the Santa Monica Bay Area our home Karon and I made a conscious effort to find a place we wanted to live and work. We made a trip in Black Beauty all the way to San Francisco and checked each major city near the beach all the way to San Diego. We looked over San Francisco, Santa Cruz, Monterey, Carmel, San Luis Obisbo, Santa Barbara, Ventura, Malibu, and Los Angeles Bay area, Newport Beach, San Clemente, Oceanside and San Diego. After examining all the communities, we decided to live and work as near to Malibu as was possible. Malibu was our choice and not far from Santa Monica Canyon.

We felt the large city of L. A. would, as time went by, expand northerly up the coast into Malibu and it would be a good place to practice architecture. Malibu was close to the sophistication of a big city. It was ripe with unbuilt lots. There were no tracts planned, and I didn't do tracts anyway. It had a romantic history. It was known throughout the world. We both loved the beach and nurtured the idea that one day we might be sailors. In the meantime I wishfully dreamed of getting a small rowboat and dropping a fishing line in the calm kelp beds of Coral Beach, much like I had in La Porte, Indiana. Malibu beach was body surfing country. That appealed to us.

MALIBU OFFICE

Two-thirds through 1957 Dick had a notion he would like to open his own office in Malibu and asked me if I wanted to share. I thought it a great idea. I hadn't the foggiest idea of what I was going to do after the Cliff May job ended. Perhaps if we opened an office together I could try real hard to get work. If Dick had work he seemed willing to pay me to do some drafting. Of course he could do drafting for me, too, if ever I were lucky enough to find my own jobs. I was at present *lost as a sweet babe in the woods*, going on desire, not knowing what else to do, going on guts, going to avoid the unpleasantness of working for other architects. I was doing what came next. Or I was *reacting* to what came next, or, in fairness to myself, both, *reacting* and *acting* on what came next. We agreed to try to find and share an office to do our separate work.

The following week Dick came up with an office in a partially completed two story building on the beach for $160.00 per month. It was over the Chris Craft building. *(Now the Tide Pool Gallery.)* *"Wow! An office on the beach in Malibu!"* Being in Malibu fit with Karon's and my planned discussions about where we wanted to live and work. We were on course! I was excited about the place and talked with Karon and we both decided I should throw in with Dick and see where fortune took us. I scraped up $80.00 for my share of one month's rent from the Cliff May job, as probably Dick did, and we gave it to the man.

CHRIS CRAFT BUILDING

Maureen O'Sullivan and her husband, whose name, with apology, I have forgotten, owned the Chris Craft Building. Maureen O'Sullivan made her name in the motion pictures playing Jane opposite Johnny Weismuller's, Tarzan. I never met Maureen or her husband but instead did business with a likable, short, skinny, gray haired chap, who wore a captain's hat. He was called Cap and for all intents and purposes, he was our landlord.

The yard in front of the small two-story structure was filled with a transient display of 3 to 6 large powerboats of all makes. They were of all sizes up to thirty feet long, mounted on movable trailers or wooden frames. Most were new but a few, used. Cap was a congenial fellow about seventy who sat in the office or walked in the yard, or showed brochures, or talked prices and financing at his desk with prospects. We immediately became friends and our rent helped pay Cap's rent.

The space wasn't much for $160.00. Once upstairs, we entered a foyer, which wasn't large enough to hold more than a desk and a little storage. The space was too light. The large window facing up the coast lit too small a space. Through a door and behind the foyer was a larger office about 10 feet x 14-feet. It was too dark. It may have had a window toward the rear. I don't remember.

In the larger office, we set up our two drafting tables made from hollow core Masonite doors carried on 2 X 4 frames and covered them with white linoleum as the drawing surface. On the tables, as before, we clipped black swinging drafting lights. Our layout tables were similar without the linoleum and mounted lower for ease of layout and viewing. We installed our parallels and had gray plastic silverware dividers to organize our drafting equipment such as erasers, pencils, scales, lead, and compasses. Our triangles and electric erasers rested on our tables. We got concrete blocks and ten-foot white pine boards and made ourselves bookcases to organize architectural brochures and magazines. We loosely filled a four-drawer filing cabinet and had a telephone installed. I think the number was EX 6-8519. *"Voila!"* *We're* in business!

87 - Karon in front of the Chris Craft building designed by John Lautner and owned by Maureen O'Sullivan.

(As I later found out, an architect, (then a designer) had designed the building by the name of John Lautner. If you are unfamiliar with this name, John had worked with Frank Lloyd Wright until he decided to go into business for himself. When he did, his work was highly publicized in major periodicals. One of his most popular works, then, was a crazily designed Hollywood fast food restaurant named, "Googie's." He became quite famous as one who did expensive, outlandish and daring forms for his residential client's. (Did Maureen O'Sullivan and her husband commission him? Why was the building left unfinished?)

WHERE'S THE WORK?

Bill Scott sailing his catamaran off the Malibu coast.

Karon and I had been invited by Bill and Terri to enjoy the beach next to his apartment building. Bill was a carpenter-contractor who also built and sailed Malibu catamarans. He and Terri had been able to pick up a couple of zoned R-4 beach lots, and with the lending institution and their own efforts, built themselves two four unit apartment buildings on the beach. Now living in one of the units, the remaining apartments modestly supported them. They had no children and since they had come to Malibu in the early 50's, were socially active and seemed to be friends with everyone.

Bill suggested I join the Chamber of Commerce to meet people and to see Reeves and Eileen Templeman who owned the Malibu Times. Perhaps Reeves would run an article about my new business. He advised me on the meetings and activities of the Malibu Township Council. In fact there was a meeting on one current affair or other at Webster School next Friday. Why didn't I attend? He would go with me!

Then I'd return to the office and answer another call or two for Dick. There weren't many answering machines in those days and we couldn't afford to pay the just started Day & Nite Answering Service in Malibu. Answering the telephone for Dick became annoying and reminded me I had *no* work and Dick *did*. I was a *failure* and Dick was a *success*. I had *failed* in an office with Dwight. Now I'd *fail* while *Dick* was watching.

As the month was coming to a close, the unimaginable happened! Dick informed me he was pulling out of the office. He was sorry he wouldn't be able to share the rent, but that's the way things were. He no longer needed the Malibu office. I was left to reason it out. Either he didn't have the rent money, or decided he had a perfectly good place to work at home, or had discovered it was hard to pick up architectural work, especially if he wasn't licensed. Maybe he picked up a good job and didn't want to share it and decided to do it at home. I couldn't reason it out. I just took it as a personal setback fearing for the loss of my beloved new Malibu office. I was upset at having to tell Karon and worrying about the demise of our well-laid plans. I couldn't afford $160.00 a month. What was I going to do?

WHAT I DID

I told Cap the story. I didn't want to move. I'd try to find someone to share the office. I couldn't pay him the full $160.00 a month. Surprisingly, he was more amicable than I'd expected and agreed to accept my $80.00 on the condition I find someone else to share the office and pay the additional amount. I was delighted! During the second month I began to look in to Bill Scott's suggestions. I hung out my *shingle*. A redwood board with some plaster letters in the modern Arial Style spelling out, *Douglas W. Rucker - architect*. I used the small "*a*" for architect because I thought it was more *designee* and modest appearing. I would be a *modest* architect.

Then I came to know I had to look in the phone book and contact every contractor in Malibu, Santa Monica, Pacific Palisades, West Los Angeles and Brentwood. I called some of them and discovered they were no longer at that location, or they worked days and wouldn't be in, or they were there but didn't need any drawings right now. I made personal trips to Santa Monica and Brentwood and dropped in on the contractors to see what their offices were like. I spent all day alone in the car. Sometimes I'd pull under the shade of a Brentwood tree to eat grocery store food while I looked up my next prospect. Nothing was happening! No man! Nothing was happening,

89 - Doug and Dad beneath my new "shingle." It said, Douglas W. Rucker, architect. (No capitalization for architect.)

IRWIN AGAIN

Irwin came by and wanted to go for a walk. I said, *"What's up?"* We went downstairs and started walking on the sidewalk on the ocean side of Pacific Coast Highway toward Santa Monica in the shade of the apartments. He wanted to resume sharing the office with me during the coming month. To me this was a shock. I'd spent a month in mourning, watching my plans for the future going down in flames. I felt caught flat-footed. My head spun. *I asked myself how serious he was. I thought it over quickly. My inner self knew the answer. My outer self had trouble saying it.* Finally I said it was my preference to keep the office for myself - alone.

He seemed surprised and didn't say much. I expected he wanted me to explain myself. I expected him to explain why he wanted to return. He offered no reason except he'd decided to. He may have known he was in a difficult position with me because of leaving me in the lurch. He'd run out on the second months rent. I wanted to tell him how hurt I was that he'd moved out after the first month, but couldn't find the courage. I said I'd become used to being by myself. He probably inferred, *"Doug thinks I'll run out on him again"* Of course that's exactly what I was thinking. The rest of the walk was particularly uncomfortable for me and I'm sure for Dick as well. I'd made a stand. Dick didn't argue or reason or complain or object. I was left thinking he probably had no reason to want the office and would leave again for no reason. I guess we returned to the office and he went away, presumably disappointed.

I suffered from a guilty conscience. After all, Dick had found the office in the first place. How could I be such a cad as to refuse his return? I suffered for a long time. In fact I still suffer about it. It was not a kind thing a nice guy would have done. My actions were surprising to me. I only rest on the knowledge of Dick's character. Dick was not one to be steady. He seemed restless and moved around. Evidently he was talented enough to do so. As far as I could see his schedule was arbitrary, and I'd never seen him make a plan and stick to it. I didn't like to take his telephone messages. I still feel I did the right thing. I didn't see much of him after that. I don't know what his life story was after we split up. We each carry our burdens.

MRS. GORDON McCREA

I dropped in every real estate office between Topanga and Heathercliff Road and told them I was in business and to let me know if they had any work. I dropped in at the Building Department in Malibu and checked it out. If I was lucky, I might get to go in there for business reasons. I cruised the streets, the Point, the Retreat, the Knolls, Morning View Drive, Piuma, Monte Nido and other Malibu areas.

I met and spent time with Mrs. Gordon McCray, a short, stout woman of about 62 who strolled her property with tennis shoes, denim pants and windblown gray hair under a floppy hat. She owned

40 acres at the upper end of Las Flores Drive that was for sale. We walked the property together and talked about her plans. I gave her the notion that I, myself, was looking for just such a property, but at this time didn't have the money and hinted that if she'd just give me a part of it, she could consider herself a principal aid to the less fortunate. I fantasized perhaps she would consider me the bright, young, career-building son she never had, that being so, maybe in the future I could do something for her. I kidded myself for while she might be my benefactress, alas, she was spending time with a young architect hoping I would know someone who might buy *her* property. I was familiarizing myself with Malibu.

Three quarters of the month was over and another $80.00 would be due for the rent. I also had normal household bills including a mortgage, car payments, gas and oil, insurance and taxes. Thank the stars for Karon who had a steady job. If it had not been for her income, I couldn't have considered an office of my own. What more could I do to get started? I was acting on some kind of plan, but was continually worried and anxious

KOCH

Before the month was over I got a call from a contractor named Bruce Koch and he presented me with my first architectural job. He asked if he could come up. I said sure. I don't know where he got my name. It is probable that Bill Scott told him about me or Bill's brother-in-law, another contractor I knew, might have told him about me. Maybe he saw my shingle. I put vellum and eraser crumbs on my drafting table to look like I was busy.

Bruce was a gangly guy with light work pants and work boots, flannel shirt and a mass of dishwater blond dusty hair dangling off to one side. He looked dusty and lurched around, finally sitting down, and spoke with a nasal twang. He'd been a plastering contractor *(even then he looked like he'd just come off a plastering job)* and was getting into general contracting. He had a set of plans for a spec house done by a drafting service. The permit was obtained and the foundations were in, but he was displeased with the exterior and wondered if I could fix it. He'd pay me three hundred dollars. That's all he could afford. I could take it or leave it. Of course I'd take it. I thought to myself, even if I couldn't fix it, I'd fix it! I thought, *"This job could pay a months rent."* I said, *"Sure!"* took his hundred fifty down payment and after seeing the site, started the drawings.

Bruce did the house. I made as many improvements as I could think of. I'm not thrilled with the overall design, but I'd taken an existing structure and done the best I knew under the circumstances. I was not displeased with it either. After 40 years the yellow stucco house with wood trim is still there. It looks the same. I never visited it after it was sold over forty years ago.

QUIROS

Cap came up with somebody! Mario Quiros, the newly arrived land surveyor, was looking for a small office. I liked Mario at once and was enthused to have him share the rent. We made a deal. Mario had received his education in Costa Rica that, by the way, is rated scholastically better than the United States. He had an excellent English vocabulary that he delivered in a Costa Rican accent. God was watching over me. Mario would take the little office up front, the one barely big enough for a desk, the one *light-shot* by the west sun blasting through the big window. He'd need a shade. He said he would put a phone in the office and use it as his Malibu address. He was gone every day anyway surveying jobs. Mario and his Spanish speaking helper set up a small drafting table in the bright light with a shade to produced drafting work. They operated in this tiny space for several months until changes were made.

KOCH AGAIN

After Koch got going with the new plans, we became friends. Bruce was doing Spec houses. He had four lots on the bluff overlooking the ocean and Malibu Cove Colony. *(The Cove Colony on the beach in 1959 had been subdivided, but there were only a few houses built.)* One of Bruce's houses had been completed and sold. He was now working on the second house and felt he should be getting started on the third. Did I want to do a new house overlooking the ocean? Boy, did I!

I thought to myself, *"I'll do it at any price"* and agreed on plans for the whole house at $600.00. Remember, prices for construction were very low late in 1957. Contractors were doing houses for about $10.00 a square foot. A house of 2,000 square feet would build for $20,000.00 and architects with a compensation of 10% would be getting $2,000.00 for a complete service. My philosophy was simple. *I had to keep my Malibu office open.* A builder didn't want a full service. *Hell, he knew details.* He just wanted a permit so he could get going. Bruce only wanted $600.00 worth. I gave it to him. I made a preliminary on a post-and-beam that Bruce accepted without comment and began the working drawings. It is probable that Bruce was so new and so naive about houses that he didn't know a good one from a bad one. Or it may have been possible that starting out and working on such good lots, he wanted something special. To me, this was a month's work. I thought to myself, *"Now I might even be able to pay for the third month's rent."* I began happily working away.

ROUSH HOUSE

*W*hile Bruce was working on his third property, he sold his fourth property to Mr. and Mrs. Roush. He was facilitating the sale and had talked me up to his buyers. I reasoned, if I give them a reasonable price, they would use me as their architect. The Roush's were an amiable elderly couple and we wrote a program for their house. They didn't want a house in the traditional style and I certainly didn't suggest one. My fee would be $800.00. I was whaling!

Their house was to be built right on the bluff, so close to the edge, the engineer who worked for Bruce and other builders in the area, designed the foundation on long, thin, 8-inch diameter concrete friction piers at eight feet on center. They were narrower than those of today. There was no Geology or Soils Division in the Building Department enforcing strict laws. Only good engineering practice governed. Above those piers were reinforced concrete grade beams and above those, posts and cross-braces supporting the one story building. A twelve-foot long cantilevered deck supported by tapered laminated beams projected seaward over the bluff. For Malibu it was quite daring.

SLIDE

One bright and early morning late in 1957 I slipped out of my carport in my new MG dressed for work in Malibu. I drove the remaining curves down Amalfi Drive to West Channel Road, turned right and pulled through easy traffic to Pacific Coast Highway. Having the light, I swung a wide right turn, heading up the coast, catching a glimpse of what I thought to be a policeman on the far side of the street. When I made the turn, I didn't think a policeman was peculiar. Thinking about the day ahead, I had been moving, jaunty-jolly, along the coast for a half-mile or so when, to my astonishment, Pacific Coast Highway vanished into a hillside! The pavement was cut of by a mountain.

I thought twice and hit the brakes. How could this be? The tail of the slope extended almost to the ocean and the sloping top, perhaps a hundred fifty yards long, was sixty feet in the air. A policeman came out of his car and waved me into a U-turn. I was forced to return the way I came.

I took the highway back to Chautauqua and came to work by the Sunset Boulevard route. I heard I'd run in to a big coast highway slide somewhat larger but similar to those that have plagued Malibu since the turn of the century. This one had buried a luckless worker who died inside his van before he could be reached. The slide had left a huge escarpment and it was months before Cal-Trans removed the tail of the dirt to construct what was thought to be a temporary highway. Paving was constructed around the ocean ward tip of the shortened slide and later Pacific Coast Highway itself was adjusted ocean ward to fit the more relaxed contours of the temporary route.

The press called this one the *Killer Slide* and generated many articles about their prevalence and the necessity of keeping Pacific Coast Highway continually open, especially for mass evacuation.

I won't forget my surprise at seeing the highway end abruptly against a mountain.

SELF-PROMOTION

I went to the Chamber meeting on the second floor of a building on Malibu Road near Webb Way. The one that used to be over the

California State Highway Patrol office unmistakable for it's series of overhanging arches and it's expanse of windows facing both ocean and mountains. There I was introduced to about 15 or 20 good old boys. It certainly was an organization to promote business and I was immediately selected for a committee.

After attending a few meetings, I met a sharply dressed, retired military officer named Nick Schiro. Since his retirement he had become a general contractor. Contractors come from basically two sources. The first were usually trained as carpenters by their fathers and grew up with contracting in their blood, or second, a group that usually had no special training, but decided later in life that contracting is what they wanted to do. The assumption was they can organize the subcontractors as well as anyone else, if not better, and might as well make a profit doing so. Contractors of the second group, the ones who didn't also work on the job, are sometimes called *telephone contractors*. Nick was definitely a *telephone contractor*.

I liked Nick. He seemed a forthright sort of a guy with a personal dignity. I felt him a caring person. I apparently appeared to him as an eager, trustable young person. Nick, with his boyish spirit, asked me if I would help him by doing a small remodel job for him and for a client of his named, Shafer. I responded with an enthusiastic OK and was paid $300.00 dollars to rework existing plans. The job was successful and though I didn't make a lot of money, it allowed me to keep my doors open for another month.

I went with Bill Scott to the Community meeting at Webster Elementary School and learned nothing that I can remember except the importance of the meeting for the community. Then, following Bill Scott's suggestion I went to see Reeves Templeman, owner of the Malibu Times. On March 7, 1958 Reeves included an article on page three about Malibu's new architect.

DOUGLAS RUCKER, ARCHITECT, OPENS OFFICE IN MALIBU.

Realizing a dream of long standing, Douglas Rucker, architect, finally opened his office in Malibu and hopes to prove to Malibuites – for the sake of both a living and career – that he's a pretty darn good architect.

Although he has been ensconced in the Chris Craft Building, 22762 Pacific Coast Highway, for a scant three months, the mark of his talent has already been expressed on the Jay Roush home; now under construction by Contractors Roland Powell & Bruce Koch; the Vladamir Ourousoff home on Broad Beach Road (actually in the Sweetwater Mesa area); the Philip Zenn house at Sycamore Park; and the Shafer home constructed by Nick Schiro.

Mr. Rucker who lives in Santa Monica Canyon at the present time with his wife, Karon, graduated from the school of Architecture at the University of Illinois, eight years ago. His wife is active in theater arts at UCLA and has directed and appeared in productions there.

"I fell in love with Malibu when I first came to California and have always wanted to live and work here." said the enthusiastic young architect. "Malibu deserves the best efforts of any architect. I love my work and hope to have a part in helping to build this wonderful community."

Then, as a result of the Pacific Coast Highway *Killer Slide* near Santa Monica Canyon and the continuing brush fires, both of which caused highway bottlenecks during their sliding for users of the area, and particularly Malibu residents, Reeves began promoting the idea of an Express-causeway and wanted me to do a sketch for his paper. I of course agreed. His article was as follows:

"Express-causeway at Castle Rock (Will Rogers State Beach) running out over the bay, approximately one-sixteenth to one-eighth mile off shore, and re-entering 101A at the Los Angeles City Beach property just south of the Chautauqua intersection" - - -" Florida's miles of causeways, Miami to Key West, as an example, withstand the terrific Atlantic Ocean fury and hurricanes which are common most of the year - - - Our magnificent State of California is not subject to these conditions"

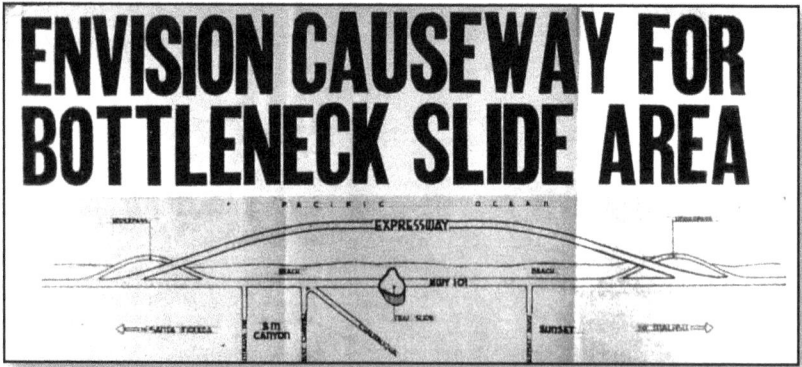

90 - *Original Causeway sketch in the Malibu Times, Reeves Templeman, editor, April 4, 1958.*

Several months after this publication I did a perspective of what the causeway might look like. After much feedback from his readers and public talk about his idea, the idea was expanded to extend the causeway to Las Flores Canyon.

At Reeve's request I did a pen and ink perspective of how I thought a causeway might look. This time it was envisioned much farther out to sea and extending to Las Flores Canyon. The idea appeared to be turning into a pipe dream.

As I saw it the ten mile long six-lane highway would be supported on concrete piers sunk through fifty feet of water and thirty feet of subsurface bedrock and stressed to withstand the terrifying lateral stresses of storm winds and the surge of powerful high tides and waves. My thoughts:

"How would I like to be coming home some black windy night with a few beers? I'd be traveling on this thin ribbon of road, a mile or so out to sea with nothing but the black water raging beneath me, driving through pelting rain hitting me from the side? I'd roll up the windows, turn on the radio and struggle my anxious way! How would sailboats go under? What if a truck crashed the railing and plunged upside down to a watery grave? If I were a beach homeowner I'd look out and see a stream of traffic! What about a Tsunami?" What a great place to watch Malibu burn!"

MALIBU OFFICE

COMPETITION

Let me say that I have never considered myself in competition with any other architect. It seems we architect's have a strata of clients that we attract and a client of another strata rarely crosses over. While I was in Malibu, there were other designers and architect's working in area, but none of them took jobs from me nor did I take jobs from them. We were selected by our own abilities, character, and personality to our pre-fixed strata. Clients of similar character followed us there.

CHARLTON

Jim Charlton was a practicing architect in an upstairs office across the highway. Out of curiosity I visited him. I found we were kindred spirits and liked each other in our self-concepts and philosophies. He showed me a contemporary residence he had on the board. Later I met his clients, a couple with no children, but planning to have some when their house was completed. Educated, artistic and sensitive, they were typical of many young couples desiring to build in this suburb of Los Angeles. They were reasonably well off financially, like Karon and I were struggling for a cultured home in which to raise their children, with books, art, music, decent furniture, and the good life. Jim Charlton's long-term plans were to live and work in Hawaii. He eventually achieved that goal. To my knowledge, except for Jim, I was the only other practicing architect renting office space in Malibu.

WATERS

Terry Waters was another architect in Malibu, working out of his home. He had studied with Frank Lloyd Wright and had worked intimately with John Lautner, the person who had designed *Googie's* and Malibu's Chris-Craft building. During World War II he acted as Malibu's Block Captain and if we'd been attacked, would have led residents to emergency shelters, or organized special help citizens groups for care of the injured, or be the one in charge of emergencies. Even in 1958 Terry drove around with bottled water and dehydrated food in his trunk along with survival tools, foxhole shovel, and extra gas. He was one of the few prepared to *get-out-of-town* in case of nuclear war.

His designs were extremely contemporary and might even have been considered wild, but his practice was slow. Like Frank Lloyd Wright, he seemed to have few clients who would deal with him on his rigid design terms. Some time later he invited me to see his office that was high in the hills overlooking the magnificent ocean and sky with the flowered rolling hills of Malibu below. I didn't go, but he explained to me how he had struggled to find an inspiration for the office design. Then one sunny day he was sitting on his cliff-site when a hawk appeared gliding lazily into view. As it made it's broad, calculated arcs in the calm and steady way hawks do searching the natural growth for a mouse or small snake. Finding nothing, it lifted a wing and soared smoothly and silently down the hill and out of sight. That was it! Terry was inspired! The idea was full-born! The office would be in the shape of a hawk's wing lifted on the wind. Although I never saw his office, he built it this way. This is not the quintessential Terry Waters story but just an episode illustrative of Terry's character.

Terry felt, as I did, we had things in common. We were able to talk architecture together. We agreed on the contemporary approach to design. Though I didn't seem to have any, Terry had many fascinating stories to tell about Lautner and Wright and Neutra and other architects who had made significant contributions to architecture in Southern California. He was filled with philosophy and inspired by life, a rare enough architect to have the courage to tell it like it is. I enjoyed Terry. In his later life he enjoyed health foods and continued with a vigorous swimming regimen that kept him healthy in mind and spirit for a very long time. I still admire him and consider him a close friend.

REID

Bill Reid, our neighbor and son-of-silent-movie-star, William Wallace Reid, was a design-oriented contractor who had been leaving his contemporary mark on Malibu for years. He was continuing to do so. Bill was a lean six-feet-six-inches tall and worked from his office cut high into the easterly bluff of Santa Monica Canyon. One New Years morning, after Santa Monica canyonites had fallen exhausted into bed at 2:00 or 3:00 A. M., loud bells gloriously ringing in the New Year awakened us before dawn. Through huge commercial speakers set up in his back yard and pointed up and down the canyon at 1400 decibels he clanged, *Oh Little Town of Bethlehem*, *Away in the Manger*, and *God Rest Ye Merry Gentlemen*. Resident's buried their heads under pillows in an effort to escape the glorious sound. The bells could be heard for miles around his lower Amalfi home. The next time I saw him he was quite unapologetic. I was probably one of the few who thought his idea funny. It was like everyone got drunk, did devilish things, and was awakened to ethereal bells tolling their after-life. Our paths crossed many times during my long stay in Malibu. I liked Bill and considered him a close acquaintance until his plane crashed in a thick fog over Santa Monica Bay that caused his death in the 90's.

CATHCART

Bill Cathcart was doing his first work in Malibu, mostly apartments on the Coast Highway and residences back in the hills. Having lived in Santa Monica Canyon with several children, he eventually became divorced and spent several years in Carmel doing oil paintings and architectural works in the Sea Ranch style. When he returned to Malibu, he did what I thought to be decidedly better architectural work. His style had been altered by his Monterey-Carmel experiences.

Bill Cathcart and Bill Reid were friends and they were both friendly to me. Our architectural paths rarely crossed

MATT KIVLIN

Matt Kivlin whose office was in his home also lived in Santa Monica Canyon and was working minimally in and around Malibu. Our architectural paths never interfered and we have remained friendly and non-competitive.

DORR HOUSE

I was interrupted from drafting on a minor job when John Dorr entered my office. A large man with a shock of light brown hair slanting boyishly across his forehead, he exuded massive energy under a pleasantly controlled manner and was here to see me about building a house for his wife and children. The family consisted of John and Mary and their children, a daughter *(15)*, son *(John Junior)*, *(13)*, another son, Lennie *(11)*, boy twins *(both 8)*, and a grandmother. I soon learned he worked for IBM and only later found out he was considered number 3 man. IBM had transferred him to Los Angeles and was supplying whatever additional funds were necessary to build the Malibu house after the sale of his house in Oakland.   Like   my dream come true, he loved the post-and-beam style that I accepted fully as my own and intended to pay the going rate for my services. I quickly re-thought my position from compromised charges with Bruce to dealing with a bona fide client. Compensation in the American Institute of Architect's manual for residential services at that time was 10% of the construction cost. I would be giving him full services including supervision, why shouldn't I charge him the standard amount? We drew up a contract at 10%.

His family was still in Oakland and it would be a while before I'd meet them, but seeing eye to eye, we visited his beautiful 100-foot wide by 700-foot long bluff lot he'd purchased overlooking the beautiful blue Pacific on Pacific Coast Highway. It was treeless, covered with flowing rye grass and mustard weeds that sloped gently toward the ocean. I was blown away. I tried to keep cool. This was my first real job.

He quickly sketched a program for me, including a room for each of the kids, a master bedroom and grandmother's quarters. He wanted me to work fresh from the beginning with a landscape architect. I thought immediately of Eric Armstrong who had helped us with our landscaping in Santa Monica Canyon, even though he *had* specified the horrendous Wigandia Caracasana.

Eric was doing significant work in the landscape field and was in great demand, however the site and client spoke softly in his ear and he was instantly available.

THE DESIGN

Eric was a big unmarried man with a strong voice that boomed with laughter at times and an ego as big as the whole outdoors. He would have had a heavy beard had he not meticulously shaved. He wore glasses, smoked a pipe, and knew about operas, plays, history, literature, art, modern furniture, architecture and current events. When he silently pulled up in his yellow Jaguar convertible sports car with the top down, shut the door gently with a silent click, and approached, one would see a casually dressed person of great confidence, high intelligence and immense talent. We learned he had earned the *Prix de Rome* scholarship to Rome from Southern California University to study a year. The fact that he had done so added worldliness to his presence.

His main office was downtown with several draftsmen, but he worked in a marvelously conducive space at home, usually to Mozart playing in the background. There were times, he said, when designing he needed to be alone. I could imagine this highly talented artist getting deeply into his work, creating beautiful, mysterious and magical things. When asked his hourly fee, he would say that while he was designing he charged $90.00 an hour, but of course, if he were traveling to and from the job, his fees were still the same. If one were interested in cost savings, he would have to travel to Eric. He assumed anyone who hired him to be immensely fortunate, and then he'd laugh at his own presumptuousness. People believed him and he was able to deliver.

His house had been remodeled in the contemporary style with floor to ceiling glass facing an intimate, landscaped patio with stonewalls and dripping fountains and little pools with floating lily pads and colored fish. I pulled my butt up on the guest stool and we set to work. Before asking how I intended to design the house, he took a sheet of tracing paper, laid it over the survey, and with bold, confident strokes, drew an L-shaped house and said, *"After all a landscape architect needs to work against a plan of some kind."* I sat there as if someone were finishing my masterpiece, except I hadn't started yet. I watched in a stupor, not knowing what to do. Eric said the L-shape would offer the best opportunity for landscaping inside the *"L"* with different levels, *(he sketched),* a series of 5 specimen trees, *(he sketched)* little entry pathways and boulders, *(he sketched)* and so on. *"Within the 'L,' he said, the landward wing would be the bedrooms, the ocean ward wing would be the kitchen, dining, living, and garage areas. It was all so logical."*

What was I going to do now? I had expected to make a project out of the design. I had intended to search through architectural magazines to find an answer. I'd expected to cogitate, deliberate, calculate, and stay up 'til 2 in the morning and with no sleep and beads of sweat pouring down my temples, present an amateur design, somewhat past the deadline. Now look what he'd done. He'd already designed the damn thing!

What did he expect me to do, put it together like a drafting service? I was very let down. *I was disillusioned! I gained maturity!* I dreamt of falling into my own magical space, listening to, maybe Beethoven, and struggling to my own creative solution. Now Eric, thank you very much, had done it for me.

I went back to my bare little rat's hole with no windows and developed Eric's scheme, adding as much of myself as possible. Eric then completed his landscaping and we both presented the preliminary to John who was delighted. He returned to Oakland, showed his family, and gave me orders to begin the working drawings.

OCEAN ROOM

While drafting the Dorr job, Cap had moved his collection of junk out of the empty seaward office with the floor-do-ceiling ocean window and fireplace on our second floor. Mario needed extra space, my old one, and would pay more rent. I was overjoyed when he agreed and I found myself with my drafting table and stool in the spacious room next door with brick fireplace, floor to ceiling plate glass, and the surf breaking below.

It was Harry Heckendorf, the contractor who built the Zenn house, who donated a conference table made from a 1-3/4" thick solid core oak door. Harry framed it in Douglas Fir and I gave it a natural finish and put it across two sawhorses. I felt I was coming up in the world. The new conference table dressed up the place and though not perfect, made the office look pretty official. I don't remember chairs.

91 - Doug's first office. Second floor, Chris-Craft building.

At any rate, while drafting, I could turn my head ninety degrees for an intimate view of what was happening in the ocean: storm surf, the flat purple look of the ocean during a Santa Ana wind, regular westerly swells, the fishing boats, fleets of racing sailboats, long distance swimmers, board-surfers, the pier, catamarans, wind, cloud formations, tides, the whole enchilada. During high tide and high surf, massive sections of dirt were pulled into the ocean from beneath my floor. It was good fortune the building was on solid wood piling driven to point of refusal. Though I could feel the building shake, I never had to worry about it's collapsing. Mother and Dad visited me while I was in this office. I was very proud.

MORE FIRST JOBS

The move into the office with the fireplace and big window facing the ocean seemed to be a turning point in my architectural practice and therefore for my life. Not only was I in love with the space, but others seeing my layout seemed to enjoy the space as well. It was fun for them to drop in and see their architect drafting comfortably in front of his fireplace with the ocean so intimately a part. While I was doing the Dorr job, other jobs began arriving. One of the first was the Clark House.

CLARK HOUSE

A young man about 32 came sauntering in to my office. He was shorter rather than taller, thinning hair and wearing everyday clothes with gym shoes. He was not in especially good condition and was not a builder. I saw him to be financially needy however he seemed highly motivated. His name was Bill Clark and he wanted to build a house by himself and sell it for a profit in the little community of Monte Nido. Monte Nido is located about four miles inland along Malibu Canyon Road in the shadow of the three thousand foot Santa Monica Mountains.

Though one might think my career was thoroughly launched by the Dorr job, I really wasn't that optimistic. I was hungry to take anything that came through the door. At least any *post-and-beam* house that came through the door. We talked. He had little money and to keep architectural expenses at a minimum I agreed to draw the plans with minimal if no supervision. I think my total compensation, again, was $600.00. He was a young owner who in addition to his main job had the idea of making additional money by building and selling houses. It was an idea that crossed a lot of minds during that time because land was relatively cheap and lending institutions were generous.

I designed a standard small house, three bedrooms and two baths with kitchen, dining and living room in one space. I enjoyed looking at his site, as I have enjoyed looking at all sites with the possibility of expressing my imagination. The site was rural approached only by gravelly, private roads among and through a live oak forest. He owned an acre or so with one-half relatively flat and rolling, the rest sloping steeply to a wooded dry creek. There was little natural growth on the flatter portion, but a few live oaks on the slope and below.

I placed the main house on the flatter portion and cantilevered the living room over the cliff. The separate garage was nearer the road with a long walkway to the house. Bill began to build the house from my plans and worked diligently in the evenings and weekends. I checked his job enough to be informed of its progress that was very slow. Bill had a day job and little time to work on the house. In addition he seemed to be having marital problems. The house went on the market before it was finished.

It sold to a nice vegetarian couple that ate only organic foods. They completed it the following year and moved in. As a visitor, one time, I saw an opened ten-pound bag of shelled organic almonds lying on the floor against the vertical siding of the entry wall. The mode of dress of the owner: open shirt, jeans and go-aheads, plus the large sack of open almonds, gave me a superficial insight into their style of life. The new owner wanted me there because one corner of his cantilevered living room had dropped an inch or two below the other. I had cantilevered one support beam farther than the other and the longest one deflected. I recommended he shim the house, put a support under the deflected beam to match the opposite beam. It wasn't that easy, but somehow I'd answered his question. I don't know if he fixed it or not.

The Clark house became a subject for publication. With me as his assistant, Dick Gross, a Los Angeles Times photographer and later a close personal friend, photographed the house for the Los Angeles Times. Several years later Mary Buchanan purchased the Clark House. Later I was lucky enough to do her house in Malibu.

ADA MARIE BOWERS

Then one day a handsome, well-educated woman walked into my office to inquire about services. We sat facing each other over my naturally finished oak door conference table. Neither fat nor thin, she was a strongly built and a highly individual woman of middle age. She was a strong character of a woman who wore no-nonsense clothes and kept her graying hair short. She peered at me through stylish metal-rimmed lasses and lit a cigarette before coming down to business. She was in investments and perusing real estate and in the Malibu-Los Angeles area interviewing architects. Evidently she lacked faith in the ability or design philosophy of those architects in Santa Barbara. She wanted to build an eight-unit apartment building for the students of UCSB, *(University of California at Santa Barbara)* in Isla Vista, the village northerly and adjacent to the University,

After a week or so from our conversations and negotiations, and while she returned to Santa Barbara to check with her banker and partners, it was determined I would be architect on her eight-unit apartment building.

I agreed to do the design and working drawings and, since the project was quite a distance away and since a personal friend of hers would be the contractor and therefore honest and operating within her control, she would not compensate me for supervision.

The site was a hundred feet wide and a hundred feet deep. The design was two, two-story apartments facing each other with four units each side making eight in total. Two bridges were to connect the top floors and Ada Marie was to plant a two mature mulberry trees in front of the apartment giving it her special apartment name, The Mulberry Tree.

The project took about a year or so to complete and I made several trips at my own expense to check the progress. I enjoyed working with Ada Marie and wasn't to see the last of her.

BOB'S 2 DUPLEXES

Bob Olshausen gave me my next opportunity. Karon and I met Bob at a beach party given by Bill and Terry Scott on Malibu Road. Bob was unmarried at thirty-five, five foot ten inches tall and though prematurely balding, was handsome. He had graduated with a B. A. in Business and owned two 50-foot by 100-foot lots near Ada Marie's in Isla Vista. We got to know each other and he learned of my activities there. I gave Ada Marie as a reference and he visited her. Eventually he hired me to do a duplex on each of his lots. He would be renting to students.

I was overjoyed to be working in Santa Barbara so soon again, and within another year his units were built. I had done three jobs in another city. The work was interesting to me because the three Santa Barbara jobs were a success because they were architecturally different and they made money for their owners.

BARSTOW

Then a friend of Karon's who had graduated in Civil Engineering a year or two prior at Pomona Men's College was working as Chief Sanitation Engineer of the Barstow Sanitation Department. He recommended me to an older friend of his, Gale Kenyon, who was the City's Chief Civil Engineer. Gale visited me in my little office with the natural oak conference table and old hollow core drafting board by the window overlooking the beautiful blue Pacific. He talked to me about doing a three-classroom addition to the Barstow Elementary School. This sounded like *big time*. I was excited by this turn of events and reported I'd been one of the two draftsmen on the Kenter Avenue High School in Brentwood when I worked for Ray Jones and that I was familiar with the State's special Governing Rules.

It seemed I was the guy. Presently a contract arrived and after making a visit to the Barstow site, I found myself in the glad possession of a Barstow Elementary School addition. There was a deadline for completion. I had enough to do without the school addition so I decided to hire a draftsman to help me do the Barstow work. With calls to Frank Young, Hap Gilman, and Hal Whittemore, a successful church architect I'd known in Pacific Palisades, I was able to locate a pleasant, tall and eager young man. He was a glib and slick sort of twenty-one year old who, if he didn't know what he was about, sure talked like he did. I was shaky on architectural details and felt he could help me with them.

The three classrooms were very straightforward and we finished them with a minimum of trouble since Gale Kenyon was doing the structural calculations and handling the Building Department corrections. I was paid the standard eight percent compensation and the job established me as a *no foolin'* architect. It also broke new ground, in that it gave me a new experience in processing and hiring a draftsman and gave me greater confidence in my ability to deliver the work.

There was more to the Barstow job than I have related, but there is a relationship between the rest of the Barstow story and our home activities with a very special friend, Ricky.

RICKY VOLKMAN

*R*icky was a five foot six inch, longhaired brunette with deep brown eyes, thick lashes and a personality that bubbled with a zest for life. A slim young woman in clean summer dresses, bare legs and sandals, with eyes and mouth always on the brink of laughter, she was getting her Masters at UCLA in Sociology. Ricky was a young man's dream of heaven. Karon met her at the University and they adopted each other as close friends.

I was attracted to her as any man would be but reminded myself I was a one-woman man and that I should only have eyes for Karon. Ricky was Karon's luscious, intelligent single friend.

Ricky, Karon and I were close friends for about four years, going to the beach and taking driving adventures, but mostly we had her over for dinner, wine and long conversations. Being the therapeutic type with a strong curiosity and a tendency toward introspection, Ricky liked to talk. She appealed to me because I had the same tendencies. After dinner we sometimes found ourselves analyzing the wonders of the universe at 11:00 P. M. while Karon had long since fallen asleep on the couch. I loved Ricky as a friend, though I have not seen her for over 43 years, and still do. It was understood she had her romantic world and I had mine.

Doug, Karon and Ricky Volkman in Amalfi house entry.

In 1958 Ricky met a wonderful person, Gene Grounds. Gene, six feet four and a champion long distance swimmer and surfer from the University of Southern California, was lifeguarding at State Beach, only a ten-minute walk from our house. She thought Gene a handsome hunk and as sometimes-young women do, flirted with him at the beach. After laughter and conversation around the guard tower, they started dating and became more than friends. Gene was to become a particularly close friend of mine for the next decade and remains so to this day.

Gene invited Ricky to Hawaii and when she got there, she was astounded with the beauty of the Islands. She wanted to save every shell on the beach and began a collection but soon had too much to carry. She wanted to take the sand home because she loved the tiny white shells out of which it was made. Her naiveté and girlishness were attractive to Gene who knew and loved the Islands and according to Ricky, Gene took the white and tan shelled sand and threw it in the wind to show her there was no way one could own so much beauty, particularly if it was so readily available to everyone. The sand was already where it was supposed to be, he said, on the beach. It was so simple. She understood she couldn't own the sand any more than she could own the trees or mountains or a wonderful day. She already owned all the sand as everybody did

The pair didn't end in a permanent love match because they eventually decided their life goals were different. They agreed to see each other less frequently and to remain just friends. Later, Ricky found someone she loved and married, Art Volkman, which is, perhaps, another story.

The sociologist, Ricky, invited us to Synanon Foundation's Friday Night Open House that changed us deeply in our attitude toward problems of the addicted.

SYNANON FOUNDATION

Ricky was doing her UCLA Sociology thesis on *The Synanon Foundation*, popularly known as Synanon. Synanon was a self-help organization of 50 to 60 live-in persons carefully selected to make the group work. Located in an old four-story brick building built on the beach as an armory during World War II, it was on the beach side of Pacific Coast Highway below the bluffs in Santa Monica. Accepted methods of getting addicts off drugs were available from the State and County but had only a 3 percent success rate. Synanon boasted a 40% success rate. Chuck Dederick, the chief organizer, was a 55 to 60 years old former alcoholic who had devised a new method of getting addicts off drugs. His idea was to provide a live-in situation where residents had regular sessions of psychotherapy conducted by Chuck and a few chosen former addicts. Between therapies live-in members who had been clean longer would positively influence the session's newcomers. So-called *clean addicts* would be therapeutic by example. Emotional help would automatically take place while doing chores like mopping, vacuuming, making beds, dusting, repairing, shopping, cooking, and cleaning up. Empathy, exchange of experiences, knowing that one was not alone, would take place during the live-in situation when residents were not in their sessions.

At one time there was an unwritten contest on who could read the most self-help books. Information on the affects of addiction and psychology was available from their small but growing library. One member read over a hundred self-help books, another 75, another 51, and so on. .

As Chuck and his former-user friends knew, it was in the nature of the addict to be a liar. It was difficult for an addicted newcomer to enter the facility. *"A user will tell you anything whether it's the truth or not."* Chuck said. A prospective member had to be off drugs for at least a short period of time before he would be interviewed. A jury of Chuck and about 3 or 4 respected members would decide whether or not to dedicate the time and money to accept the responsibility of a new member. Chuck was harsh in his choices, but dependable once it was made. An addict, however, one who had *"split"* or decided to leave Synanon, was seldom allowed to re-enter.

ATTACK THERAPY

Twice a week the live-in addicts conducted what my friend Rick Davidson called, attack therapy with the newest members. It was a stiff session for a newcomer. The older members held nothing back in expressing their contempt for the self-deceptions and lies they to which they were subjected

I can only imagine what went on in those meetings. Rick, who actually took part, said *using* addicts lie to themselves as well as others, to get a fix. A live-in addict, who has been working on himself for over a year, can instantly catch a newcomer in a lie because he's been there, done that, and found it leads directly to a painful and demoralizing death. He attacks the newcomer mercilessly because he knows that understanding and sympathizing with a liar he becomes an enabler that allows the newer member to continue their habits of self-destruction.

Synanon is like AA. Both are self-help therapies. As alcoholics treat alcoholics in AA, addicts treat addicts in Synanon. Former addicts know what the newer members are up against. Non-addict psychotherapists who work in governmental programs have not experienced the addict's horrendous difficulties so it is impossible for them to completely understand. Some newcomer addicts upon finding their lies transparent and feeling demoralized, and therefore in need of a fix, would walk out of the meeting and out of the building. If they did so, they were not invited to come back. If a newcomer addict managed to sit through an attack therapy meeting and have his lies thrown back in his face and yet had the fortitude to continue, he found that once the session was over he was released into an extremely loving environment. His fellow live-in addicts showed sympathy and would relate their similar tales. If the newcomer did his honest share of chores and was just part of the group, he would get unconditional love and healing would begin.

Disillusion equals maturity. When one is disillusioned, one gains maturity. Expect to win the race. Come in third. Realize you are not the best. *Gain maturity.* In an addict's case, lies no longer work nor does his everyday approach. He faces truth. *He is disillusioned. He gains maturity.*

Synanon forced members to see the truth and showed them a better way. You might ask, when are they cured? Never! Like an alcoholic, they're always addicts but they can stay clean. When do they move out? Perhaps never, but considering the alternatives, isn't that all right?

FRIDAY NIGHT MEETINGS

Friday nights were open house to any guests who chose to attend. There were usually about ten. The open house was to teach the public about the community's social problem, to show them the blatant effects of such a debilitating habit and the immense difficulty of getting rid of it, to familiarize the public with the variety of people who have fallen into addiction and that Synanon had nothing to hide but something to teach beneficial to society. Friday night meetings were also to show the addicts another way of life, the *"square"* life, to demystify the straight person, to show them the *"squares"* were not too different from the *addicts.*

The meeting was held in the large living-dining area on the second floor of the former Armory. Former addicts who had been clean for at least a year and supervised by Chuck and two of his trusted former addict friends led it on a rotating basis. Guests were invited to comment and give their opinions.

The large room usually had one or two persons who appeared to be unconscious lying face down on the couch. He or she would be quitting, cold turkey, the only way allowed in Synanon. Old timers and newcomers who would form the main audience lounged on donated sofas and threadbare easy chairs and a variety of used straight-backed chairs around Salvation Army type dining tables.

They discussed the meanings of anger, frustration, caring or a lack of caring, what they did for a fix, how they felt about themselves before and after becoming clean, their former attempts to stop using, outrageous lengths they'd go to get dope including prostitution, thievery, embezzlement, forgery and credit card fraud. Many had spent time in jail, some as long as twenty years, and learned tricks from inmates. They related the ineffectiveness of the State methods of curing, the impossibility of trying to quit without help, their attempts at self-quitting, types of quitting with lighter drugs, or cold-turkey, and all the emotions, ramifications, differences and nuances encountered while doing so.

During the Friday night meetings the members chained-smoked until by the end of the session the large room was blue and the foul air stung our eyes. Members drank cup after cup of real coffee. Apparently they had to be addicted to something. At times the discussions were passionately expressed with different points of view, then things would settle out and another would tell her tale, then his tale, then another, and another, until the subject had undergone a mutation from the original topic. After a couple of hours, all particulars would have been heard and with some closing announcements the meeting would be adjourned.

Chuck would then invite members and guests to have soft drinks and a selection of cookies and cakes that had been set out and baked by the former addicts for the meeting. During this social time, Ricky, Karon, I and other guests and addicts were able to talk face-to-face and one-on-one. We discovered our likeness to one another.

I learned there wasn't much difference between an addict and me. Addicts were unhappy people, their habit being a hell on earth. I felt, *there, but for the grace of God, go I.* The experience was humbling and took the mystery out of addiction. Because I learned why addicts are addicts, I became more forgiving and my perspective was widened.

While I was in their space, love was thick enough to cut with a knife. I have never felt so much love anywhere in the world. Why?

Because there was no one there who hadn't done things many times worse than I have done in my wildest imaginings. I discovered I wasn't evil. That evil was relative. There were good reasons why people were evil. Thereafter, I didn't see the addicts as evil, particularly in the light of their heart-rending remorse and their super human attempts at self-cure. I could now see them as people doing the ultimate to live their best possible lives while reacting to impossible circumstances.

THE END OF SYNANON

For me Synanon only existed between 1958 and 1968. Later, members tried to form an organization in the Big Sur area and other places in the country. I knew little more of it after my visits ended. Rumor had it Chuck had begun drinking again. Some argued why should a former *alcoholic* be the head of a *narcotic* self-help organization? Shouldn't a former narcotic addict hold that position? There was negative media notoriety of a rattlesnake in a mailbox. There were rumors about arguments over who would form Synanon's policy. Chuck Dederick was adamant in his views and I have heard he tried to affect multiple sexual relationships between the members, even between married couples. Many objected to his changing philosophies and tried to open their own organizations. Synanon was controversial and always in the papers. Several books were written on Synanon. To my knowledge, the wonderful idea of Synanon petered out in a mass of deception, betrayal, disagreements, arguments, lack of loyalty, getting too big, and not having a mature and reasonable growing edge. I lament its demise.

REST OF THE BARSTOW STORY

The Barstow Elementary job came with what Gale and I thought to be other opportunities. Gale asked me to do preliminaries on four major Barstow City buildings, a City Hall, an Auditorium, an Administration Building and a Police Station. For promotional purposes, I was to do exterior sketches only. If this went through, I could be in the big time. I had worked successfully for Barstow's School Board that had reflected favorably on Barstow's Chief

Engineer and after being recommended by the City's Sanitary Engineer, I was politically in.

93 - Proposed Barstow City Hall.

I burned the midnight oil doing the preliminary sketches. Since all the buildings were to be seen together, I tried to make them compatible. As a group they had to harmonize. I had to get my feeble, ill-formed brain to make a decision. I was afraid of failure. I had to become instantly brilliant. I looked in architectural magazines to see similar work and asked myself, what would Neutra, Craig Ellwood, or Thornton Abell do with these jobs? Studying was no help. After studying, I still didn't know. I ran out of time and went with whatever gut was in there. I designed it myself.

94 - Barstow Auditorium.

95 - Proposed Barstow Administration Building.

The Police Station would be the first to be built and because of my own personality and because of the softening I had gained about the formerly incarcerated addicts, I entered this design in a state of conflict. I didn't want to become an expert in incarceration. I didn't like police stations. I'd spent my life avoiding them. I didn't even like the DMV. I realized their necessity, but after my Synanon experience, I wanted therapy for the criminals. After all criminals are people.

96 - Proposal for the Barstow Police Station.

In an emotional state because of my Synanon experience and because I felt the work was beyond me, designing the Police Station had me in a state of emotional turmoil. I drove into the desert to meet Gale to examine Barstow's police station recently constructed for Palm Springs. After touring the entire facility, I gathered much information there. Returning, I wrote my own program and examined sketches of the Palm Springs Station. I made my own plan and thought if I knew what the inside was like, I would be able to design the outside. After all, hadn't I designed a train station for my

State Board Examination, and at Illinois University an Archeological Headquarters for digging up ruins in Egypt? This project was only four big commercial buildings. AAAHHHH!!!

I produced preliminary plans for the Police Station which included barred jails, bugged interrogation rooms all with one-way glass, general and private offices, showers, a public reception area, and parking for public and police cars.

When the preliminary was done and sort of staring me in the face with the real chance the job might be built with my name on it, personal issues on law enforcement were raised. After my Synanon experience and during this period of time when Jack Kerouac and Allan Ginsberg were leaders of the beat generation now in progress, I wasn't clear as to how I felt about law enforcement, or bugged interrogation rooms, or barred jails. Should I put TV's in them? Where are the interior gardens? Shouldn't we have skylights for the cells so the inmates could know if it's raining out? Shouldn't there be a library? Was incarceration the only solution for wayward souls? Wasn't the Barstow Police Station the dignified name for the Barstow jail? Shouldn't America be building Recuperation Centers rather than jails?

I sent off my drawings. Gale presented them in front of the Barstow City Council. They took it under advisement and that was the last I ever heard of the four projects.

DAVE RICH STORY

I was envious of Dave Rich because he was doing beach houses in Malibu and I wasn't. When I first heard of Dave he was legally a Designer, the name given to unlicensed architects, and was doing numerous beach-lot spec houses for contractor, E. M. Powell on Malibu Cove Colony Drive. I couldn't admire Powell for what I considered his fake post-and-beam work, but can say he did his best to make a buck. Malibu beach houses sold for higher prices because they were on the beach and it was economically feasible to hire someone of better talent who fit that description, like Dave Rich.

Then one day Mary Gonzales invited me to do an upstairs bedroom-playroom over her Malibu Road beach house. Mary, with two small children, was generous, outgoing, full of laughter, and one of the young housewife Pro-Malibu women. She was celebrated in the community because of her positive nature and through her hard work with the school and various public women's organizations. A few weeks later she apologetically told me that Dave Rich would be doing the job instead of me. She explained Dave was a fraternity member of her husband, Manny, and fraternity member's stick together. I watched her building activity and eventually discovered Dave's solution, an attractive second story A-frame building that was outstanding compared to its neighbors.

Eventually I got to meet the famous Rich. Karon and I were invited to a party by the owner of one of two good-looking houses Dave Rich had designed that faced each other on two La Costa bluffs. On the high cantilevered deck overlooking the ocean at twilight there was loud chatting, beer and wine, party snacks, and private discussions. Dave, the architect for the two houses, was the guest of honor and the center of attention. He laughed and told jokes and drank beer and was not only a bright young man, but also a boisterous one.

Then someone asked Dave if he'd play. He didn't seem shy while taking his golden trumpet from its case. I thought, *trumpet, eh? I knew trumpets. My brother, an all around stud also named Dave, was also a trumpet player, leader of a high school jazz band, and performed in Nogales for beer.* Dave Rich quieted the party when he played a few short jazz tunes. He was good and also a stud.

We met, we chatted, and we were friendly. I was thirty-three, in my own business for four years and supposed to be the more experienced. Yet I questioned myself, *would I have had the audacity to come up with an A-frame type building. These two houses on the bluff weren't bad either. Was Dave Rich not only younger, but also better than me?*

Then I discovered Dave was building a catamaran of his own design in back of Tom the Surfboard Man's store. He had worked on the hull elsewhere and had gotten permission to join it together next to my office and fiberglass them in Tom's fiber-glassing yard.

Not only was Dave younger than me, doing houses on the beach, and two on the bluffs, and was a great trumpet player, and had stolen away one of my additions, but he was also a boat builder. I felt inferior. I consoled myself when I remembered Dave wasn't married and hadn't built his own house.

The boat building went on sporadically between his architectural work and I saw the catamaran begin to take its final shape. The bow looked small and the mast looked too tall.

Then one day on the sidewalk, while he was walking past my office and I was going the other way, I said, *"Hiya, Dave!"* he dropped his head and refused to speak to me. Seeing him numerous times over the following year, I would start to say *"Hi! Dave!"* then stop myself because Dave always lowered his head avoided my gaze. It was as if to tell me our conversation was not an option. I felt hurt. I was a loving, people kind of guy and this had never occurred before. *(Or since, I might add.)* His refusing to answer me weighed for years on my soul. Why wouldn't he speak to me? Why was he cutting me dead?

It is possible Dick Irwin, also in the architectural world, may have told him he'd been the one who found our Chris-Craft office, then after a month, left for a month, and then decided to return and I refused to let him. What was Dick's message? I was a scummy guy. *Doug wouldn't continue to share even though Dick found the office.* I felt this guilt myself, yet I feel in the long run, I did the right thing. Then, again this may not be the reason he refused to speak with me. If dropping his head and refusing to speak was not about Dick Irwin, then what?

A few years passed and from time to time I'd see Dave in odd locations and start to say hello, then catch myself when he averted his gaze. But then one day he walked right up to me and acted as if nothing had happened. We began a pleasant conversation and I returned the talk, delighted that things seemed to be straightening out. A week later he called me on the phone and invited me to see his new office. He'd gotten his license and was practicing near the corner of Sunset Boulevard and Pacific Coast Highway. I agreed to see him on a convenient day and visited him. His office was acceptable and he seemed to have enough work. In fact he was doing an immense house for basketball star, Wilt Chamberlain. He asked me if I wanted to go into partnership with him and share the design and profits fifty-fifty. I was flabbergasted and asked him to give me a few days while I thought it over.

That night I told Karon and we talked of the irony of the thing, that after cutting me dead for two or three years, he would now invite me to go into business with him as a partner. I of course had had the partnership experience and didn't find it to my liking. I called him a few days later and said regrettably, I had too much work and wanted to continue alone in my own business.

Later it was rumored he had trouble with his catamaran in the heavy winds because the tall mast and huge sail caught so much wind it exerted too much pressure on the narrow bows and they submerged. His boat required additional engineering. I haven't heard from Dave since our last meeting where we discussed the partnership. I understand he completed the Wilt Chamberlain house and I presume continued with his practice. He is no longer near the corner of Sunset and Pacific Coast Highway, and so much for the Dave Rich story.

STATE OF THE WORLD – END OF 1958

American architect, Frank Lloyd Wright dies at 89 and his Guggenheim Museum opens in New York. Cecil B. De Mille and Billie Holiday die. *(Billie at 44.)* Alaska becomes the 49th state and Hawaii becomes the 50th. Rogers and Hammerstein write Sound of Music. James Michener's, *Hawaii*, is published. Rod Serling hosts Twilight Zone. Mattel introduces the Barbie Doll. The Saint Lawrence Seaway opens. Marvin Gaye, Diana Ross, and Stevie Wonder star for Motown. Nixon and Khrushchev engage in the *"kitchen debate"* Communism vs. Capitalism. In Antarctica scientists discover a gaping hole in the ozone layer.

I paid no attention to the above. I had my work in front of me. I was beginning the career-building phase of my life. The world was doing what it does; I was doing what I do.

DORR & OTHER JOBS

DORR HOUSE CONSTRUCTION

The permits obtained, I was fortunate enough to get the contracting firm of Butte and Laughtenschlager to do the work. Bob Butte would do the bulk of the work because he lived in the Brentwood area on Tigertail Lane that was closer to Malibu. Laughtenschlager lived in Venice and handled that area.

The L shaped house was designed on a slab using the normal Douglas fir studs and posts, but the roof planks would be entirely unique. John Dorr made arrangements to buy lumber from an old Mill being torn down near Eureka, California. He was able to obtain ancient 4x12 redwood boards formerly cut from old growth redwoods and have them shipped to Los Angeles where they were milled on four sides and delivered to his Malibu job. These 4x12 redwood beams would form the tongue in groove plank ceiling.

When the planks were delivered I found the old redwood was so dry and light I could pick up a 4 x 12, eighteen-foot board in each arm and easily walk around. Like balsa wood after being in the dry mill, they were featherweights. Later, after the 4x12's were in place, the stains created by boltholes still penetrating the planks bothered John. He elected to cover them with solid, clear heart redwood, ship-lapped boards. The ceiling was clear, red, uniform unusual and stunning.

97 - The Dorr house under construction seen from the ocean bluff.

The concrete floor slabs in the living-dining area, where not carpeted, but covered with flat Bouquet Canyon Stone that ran through the floor-to-ceiling glass doors in and out of the house. It had the classic indoor-outdoor feeling.

FLYING

During the course of our many discussions I found John had been a flyer in the Navy and owned not only a twin-engine Beechcraft, seating about six people, but also a PBY four-engine aircraft with an upper wingspan of one hundred four feet and capable of carrying about a dozen people. The huge, slow flying airplane had a cruising speed of 110-miles-per-hour and was useful in wartime for high altitude reconnaissance.

John also owned half interest in a four passenger Cessna and two Naval Grumman, F-8's. The F-8's were the fastest propeller driven fighter planes ever made and the last ones built before the jets. John let me sit in one after returning from a Beechcraft flight I'd made with him. The F-8 had much too short wings compared to the immense size and weight of its body. I put my fingers around the thick, black rubber joystick and thought I was in a chunk of steel that would never get off the ground. But get off the ground it did, with heavy counter-rotating propellers revving up at an unimaginable acceleration. It took off at a terrifying speed and was able to climb straight up to magnificent heights, above the clouds and into the stratosphere. I would have been afraid to ride in one. John flew them in the Navy for years.

According to a story John told me, while flying an F-8 in the Navy, he and his co-pilot took off in questionable weather at twilight from San Francisco heading to Los Angeles. Around San Luis Obisbo, perhaps an hour into the flight, the rough weather turned into a cloud that extended to the ground. The visibility was zero. This was not supposed to be the time for a problem with the fuel line, however the engine was acting as if it were not getting enough gas. F-8's do not glide well. Both men were aware that if the engines lost fuel, the plane would plummet like a stone. Yet the engine continued to miss, threatening to stop. John, who could not see the ground due to fog and darkness, but through reading his altimeter, brought the F-8 as low as he dared. The two of them didn't know whether they were over land or ocean, but hoping the engine would continue to function were flying by compass, dead reckoning and intuition. Soon the emergency was at hand! Thinking quickly, John headed the plane toward what he thought was the open ocean and in the pitch blackness, ordered the co-pilot to bail out, then bailed out, himself.

John's chute opened and delivered him into the icy water, where through courage, physical strength and blind luck, he managed to drag himself ashore and walk for help. The Coast Guard and Navy made a long and thorough search, but never found his co-pilot.

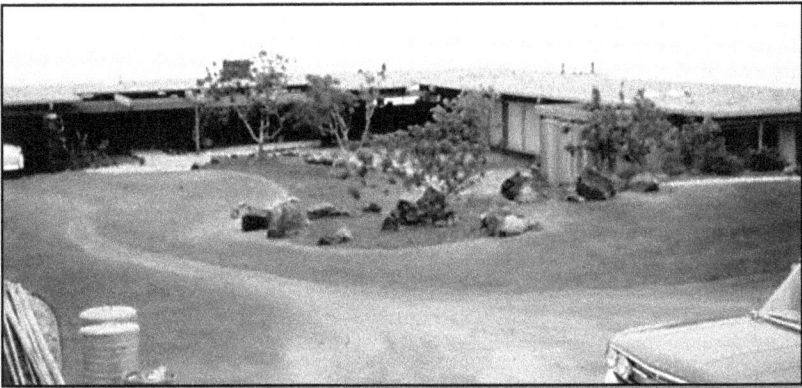

98 - The Dorr House.

LAVA ROCK

Before completion of the house, John, who was filled with creative ideas as a matter of course, invited Karon and I to travel 200 miles to the middle of the Mojave Desert near the little town of Amboy, California. His idea was to build large areas of black volcanic lava rock on two eight-foot high walls, one inside the house and one outside. Amboy was near two natural cinder cones and the surrounding sandy terrain was abundant with rocky lava.

Though I was reluctant to introduce such a different material as black lava rock in one of *my* houses, especially a material so structurally weak, I rationalized, since it would be applied as a veneer to a solidly reinforced concrete block wall, the structure would at least fall under the broader category of *masonry*. The Dorr house would be made of concrete, wood, glass, and *masonry*. I reasoned it accented the entrance and black was not impossible in texture, nor did it go poorly with Redwood. Also, there was little I could do about it. It was his house and his money.

There are two kinds of problems in building. *(1) Actual problems. (2) People problems.* Lava rock fell into the latter category. It has been said, *"If you can't lick 'em, join 'em."* So I appeared to the Dorr's to agree with them in full heart, determined to let my new gift-from-God-clients have their fun. After all, they'd gone along with the contemporary post-and-beam style I'd insisted upon. Shouldn't the owner's be part of the collaboration? Besides, it would be an adventure for both our families.

AMBOY

Karon and I were to drive into the desert and meet the entire Dorr family, John, Mary, Elizabeth, John Junior, Lenny, the twin boys, and grandma who would fly with John in their twin engine Beechcraft. Early one fall Saturday morning we found ourselves bright eyed and humming along the desert highway watching the sun come up.

99 - Interior showing living room. Lava rock wall behind reflections of Karon and Mary.

After an early lunch we parked at the appointed location near a conical shaped mound of black rocks poking a hundred feet or so through the desert sand. The black cinder cone was the remains of a formerly much larger volcano, partially buried and eroded over geologic time. Nearby smaller thrusts of heavily textured black rock projected through the sand and sometimes shelves or slanting tables of rock jutted here and there casting strong shadows. Green leaves in the burning sun curled and stretched in imaginative and arbitrary patterns and the deep blue sky, black rocks, deep shadows, rolling dunes, and the random plants, made the collecting trip unforgettable.

It was a shame to remove anything from that beautiful site. But there, as the antithesis, sat the two large rented trucks with drivers ready to haul the rock away. The family and Karon and I pulled the rocks loose, or uncovered them, or broke them off the slanting shelves until, after a picnic lunch, more collecting and the first signs of darkness, the trucks were filled. It was time for them to be on their way and for us to return to a rented motel room, shower and change and join the Dorr family in Amboy for dinner.

100 - Karon in front of the entry door.

There didn't seem to be any laws against gathering the rock. I wondered who owned the property. There were so many rocks left in addition to the hundred-foot cone, that when we finished it didn't look like we'd been there. I can imagine the next desert wind blowing across the dunes and the sand covering our thieving tracks so no one would know if we'd been there. *Eternity doesn't care.* I regretted gathering the rocks, but stone yards must gather them somewhere. After all, I use lumber for my houses. Do I question who is cutting the trees? I was young and experiencing the world, coping the best I knew how, being dumb and having a new business.

The next day John flew Mary, a child or two, and Karon and I to the town called Death Valley. At Death Valley we were able to see the dry, desolate and ancient landscape of the lowest point in the United States before lunch and our flight back to Amboy. From Amboy we drove home. The black lava rock was installed in John and Mary's house and made a bold, individual, one-of-a-kind statement.

REDWOOD ROOTS

Near the mouth of the Russian River in California, John, in his travels, came upon some immense redwood roots, magnificent and alive in their contorted shapes. I assume local people who do that sort of thing had collected them, but knowing John, he could just as well have seen them at the mouth of the Russian river and had tractors pull them out of the estuary. John got the idea to trim the best parts of the roots and have them bolted to his black lava rock walls as a further personal statement. I helped him choose the locations and we installed one inside the house and one out. The size? On the outdoor wall, twelve feet long, five feet high, and almost two feet thick, on the indoor wall, ten feet long, five feet high and two feet thick.

PLAYING

I did not always work hard at architecture. The Lautner building or the Chris Craft Building, or the second floor office where my drafting table sat in front of the fireplace and next to the full length window facing the beautiful blue Pacific, wasn't really a conducive place to work. It was favorable to playing. Lautner's funny angular building that never received a finish coat of plaster or paint, nor was the minimal wood ever painted, sat to one side of a paved yard filled with new and used Chris Craft boats on trailers. Cap was an ancient, short, skinny, southerner who was married to his captain's hat. I don't think he sold many boats. In fact, in two years I don't even remember him selling one. Nevertheless, he seemed to keep busy with paperwork and between customers, had many funny stories to tell about growing up in Mississippi and about his happy, risqué association with a quasi-legitimate theater and Wingy Munione, a Dixieland bandleader,

He had a young assistant, Pat Ahern, who was 25 or so, heavier than lighter, and seemed out of condition. He had thick dark hair and eyebrows, wore dark rimmed, tinted glasses and between the few prospective clients, he dozed or loafed. Feet on the desk he'd read the newspaper or do some minor scribbling or on some days wouldn't come in at all. I'm not convinced he was necessary to Cap's business, but took him in good humor and enjoyed his point of view when

I agreed with it, or ignored it when I did not. Perhaps I do him injustice, but he reminded me of a college dropout relative at work in the Chris Craft store because *"Uncle"* Cap created a job for him. I conjectured he was there because he couldn't do anything else. Pat told ribald stories and with loud laughter, amused himself with his sense of self-importance. I laughed too, but didn't take him seriously, nor do I think he took himself seriously. We were friendly business associates, not too distant, not too close.

SAIL FISH

One day I noticed a fine little surfboard sized blue sailboat attractively assembled in Cap's store. I hadn't seen one before and was intrigued. It cost about $600.00 and had an aluminum mast, sail, guy wires, rudder, and all kinds of guarantees. This large surfboard with a sail was called the Sailfish. I thought briefly of buying one, but didn't have the money.

A few weeks later, Cap's assistant, Pat, told me he had ordered one and it would be here in six weeks. He waited in anxious anticipation for the promised time until one day a large truck dumped off a cardboard package 20 feet long, by 4 feet wide, by 18 inches deep. Pat couldn't wait to see his new treasure and opened it immediately.

I should tell you at this time that Art didn't know how to sail. I'm not sure he knew how to do anything athletic, but he probably thought if he learned to sail the Sail-Fish, he would have some of the sailing knowledge and feeling for boats and water as his customers. For instance he would be more familiar with what a mast was, or centerboard, or mainsail, or rudder. Perhaps, bow, stern, port and starboard, as well. Not only that, sailing might be fun.

He diligently opened the package, threw the cardboard in the outside trash container, and studied the direction booklet telling how to put the thing together. It took him the better part of a week to assemble the simple surf-board-sailor. But on the day he finished the surf was as high as his excitement to try out the new toy. We all warned him that with such high surf things might not go well and suggested he wait until the weekend for his first sail to avoid catastrophe. He didn't seem to hear us and Art had waited long enough. The boat was assembled perfectly, mast plumb and true, center-board in place and pulled up, rudder attached with tiller lightly wedged, sails flapping noisily in the wind with the guy wires lightly humming in the breeze. He was up for it. He was going out!

His theory was to wait for a big wave to come crashing in, then as the wave washed out again, ride the outgoing rip-tide and get sailing quickly so he could push past the next on-coming shore break. Timing had to be perfect. There wasn't a big crowd. Cap and I were the only ones watching. We saw the whole thing.

Just after the big wave crashed into shore and the moment it began receding, Pat pushed off, wading seaward along with the heavy flowing water. When he could wade no more he leapt on to the craft. He leapt all right, but the light boat dumped him as quickly back into the moving sea and he was now being pulled seaward by the craft while dragging his legs in the swirling water. The sails were snapping in the wind and precious time was slipping away. A second wave was about to arrive. It wasn't a little one!

The sea leapt crazily skyward, the front of the boat rose with it until the bow was vertical and the wave, like a waterfall, rolled over on itself rotating the boat, end for end, making a beautiful semicircle so that it was exactly upside down before slamming the top end of the mast deeply into the sand. It shuddered there for a ghastly moment until the mast buckled and the boat fell on its side. Pat's head and leg emerged here and there among the debris, until the whole bloody mess, L-shaped mast, guy wires, sail, rudder, cushion floats, packed lunch, seaman's hat and Pat came washing up on shore. The huffing, puffing, stunned body pulled itself out of the water and scrambled to shore. We were horror-struck. I ran to help the poor guy out, recover parts we could still find and swim after those bobbing or visible in the water. We sympathized with Pat's predicament and helped him assemble himself and collect parts of his boat.

I have a saying. *He was disillusioned. He gained maturity. When you can say I'll never do that again, you have met your real self and know where you stand on the subject.* I didn't say anything to Pat. I didn't need to. He was pretty depressed and very mature.

The next time I saw him with the boat was several months later. He had a new method. He was going out on a windless day with an orange life jacket. He had strapped the mast, sails, rudder, rudder, lunch, guy wires and wind jacket to the boat so it couldn't come loose. He paddled beyond the miniature swells and assembled the boat - out there. After about a half an hour drifting down the coast in front of the wind and when his sail was up and everything was in order, he pulled in the sheet and began his slow sail out of sight toward Santa Monica.

For a while I heard from friends living on the beach they had frequently seen Pat and his Sailfish about a half-mile out in calm water moving up or down the coast. Evidently he was having fun with his reconstructed boat. Rumor had it that on one of his trips toward Santa Monica Bay he was caught by stiffening Santana winds (*off shore winds*) that blew him out to sea with such force he couldn't make headway against it toward shore. My friends with binoculars watched the top of his sail disappear over the horizon line. It appeared he would miss Catalina. I suspect they called the Coast Guard and I believe he was rescued, cold, tired and saturated with an adventure and maturity.

BACK TO WORK

*Th*e Building Department was different in those days. It was part of Los Angeles County. An excellent leader named Bill Berg ran the Department. Excluding the Health Department headed by David Riggle, Bill's total staff was about four. We in the building profession were supposed to follow the County Code, but when discrepancies arose, Bill would analyze the problem and if you met the *intent* of the code, he'd approve the plans. I respected Bill, as did other honest professionals. If, however, someone were to try to sneak something through which did not conform to the code and was a health and safety hazard, Bill's personality would change. He'd adamantly deny any illegal or marginal request and would never forget the transgression. From such good and bad experiences are reputations made.

Building in Malibu in 1959-1960 was no big deal. I could draw the plans for a small post-and-beam house in a month, submit it to the Building Department, and it would be ready for corrections in less than two weeks. Architects dealt with the same plan checker and usually developed a good, if not friendly, working relationship. A day after receiving the corrections I'd have made them and our permit would have been issued the next day. Total time: Two months. Sewage disposal had a few simple requirements that were easily met. If there were a problem, I'd talk it over with Dave who was the single authority. There was no Geology and Soils Department; the Fire Department had simple notes to add. There were no energy calculations to be submitted, insulation wasn't required, only minimum engineering calculations were necessary. It was a lot less work to get a permit and build a house then, since there was more available land in Malibu, owners and builders constructed new houses with an almost cavalier attitude.

The cost of property in 1960 was less, too. An Owner could buy a 50-foot lot on Malibu Road for under $10,000.00. In 1958, Karon and I could have bought a 50-foot lot on Malibu Road for $5,500.00. We came to Louis Busch's Real Estate Office on the weekend, money in hand, but were disappointed to find the property had sold during the week. We looked at a one acre lot just west of Point Dume bluff with a hundred fifty feet of bluff and beach frontage for $3,300.00. In those days barren Point Dume was considered too far from civilization to be in demand and was almost empty of residents. Point Dume was *undesirable.*

The cheap cost of construction would seem ridiculous by present standards and owners would often ask the probable cost of construction for a small house. When I'd say probably no less than $12.00 per square foot nor more than $15.00, they'd always tell me their last project only cost $10.00 per square foot. Then we'd have a long difficult discussion on why post-and-beam houses cost more. If they thought my higher prices for a better house were worth it, they'd go ahead. If not, they'd go away.

A 1,500 square foot house then, could be built for $22,500.00, plus $5,000.00 for a garage, as mandated by the Building Department. I'd be pleased if the whole house came in under $30,000.00.

While work designed in 1959 was being constructed, new work arrived. I was becoming better known as the legitimate local architect in Malibu, probably because of Bruce Koch and his team of subcontractors slowly spreading the word and because of my installation as an active member of the Malibu Chamber of Commerce.

WOODHULL HOUSE

A young couple, the Woodhull's, fell neatly into my personal architectural strata. Joel and Beth were a forward thinking couple, each slim to the point of skinny and very much in love. Fresh, young, and moderately attractive upon first meeting, over time I found them to possess lasting and wonderful qualities. Joel and Beth were enthused about planning their unusual home in a remote place a couple of miles up Topanga's, Monte Vista Drive. The Drive and property are high above The *Inn of the Seventh Ray,* a popular natural food restaurant located along the Creek near the Old and New Topanga Roads intersection. The Woodhull's were from the northern mid-west and Joel worked in something like energy conservation while Beth was in something like elementary school teaching. Both in their early thirties they were good with their hands and planned to do a lot of the construction themselves.

Their land was a mile up a narrow, single lane road full of dusty potholes that led to a dirt driveway and their acre property. Coming up from the road and meeting a car or pick-up coming the other way necessitated pulling into the infrequent shoulders and sometimes braving billows of dust to let him pass. The property sat above and on the brink of what was later found to be a three-mile diameter ancient, but so far inactive, landslide. The site for the house would be in the leafy shade of old live oak trees. Of course the oaks were to remain untouched. Around the site, in the middle of a what seemed to be a poison oak sanctuary, were thousands of tiny black, meat-eating flies that buzzed around my face, and in the rocky crevices black widow spiders, and under every fifth boulder was a rattlesnake. In a large open meadow on the other side of a chicken-wire fence and close to the house site, grazed a dozen cows, guarded by dogs and a mean looking bull. The house was to sit on six or seven *never-to-be-defeated* anthills while the disturbing cries of young coyotes punctured the night with a suddenness that confirmed the Woodhull's were in *their* territory. The couple seemed delighted with their chosen area.

The neighbors farther up Monte Vista Drive were an old and well-established family called the Wiley's_who in recent times had owned an immense portion of Topanga proper, but out of economic necessity, relinquished many acres.

Naturally, the Woodhull's were on a tight budget and thought a round building would be would be a more economical shape and not disturb the trees. In theory, they knew the circle holds the most square-footage for the least exterior wall length. Foundations would contain less concrete and walls would have fewer studs and siding.

101 - Sketch of the Woodhull house (lower octagon only.) Upper octagon built for a later owner. Builder: Harry Heckendorf.

Their reasoning was correct. We came up with an octagon house, shown as a one-story lower floor in the sketch above.

Semi-circular seating in the living room was sunk a foot into the terrazzo floor around the fireplace. The ceiling was of gently sloping, 2x6, sandblasted Douglas Fir boards with a half-inch recessed joint and covered with a Bermuda Roof. A Bermuda Roof is made of lightweight concrete poured two to three inches thick in layers two feet wide over the plank ceiling. This was the first and last time I was able to do either a terrazzo floor or a Bermuda Roof.

In 1973 the above sketch was used as an illustration for a Doubleday book written by Alice Upham Smith called *A Distinctive Setting for Your House*.

The Woodhull's sold the house after living in it for a few years and I was to do an addition, the upper octagon, at a later date for clients named Andrews.

THE GARDEN HOUSES

*H*aving built the Dorr house on it's spectacular bluff, and having been in the Chamber, I was asked by an associate Chamber member to look at some property with the idea of building some houses for sale. Two properties were in Monte Nido, four miles inland, and one on the bluff side of Malibu Road next to the ocean. Nick Schiro, at fifty, could have been a much older brother or my younger uncle even though our life experiences were vastly different. Nick had spent the bulk of adulthood in the Army and was retired as a Colonel. He was of medium height, in fair condition, and dressed neatly for Malibu in open shirt, slacks, polished shoes and sport coat. He looked mature with his dark hair graying at the temples and his trimmed mustache. He was often seen lighting his pipe or pushing sweet-smelling tobacco in the bowl with his thumb or knocking ashes out against his heel of his shoe. He looked like and everyone thought of him as a gentleman contractor, though I don't think he'd ever swung a hammer in his life.

After retirement from the service and with a fondness for making things, and because he was in Malibu with available land, hard-selling financiers, and real estate friends, Nick probably figured he was able to make phone calls to subcontractors and organize construction work as well as anyone. Honest and outspoken, his Colonel-ship proved he had leadership qualities. Nothing else in life interested him, anyway, and being energetic by nature, he thought it would be fun to build houses. Now, with this kid *(me)* he could enjoy his work. We recognized ourselves as a good team.

The Monte Nido sites, four miles from the ocean and behind the Santa Monica Mountains, were the first to be built in a newly opened tract serviced by gravel roads. The developers had brought water and electricity to the sites. Natural gas was unavailable. Forests of live oaks surrounded three sides of the tract and the third side to the north was contiguous with undeveloped, bare, rolling hills. The third site was located in Malibu two hundred feet from the shoreline on a low bluff lot, forty feet high, overlooking the ocean and Malibu Road.

Nick did the proper surveys and we wrote his program. The project was to build the standard small Malibu house in the post-and-beam style, 1,500-square-feet, three bedrooms, two baths, and kitchen, dining, living room, with a two car carport. I tried to be creative and looked through magazines to get ideas for small houses. If a house was published, I thought, it had to be better than anything I could do. *Nothing in the magazines clicked! I would have to design the building myself.* I would do three *garden houses.* The garden houses would have interior gardens under a large skylight so trees and plants would grow inside As it turned out, only two houses had interior gardens. The first did not.

GARDEN HOUSE # 1

The first house had no interior garden. I should rationalize. A garden house could be *in* a garden or could be *near* a garden. Technically, perhaps, it wasn't a garden house at all but just a house in a garden. An all-exterior wood-sided house with interior beams and exposed tongue in groove wood ceiling, it had great quantities of glass, as did all post-and-beam houses in those days. It sat attractively on small bluff overlooking forests of live oaks.

When it was almost finished, Nick got an offer from his painter he couldn't refuse. His non-refusal spoke of his lack of understanding of what I was trying to do architecturally and appealed to the standard desire of getting something for nothing. The painter offered to charge half price to spray all the wood white if he could work over the weekend. He said the natural wood house looked unfinished. Nick, used to building a more normal house, agreed with him. Over the weekend the painter sprayed the natural ceilings of the wood house, inside and out, *white!*

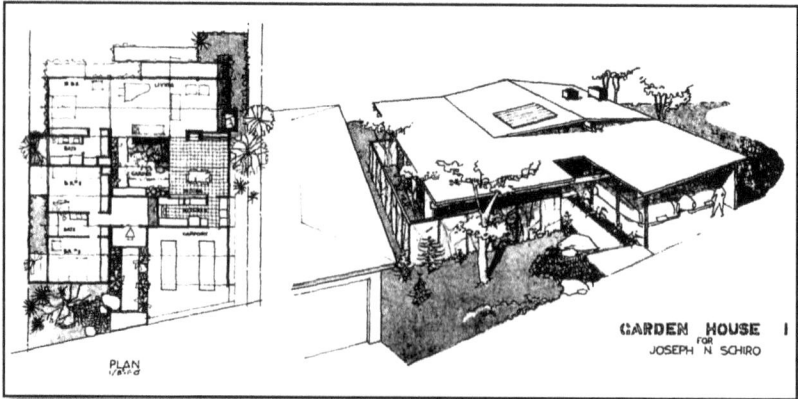

102 - Garden house number 1.

What blended with nature now stood out by itself and *alone.* What used to be artistic subtlety was now crude ostentation. The house didn't look so good with so much wood painted white. Nick realized he'd made a mistake and when he called me, I was shaken! He'd spilled ink on my fine creation. *I explained the variations in natural wood such as knots, slivers, checks, grain and joints, could be seen as imperfections. Those imperfections were minimized by the unifying affect and subdued tone of the natural wood's tan color. When wood is painted white, the imperfections, knots, slivers, checks, grain and joints become highly visible. They are no longer harmonious, subdued, and minimized, but are now accentuated because white creates unpleasant contrasting shadows that stand out against the remaining plain surfaces.*

Nick was reluctant to remove the white paint and grumbled and knocked his pipe against his heel and took off his hat to scratch his forehead. Nevertheless, it looked like the painter had shattered Nick's hopes for a profit. After hours of discussion, with no lunch, he asked for an alternative. I said he'd have to sandblast the white off! All of it! He had to get it back to the natural color. The following week he did just that, but all the white wouldn't come off. White paint clung tenaciously to the wood's soft spots. We elected to finish the job with a transparent, wood-colored stain to kill the white spots. That is to say, we had to re-paint the house. It worked reasonably well and to the eventual buyer it was no problem. Nick made his profit.

As a side note, the eventual owners also became owners of a

unique new-age bookstore called *The Bodhi Tree*. I admired their collection of poetry, philosophy, psychology, new-age books, and became an admiring and willing acquaintance.

(Note: In the above Chamber chapter, I was asking, what was my point of view? Working with Nick Schiro on the house accidentally painted white, I found I <u>had</u> a point of view, even if it was only about <u>not</u> wanting to paint a natural wood house, white. Circumstances forced me to figure out how I could stick to my guns. By verbal persuasion! I felt I was able to state what I thought to be true convincingly, and realized that it was important to be able to explain my point of view, whatever it was. If I couldn't explain it, I'd better think about it until I could.)

GARDEN HOUSE # 2

Garden house number 2 actually had an interior garden. The fifteen hundred square foot house was also located over the hill and around the bend from the first. It was on a level site lower in elevation than others in the tract. A three-bedroom house, its main view from the kitchen, dining, and living area was south, also facing a tall live Oak forest.

I have always thought of myself as a sensitive architect. At this time in my career, I was in the process of developing an architectural philosophy. I agreed with Frank Lloyd Wright's premise, *a house is first of all a roof*. A good roof drains rainwater, sleet, snow, hail, shields from the hot sun, and gives partial protection from the wind. Alone in the world with bad weather, if all I had was a roof, I'd go there! For protection and delight, what better way than to have a double hipped pavilion.

Garden house 2 was the opposite of a double-hipped pavilion. It had a butterfly roof, that is, a house with and an inverted gable. The roof sloped up toward the view and down toward the center of the house. In the lowest portion, the center was the garden. Over this was an eight-foot square skylight pitched in the standard gable form to drain rainwater. I have done several double-hipped houses with the skylight at the peak, but only once could I justify one in the valley.

103 - Garden house number 2.

In this case, the best view from the kitchen, dining, living room, was up and into the mature oak trees with their gnarly trunks and branches, rich and black, against dark green leaves. Normally, to face the roof up to the exterior is to allow the overwhelming sun to penetrate deeply into the structure. The large oaks prevented this and gave, instead, a shady and unusually striking view. In this *one* case I think the butterfly roof was worth it. The owner's feel especially proud living around a garden under a well-designed inverted gable.

GARDEN HOUSE # 3

The three houses didn't go up all at once. Nick built them consecutively with time lapses between them. Though we had plenty of room on the acre sites in Monte Nido, by comparison the Malibu site felt cramped. The house was to occupy a site fifty wide and 60-feet deep. Being in Malibu it was profitable to build a larger house because of Malibu's prestigious name, the proximity to schools and services, and of course, the ocean view, the biggest sales point of all. I had to design a *bigger* house on a *smaller* site.

Still in love with the garden idea, I made a low-pitched roof with gables facing both toward the ocean and mountains. My idea was to make a big garden in the center of the house with a beautiful tree spreading upward toward a large skylight. The tree would love it. Occupants would pass through the garden with plants and boulders under an elegant tree to get from room to room. It was a romantic idea and Nick did a good job in the execution. We loved the carefully crafted, natural wood, open beamed ceiling, and the innovative vertical grain Douglas Fir cabinets, doors, shoji screens and wood trim. The exterior and interior walls were white stucco and plaster. *The whole house, being constructed of natural wood and white, is the most cheerful of combinations.*

Slightly before it was finished, I was horrified to find Nick had sold it to a manufacturer of *plastic plants*. I thought the new owner, a 50-year-old overweight and balding bachelor, was eager at finding the perfect environment to display his *plastic plants*. He immediately called his decorator and they decided to do a *faux* color for the ceiling. *Faux* means *false* in French. He would make the real ceiling look *false*. He used a new method of staining wood, black creosote as an underlayment with white paint over. Soon the creosote would bleed through the white paint and give the room an old, deadened look some called avant-garde.

This was an unmitigated travesty! If parts of a building could show emotion, the white walls, the Douglas Fir paneling and trim, the indoor trees and plants, the harmoniously colored and textured carpet, would weep tears of grief for their mother, the natural wood, so thoughtlessly and blindly distressed. The fundamental beauty of the house was killed!

Garden house number 3.

This wasn't enough. Contrary to my expectations about the owner using *plastic* plants, he brought in hundreds of *real* plants in dark green plastic containers. I momentarily felt relief and thought he was going to landscape properly, but it was not to be. Vegetation of all kinds, in one gallon, five gallon, ten gallon, and twenty-gallon containers were placed everywhere there was space. The center tree was placed in a tan fifty-gallon plastic container. The plants, none indigenous and intended to be planted in real earth, were distributed without thought to location all over the house. The interior was obscured by hundreds of species of leaves, vines, trunks, branches, in positions sitting on the planter dirt, concrete floor, outside in rows, around the foundation, hanging from the destroyed beams, inside and outside. Potted foliage was located anywhere and everywhere, compulsively and neurotically overdone. What's more? He never *planted* the plants! For over two years they continued efforts to grow in their crowded plastic containers.

Apparently, Nick and the owner got into a lawsuit. The owner wanted *resolution* before continuing *life*. Perhaps he liked living surrounded by hundreds of arbitrarily placed potted plants. The cause of the lawsuit was because the land showed signs of slippage. The front bank had fallen away leaving a small escarpment slightly closer to the house. The County required no geology reports at that time, but the owner claimed Nick Schiro knew the house was on a slide and considered himself the victim. Nick claimed *not so* and the interminable wait of the civil suit began.

Subsequently, the entire row of fifty or so vacant lots and houses showed signs of slippage. The whole tract was proving unstable with each rain, the driving force of the foothills and poorly compacted fill. Rumors were that businessmen and contractors, trying to earn quick money, created a row of bluff sites and began grading operations without a permit. Over the years the whole bluff slipped and slid and dropped away and is still slipping. After a year and a half Nick lost the lawsuit, though I don't think for a moment he was at fault. The original developers created an on-going nightmare. It is them I blame.

In the years since the lawsuit Harry Rorick and his lovely wife, Cordelia, purchased my beautiful garden house. I would imagine the couple to be now in their eighties and content in their personalized space. Harry used to be a contractor and was much interested in contemporary art and architecture. I saw the couple recently and they said they adored *our* house, including me as the designer. Their house is furnished with strange artistic items. A four foot camel stands in the planter, it's tan fabric skin decorated with miniature paintings and tiny, colored lights. An ancient round-topped wood casement showcase with leaded glass doors embellishes the entry. It is filled with more lights and inside the glass doors are about a hundred miniscule environments on customized shelves, complete with miniature models of costumed people. The Aero Saarinen classic, round, white pedestal table with matching chairs is used as an afternoon lunch and game table. A long, more formal table is covered, top and sides, with blue decorative tile. The Ficus Giganticus, *(Large size Fiddle Leaf Tree.)* has grown so big it's upper leaves crowd the skylight and a thick wayward branch covers most of the living room ceiling. Some could call the house, *The Hanging Gardens of Babylon.*

105 - The late Harry Rorick in the much loved Garden House No.3. Photo taken about June, 2000.

Before Harry and Cordelia moved in they rented the garden house to poet and novelist, Erica Jong, whom they said wanted to buy it. One of her frequent guests before he died was Henry Miller.

About 1985 another slide dropped the front bank twelve feet. Harry covered it with a deck, railings and gazebo, and made a happy thing out of the continuing disaster. I doubt if it was permitted, since the supporting posts are obviously in slide debris. Adjacent properties are in continuing stages of disarray and are quickly repaired by resolute yet enthusiastic and loving landowners. Property owners have continued trying to build on adjacent properties because of the location. I have tried to help them but have run into ongoing problems with the Building Department.

106 - Harry and Cordelia's beloved and overgrown Garden House Number 3 built by Nick Schiro. Photo taken in the year 2000.

HALLIBURTON

Surprisingly, I got a call from Sue Halliburton. She and her husband, David, had been the clients of Hap Gilman whom I'd worked for a few years back. As you may remember, I had been the one to design their original house while working for Hap. They were expecting their first child and enthusiastic about adding two bedrooms and a bath to their home. They were hoping to have the work done before the baby. The addition was to be near my office, Malibu Creek, and in the area of the Serra Retreat. They probably suspected I knew more about their house than Hap, which, having done the design and working drawings on their house and having made a few free supervision trips, I think was true.

107 - Children's bedroom for David and Sue Halliburton used in publication called The Best of Home in 1961. Photo by Richard Gross

David, a son of the developer of Texas Halliburton Oil, having requested me to do the work, allowed me to feel that, indeed, I was a respected and an up-and-coming architect. I was fortunate enough to get Bob Butte as their contractor. Bob had built the Halliburton's original house and had just finished the Malibu Dorr job. I had a good time with the Halliburton's. They paid me well and I enjoyed supervising the work.

108 - Children's bedroom. The Halliburton house. Published 1961.

Sue worked with her decorator and painter and created a colorful fantasyland for their child's bedroom. It was selected by the Los Angeles Times for publication in a small 1960 Christmas booklet called the *Best of Home.*

The reason they published it was because of the outlandish use of color that I would not have used. Nevertheless, it made and interesting and unusual photo. The addition was photogenic and Sue's idea made it a good story.

DICK GROSS

*P*hotographer Dick Gross was doing color work for the Los Angeles Times, Home section and was selected to photograph the Halliburton children's bedroom. Dick was of medium height and looked like he hadn't had a good lunch in days. He wore glasses over a narrow Eastern European face, was clean-shaven despite a normally heavy beard and his hair was dark and difficult to manage. If action is character, Dick had character. He began work immediately. We both loved the artistic nature of things and connected on this level. He asked if I'd assist him in his photography and I assured him I would. I didn't realize how much I would learn when I saw my architectural work through a photographer's eyes. I found two things: *(1) The house is one thing. (2) The photo of the house is another.*

When looking at a photo of a house it is frequently not the house you are seeing it is the *picture. A picture* is always of the best view. The colors are bright and it is artistically composed and professionally lit. If they are normally lacking, plants or furniture can be acquired. A picture is frozen in time. A room is a living thing being both messy and clean at different times. A room changes with the age and needs of the occupants. A picture is changeless, lasts forever and can be a work of art, a house, not necessarily so.

Dick was able to photograph more of my houses using me as his assistant. Meeting and working at the Halliburton job was the beginning of a long and lasting friendship.

CHICAGO TRIP

*B*ecause the living expenses were low and the place was beautiful, Duke and Lois, Karon's parents, had recently moved to Mountain Home, Arkansas, With money coming in from the Dorr House and Halliburton addition, we decided to take a vacation and drive to northern Arkansas, which is heavily forested between sparkling lakes stocked with game fish. Our first impression was Arkansas State looked run down. This was reasonable, since there were few state taxes, there were few state services. The tops of trees fluttered in the fresh, cool breezes that swept across the lakes. Sociability blossomed and every day was a good for fishing. But I wanted to tell you about an episode that occurred on our way to Mountain Home.

We were approaching Amarillo in the Texas panhandle desert late in the evening. Karon was dozing in the passenger seat and I was sleepy and not aware of cars either to the front or rear of us. To our right and off the road, our headlights revealed a parked car, lights off, just sitting there. We were traveling at an appropriate speed heading easterly down a lonely, pitch-black, two-lane highway. I was glad I had a spare tire and plenty of gas.

Suddenly two dim pink dots materialized and I became conscious they were reflections of my own headlights from an old car stalled on the highway without lights. There wasn't time to hit the brakes, but I cranked hard on the steering wheel and swerved into the empty on-coming lane. Unhurried, I returned to my original lane, heart beating and thankful at having avoided a crash.

While congratulating myself, I noted a silent ball of orange light expanding in my rear view mirror. Horrified, I discovered the stalled car had exploded and was burning, with flames leaping to the sky. Karon awakened and I cautioned her not to look, pulled off the road and began jogging, reluctantly, back toward the car, mind filled with decisions.

What was I doing? I was conscious of going! I was going to help people deal with pain, life, and death. I was going to witness a terrifying scene. I would have to help someone from a burning car. Would I be injured, myself? Dear God, why me! I was afraid. I should do this, but did I want to do this? I have never faced this kind of thing before.

As I kept jogging I noticed a police car had arrived at the scene. It must have been the car we saw parked. Two more cars had arrived and one behind those. They were all stopping to give assistance. I slowed my jog in time to see a man, pants aflame, run across the highway. I assumed he would put his own flames out rolling in the desert sand. I assumed others or the policeman would come to his aid. The car was in full combustion. I decided things were under control and a policeman was in charge. I decided to return to our car and began walking back.

While I walked I thought *I don't want to get involved. After all, I was several hundred yards past the accident when it occurred. It wasn't my fault. I don't want to be detained. The policeman has everything under control. Others were helping him.* Thus, I justified to myself why I should jump in my own car and get the hell out of there.

Afterward, and to this day, I wondered and do wonder if I did the right thing. What evidently happened was the driver of a following car might have suddenly come on the stalled car and hit it from the rear. Perhaps his reactions were not quick enough. Perhaps he had been drinking. I've always felt I was a bit of a coward and made a tough decision for my own benefit. I saw myself as a young, courageous, man and here I had not shown myself as that. I never discovered what happened to the injured. I shall always remember the burning car, the running man aflame, and assume the lives of all, except Karon and myself, were irrevocably changed. I also found out when the chips were down my action was less than exemplary.

FLIGHT TO MIDDLE FORK

During the completion of the Dorr house John and Mary invited Karon and me to fly with them for their week vacation rafting down the Middle Fork of the Salmon River in Idaho. We would be two full days on the water. We flew John and Mary's twin-engine Beechcraft hangered in Oxnard, to Boise where John loaded up with steaks, eggs bacon, pancake mix, salt, real butter, bread, corn muffins, sweet rolls and every kind of expensive food. We were *not* going to rough it.

I don't remember much of that trip except for us it was an unusual and striking wilderness adventure. For the most part, the guys stayed with the guys, and the girls stayed with the girls.

109 - John and Mary's twin engine Beechcraft.

One time John and Mary, John's executive friend, William, John Junior, *(16)* and younger brother, Lennie, *(14)*, Karon and I went hiking along a slim trail down the middle fork. An hour into the hike and at a lovely little bend in the river, John found some unusually smooth and sculptural river rocks that fired his imagination. He had to have them for landscaping his new house. The rocks were large, perhaps six inches in diameter and a foot long. We had to walk them home. What could I do as a guest? I had to help! I thought river rocks should be left near the river where they like it and not be taken away from their home, so to speak. Leave river rocks with the river, was my philosophy.

Nevertheless, I soon found myself trailing John up the middle fork with four heavy river rocks, two hunched together on each arm. Carrying only one should have killed me, but I had four! John had six. Of course he was bigger, but then I was younger and supposedly stronger. A half hour back to camp, trudging up a long hill beside the rapids, I was breathing hard and sweating. I came to the notion, at this pace; I couldn't carry these stones and make it all the way back to camp. I fought with myself and looked at John with his immense load.

Now John was an unusual man and I have learned a lot by being the architect for John's house. One thing I learned from him was confidence. John exuded confidence. He knew he could do *anything*. Undaunted by difficult tasks, he could run the sales department at IBM, or fly a twin-engine Beechcraft, or parachute to safety, or fly a Bonanza, or a Grumman F-8. He could even fly his 104-foot wingspan, twin-engine, PBY-5, the slow amphibious aircraft once used for military reconnaissance.

Convair
Catalina, PBY-5

110 - John and Mary's PBY. (Imagine with 4 engines.)

He could build a house. He could pour concrete or lay tile or host large parties. He knew how to raise a large family and keep a professional wife happy. At 47 years of age, John had proved he could do *anything*. He was a hero to me. I had to ask myself, how on God's green earth could he carry all that weight for a full hour up hill without resting? I followed his heels and watched him walk.

Each step was taken with deliberation. He paced himself to maintain his load. He neither hurried nor rested. He was self-controlled. Not making it ever entered his mind.

Perhaps he was more motivated than I. I didn't care about the damn rocks. I didn't need them for souvenirs or to decorate my garden. John did. He cared. We both made it for the full hour and dumped our stones where it would be easiest to load on the plane. Mary and Karon and the three guys arrived some time later. I became reacquainted with the turtle and the hare story. *What wins is steadiness over a long period of time. The tortoise is relentless in his purpose. The hare unfocused and given to play.*

Another time we four males hiked steeply up through a tree and boulder strewn canyon and anxiously returned in the pitch dark unable to follow the trail. We made it eventually by feeling our way and making it a rule never to leave too late or to go so far as to not get back before dark.

DOYLE

*A*bout three months before the end of the year Tom Doyle came racing into my office and wondered if he couldn't get a permit to build a real estate office over his garage on Malibu Road. A Zoning change was to go into affect on January 1, 1960 and any permits issued prior to that date would be honored.

Tom was a partner of Fitzpatrick and Doyle, Real Estate Company. I had known Bob and Tom from visiting them earlier in the year while doing my own P. R. work. I presume he chose me because I was close, available and would probably be cheaper. I agreed to do the work for $300.00, completed the job and got the permit within the allotted time. Curiously, Tom became a close friend of mine over the years and later in my career was significant in getting me a million dollar house job on that very same site for Al and Bobby Rush.

1960 – VIVEKA

EXPLANATION

*I*n trying to make things understandable, I find words traveling through my head like, *while this was happening, that was happening* or *while feeling this on one subject, I was feeling thus on another.* Though life is lived simultaneously, I must write sequentially. Both work life and home life involved my whole person and I like everyone else was doing my best to live the best life I knew how in accordance with my history and under the present circumstances. Work life and home life consisted of relationships to people, sense of responsibility and optimistic dreams about the future. I hoped it would contain love in a happy marriage, children, architecture, art, music, literature, creativity, exercise, athletics, humor, and a deep sense of purpose. Thus, continuing with the sequential part of things, this is what was happening at home.

HOME

Karon and I had been expecting a pregnancy by the elimination of birth control methods. After a year of this we had become anxious and Karon began taking positive steps to assure pregnancy. She watched the calendar, took her temperature, ate properly, and got plenty of exercise to assure herself the best susceptibility. In February, after a year of anticipation, Karon announced she was, indeed, pregnant.

We were both thrilled and began reading books and taking classes on having our baby.

Karon wanted to have the baby at home without medical assistance. Natural childbirth was not being done in 1960, although there were a number of books available describing the benefits. No unfamiliar hospital setting would be required. The husband could witness and support his wife during delivery. With natural childbirth firmly in mind we went about our business. I did my architectural work anticipating a natural birth at home. I wondered how I would feel watching a live birth and how Karon would deal with the new experience. Pondering what kind of parents we'd be, we looked forward to our first-born.

LARSEN HOUSES

*B*ut in the meantime life as usual continued. Bruce Koch called me one day and informed me a client of his would be calling me soon. Within a short time, a young actor in Levi's, Hawaiian shirt, boxer trunks, sandals, and a tan-to-kill-for strolled into my intimate little office with the window overlooking the beach. The tall, athletic looking young fellow with high cheekbones, narrow brown Indian eyes and a mien of dark hair introduced himself as Keith Larsen. We sat at my solid core oak door conference table and talked. He wanted to build two small contemporary houses next to each other on Malibu Colony Road. His parents, who lived next door, owned two lots there. He would use Bruce Koch as his contractor.

I'd always considered my roll in architecture was to help young artistic professional couples build their efficient, but well-designed homes. Later these young Bohemians, he with a pipe and sweater with leather elbows, and she having just come from oil painting while listening to classical music, would add a room or two for children, and later, perhaps, a home office. Keith seemed to fit this image, though I soon found out the houses were to be income property for his parents.

I met his mom and dad, saw the lots, got the survey, and wrote the program. In my preliminary design I worked hard to make something individual yet harmonious that would meet my clients economical needs. I developed a single plan for both houses, but flopped one plan for the second house and staggered it in relation to the first. This gave each a special look while each was compatible with the other. Because they were more or less identical, the same engineering and detailing would work for both. I then did the plans, got the permit, and Bruce began building the houses.

Things went slowly. I don't know why. It may have been that Bruce had too many jobs or that the Larsen's weren't paying him on time or he bid the job too low. I don't know. It wasn't my business. But pilings were placed and the job was framed and the concrete man was about to pour the concrete for the garage floor slab. I was supervising the work and looked too young to be an architect. The cement man, overweight with a cowboy hat, boots and a belt looped tight around his protruding stomach, looked like he'd done a lot with his life and not all good. He looked uncouth and angry and probably was an alcoholic. He was the type of person requiring me to watch my words. I didn't, though. As I was leaving my supervision trip I made the mistake of telling this big bad cement man, as is done in the normal fashion, to be sure to slope the garage slab toward the street for good drainage. He glanced at me and continued forming. I left the job hoping he understood me and that he'd still like me, but I felt I'd just gone into a biker bar full of red-necks and ordered milk.

The next day I came back and the garage slab was sloped away from the street into the back of the garage. I burned in disbelief! Water running down the street would now enter the garage and puddle against the back garage wall and leak out through the stucco. I took it as a deliberate mistake delivered as an act of revenge. I told Koch. Koch said after the pour, the cement man jumped in his ancient unwashed truck and took off for somewhere up north with no return address. I don't know if the owner's or Koch ever fixed the slab or not. It was not my fault. Any job is always the contractor's, or in this case, Koch's responsibility, unless he has been given flagrant misinformation. The last time I saw the slab it was *not* fixed. This was one of many negative building experiences. *Architecture was testing me to see whether or not I could control my job.* In this instance, I could not.

WHY?

In my early practice a variety of things unforeseen happened. It is in retrospect that I know the dynamic of this one. The job came to me through Koch, so I was beholden to him. Keith Larsen had hired me and signed my contract, however, Keith got busy and his parents became the clients I had to please. They were not as enthused about modern architecture as Keith had been. The clients, living among the stars in the Colony, were amateurs regarding building and extremely conservative with their money. I don't know what price Bruce Koch quoted, but suspect he agreed to do it for less than it was worth. When a contractor underbids a job, the only way he can keep solvent is to hire cheaper, and usually less professional people. Hence, the concrete subcontractor, because he hasn't been paid, or because he also underbid his work, or properly bid the work, but couldn't collect from Koch because Koch couldn't collect from the Larsen's, had become angry! On the day of the mistake I saw the concrete man as a person not intimidated by a pip-squeak architect. One still wet behind the ears telling him the obvious. He was leaving town, anyway. Why not pay us all back.

I have learned since, *the owner, the architect and the contractor must create a single powerful force against the job's obstacles.*

The owner and architect can't team up against the contractor, nor owner and contractor against the architect, nor contractor and architect against the owner. *The triumvirate, owner, architect and contractor must be unified and on the same side of the table to accomplish their goals.* On the Larsen job I thought it none of my business who did the concrete work as long as it was done correctly. We all knew the slab sloped the wrong way and there was quite a bit of owner-contractor against architect. Or, in this case, it was subcontractor against the owner, contractor and architect. *The great triumvirate was not in place.*

I appreciated Bruce for getting me started in Malibu and because of that, shall always think fondly of him. The Larsen houses were the last houses we did together.

SECOND PUBLICATION

Under it's Chief Editor, Jim Toland, the Larsen houses were published in the Los Angeles Times Home section in November 1961.

111 - This is the exterior of one of Keith Larsen's rental houses in Malibu Colony published in the Los Angeles Times Home section in November 1961.

I met Jim, who was a modern architecture buff, through his secretary, Shirley Osborn, whom I'd met in the chorus of Gershwin's musical comedy, *Girl Crazy*. Shirley had led the female chorus and I had led the male chorus. She became a close friend of ours attending various functions at our house. After a while she came to know my work and suggested a meeting between editor, Jim, and me. I called Jim and with photographer, Dick Gross, the photos are the result.

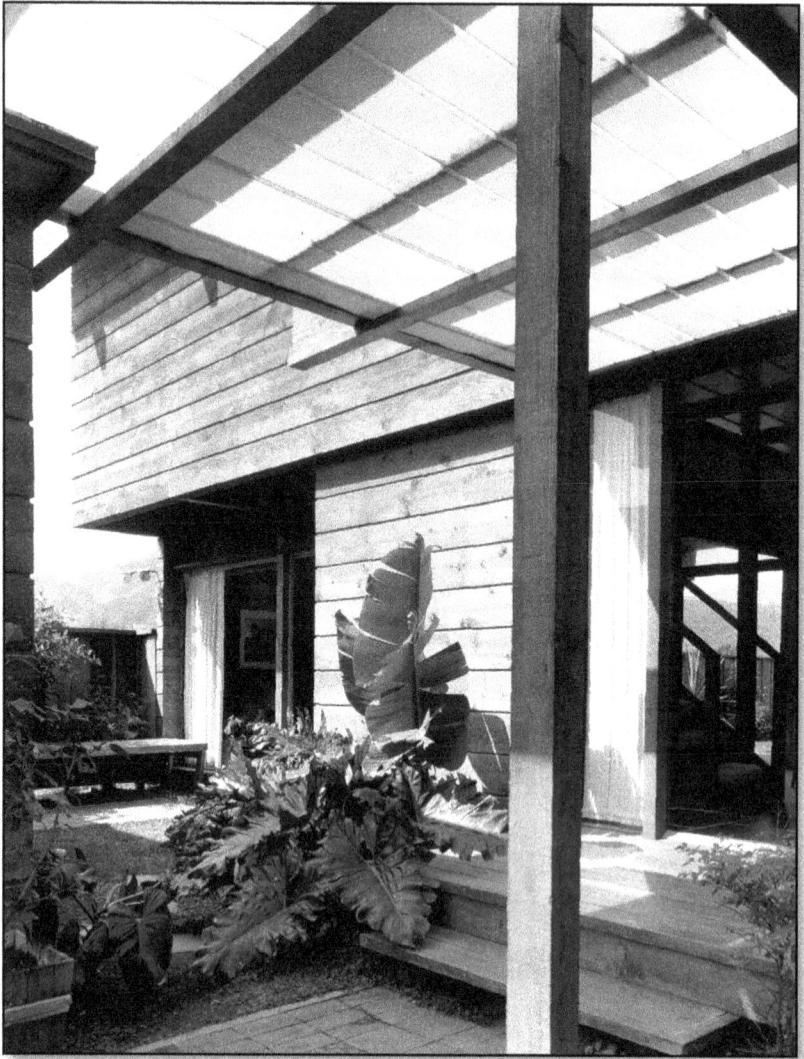

112 - *This is the entry to the Larsen house.*
All Photos are by Dick Gross. Photo: November 1961.

DISASTER

Still later *(about 1971)* the Larsen parents called and said their floor
was caving in. Alarmed, I went to the job and found the lower floor
sloping severely toward the center of the house and ominous cracks
quickly developing under the already sloping kitchen cabinets.

Observing around the house I discovered the Owner's had, with no professional advice, back-filled earth to the height of three or four feet around the house without a single opening for foundation ventilation. Moisture from the ground couldn't dry out and had seeped into the supporting girders. The earth throughout the Colony is uncompacted fill over a fluctuating fresh-water table 3 to 4 feet beneath the surface. Capillary action had brought the moisture to the ground's surface and, since the wooden girders and floor joists weren't air-dried, a perfect dry-rot condition was created and occurred.

113 - Interior. One of Larsen houses. Published November 1961.

We dug an access opening and crawling on hands and knees with flashlights, investigated under the house and found the 10 x 10 Douglas Fir girders so rotted you could scoop out handfuls of wood fibers with your fingers.

My advice was simple. Replace the girders and dry rotted boards and cross-ventilate the under floor crawl space. They did this at great expense. I learned about the devastating affects of trapped moisture and also about how important it is for the owner, architect and contractor to maintain communication. If I want the Owner's to love me, they must first trust me. Therefore I must learn to be trustworthy. *Before there can be love there must be caring, then trust.*

TOM THE SURFBOARD MAN

On the 50-foot lot next door was a surfboard shop. Tom, at about forty-three years old made surfboards and sold new and used ones as well as swim suits, snorkels, fins, spear guns, abalone knives, and other water equipment. Young surfers would commission him for a board and he'd make them one to their own and his own specifications. Short boards were not then popular. I would characterize Tom as a not-too-young, dropout on life who played the part of a former surfer when he never actually learned to ride a surfboard. Making surfboards was a good business for him. When asked his age he'd return the question and ask how old they thought he was. Or he'd tell them, old enough to know better, but *he'd do it anyway*. He joked about his age but never revealed it. Perhaps in some way he was ashamed he was making surfboards at his age and needed to play the part of a still young, partially conditioned, former surfing enthusiast. He had a trim looking girl friend, Susie, I'll call her, who dropped in now and then to help him when he was busy. She'd sell fishing spears and underwater guns, face plates, fins, swimming suits, and boogie boards in Tom's small shop with unwashed windows and sandy floors. Surfers shuffled in with bare feet, blond hair, a black and brown tan-to-kill-for, and swim shorts hanging barely off their hips.

Fortunately, Susan had a good day job. Tom and Susie were not married, nor do I think they planned marriage. Sometimes, Tom, while sanding a board, would tell the young surfers stories he'd heard, such as about the heavy old redwood Simmon's boards that were made as a forerunner to the light foam boards now used. Tales of what became of Simmon's, or stories about the daredevil big wave surfers in Hawaii. Stories of Ricky Grigg and Buzzy Trent were in the air with great frequency. Tom talked a good game, had a genial personality, a good sense of humor, and the young surfers idolized him. He sold lots of boards. I loved the water and was compatible in that Chris Craft location with Cap, Pat, Tom, and Susie.

BODY SURFING

*W*ork was over and Tom and I were body surfing the big ones on a short beach in front of our Chris-Craft business property. It was late fall when the ocean is warmest and we were surfing in the long twilight after sundown. The surf was big, smooth and steady at high tide and the on-coming mound of water would leap and dance crazily in the air before tumbling in a rush of white foam. The breakers would slide down it's own face and slam into the steep beach with a shudder and a sound that speaks of eternity. The collapsed ocean would then rush back again with equal power out to sea, and in the wake the sand crabs would surface in a multitude of little bubbles, feed and retreat into their holes before the next sand wash. The quiet, white, bubbling after-mist would hiss along the smoothing surface and I would taste the mist in my mouth and smell the salty air until on the horizon, I could be seen another big one leaping and mounding for a repetition.

Tom and I would float up the big face and decide on the spot, whether to slide down for a thrilling ride, or having made the wrong decision, go over the falls and be slammed on our backs onto the sand. We were slammed every other time, but we learned how to handle it. Anticipating a fall, we'd somersault and lie out flat, belly up, and become a victim of destiny, giving ourselves up to the crashing waves and fate. Caught in a big shore break, I'm the victim. The surf does with me what it will. I must give up control. The ocean has me. I am the ocean. The ocean is me! It feels like what I would expect being tumbled about in a cold-water washing machine. Our knowledge of how to swim in the sea, control when you can, give up control when you can't, enabled us to escape injury.

The cold sea was invigorating. The heart beat with enough power to warm the skin and equalize the cold and make the experience divine. The cold was there, but we could resist it. After an hour or so, when it became too dark to see the on-coming waves and our hearts were no longer equal to the cold and we'd had our fun anyway, we followed our instincts. They told us it was time to go in. Were I to do it over again? I would!

MOULE HOUSE

In the 1960's the Fitzgerald Real Estate Company came into existence and the firm of Fitzgerald and Doyle was highly publicized and doing well. They were located in new, semi-modern buildings located on the Southeast corner of Webb Way and Pacific Coast Highway, about where the 76 gas station is now, and maintained a new, young, upbeat establishment.

Along with their normal house and property sales was the development of La Chusa Highlands in Western Malibu. Le Chuza Highlands is located close above Pacific Coast Highway on either side of Encinal Canyon Road. It consisted of fifty or more one half acre to one-acre properties, on steeply sloping hills with magnificent views of the ocean, Catalina, Palos Verdes and on clear days, the Santa Barbara Islands.

Fitzgerald Realty Company had associated themselves with original property owner's who had the motivation, money and time to make the necessary surveys and do the proper bureaucratic work. Then they chose a couple of young builders to do the construction work and selected me as their in-house architect. I was chosen because businessmen from Malibu Chamber meetings and work I'd done with Bruce Koch knew me. There were no other licensed architects in the area nor any quite so willing and ambitious as I. Three professionals firms were required for the new idea, the Fitzgerald and Doyle's Real Estate Company, Douglas Rucker, Architect and the young Contractor's firm.

Milt Black, my next-door neighbor on Amalfi Drive in Santa Monica Canyon, was one of their first clients to purchase these combined services. He became interested in the relatively inexpensive property and bought two lots. On the lower lot he had me design a house for speculation. It was a good post-and-beam house and he enjoyed the project and sold it in a short time to make a small profit. Milt Black's house is still there and in good service, although unfortunately painted stark white.

Then Jim and Kathy Moule arrived from the Long Beach area ready to accept the Fitzgerald-Doyle lot sales program. They agreed to my compensation of 10% of the construction cost and our families became friends during the drawings and construction. On their steeply sloping property with a magnificent view and dramatic sandstone boulders, they wanted what I was most anxious to offer, a home for the modern Bohemian family. That is, an economical, contemporary, post-and-beam house, with three bedrooms, two baths, kitchen, dining, living and carport, for a cultured family.

114 - *Interior of the Moule house as published in the Los Angeles Times Home section, May 1963 with photos by Dick Gross.*

I was awestruck by the rocky beauty of the property. My enthusiasm was high. My clients seemed perfect. I couldn't wait to get into the project. I visited the site, made sketches from different angles, got the views firmly in mind and marked them on the survey. I made sure Mario C. Quiros, my office mate and surveyor, plotted the precise size, location and exact elevations of each of the huge boulders. This was to be my first *"boulder house."*

I came up with a narrow house paralleling the site's contours, with boulders close-by, framed in large plate glass windows. One boulder I left inside the building. The house was practically all glass to catch views of the fabulous blue ocean. A shed roof drained storm water and shielded the eyes from the sun. Tucking the house in the boulders and pitching the roof in one slope would protect the glass house from rainstorms and the wild Santa Ana winds.

115 - Interior of the Moule house showing the rock outside.

To hold it up laterally I used metal *"X"* brace rods crossing in front of one of the eight feet by eight feet six glass modules. In that way I could make a shear panel and in that section and not have to lose the view of the boulder or ocean. I left a large boulder inside the house in the fireplace area, 4 feet high, 5 feet wide, and 5 feet long dramatically and boldly slanting out of the ground as the antithesis to the rectilinear, Mondrian-like framework of the house. This specimen of geologic time sat with all it's burned, scarred and prehistoric presence, in a small garden and became a new kind of focal point for gatherings.

BUILDING THE HOUSE

During construction the young builder, I'll call him Sam, laid out the foundations of the house and discovered one of the extraneous boulders projected awkwardly into the building. There was no way to save the boulder and we reluctantly decided on its removal. Sam rented jack-hammers and had his laborer's try to reduce it to rubble, but the deeper into the boulder they dug the harder became the stone and after ruining a couple of dozen bits and his men's patience, called me to discuss the problem.

116 - The interior of Moule house.

We decided to blast! We called Jimmy Decker! The next highway is a mile toward Ventura called Decker Canyon Road. After intersecting Pacific Coast Highway, it runs steeply uphill into the Malibu Mountains. Up there are Decker School Road, Decker School Lane, and an Old Decker School. The Decker's lived in the Decker area since before the original Malibu property was sold to Fred and May K. Rindge and their name is historically significant in this area. One of the descendants was Charlie Decker, an elderly grading contractor who had all the equipment to grade a hundred-acre tract and get it done, not only on time, but also with a week or two to spare. He ran a tight ship with D-9s, sheep's foot rollers, water trucks, tractors, graders, backhoes, hauling trucks and all the attachments, and every other imaginable piece of grading equipment.

117 - The exterior of Moule house was published in Los Angeles Times Home section May 1963. Photos by Dick Gross

Charlie was sometimes given more to timeliness in getting the job done than having a sense of humor. His grammar wasn't the best either, but when this heavy set guy with dust on his jacket took the cigar out of his grizzled jaw, squinted through the smoke, and laid down the fact that he could grade a whole acre to an eighth of an inch, you stood in awe. It wasn't like I was going to argue with him, even though an eighth of an inch is close to perfect and what with the ability to drive that huge machine, and all .... I didn't go there.

118 - The exterior of Moule House. Photo by Dick Gross.

Jimmy Decker, whom I think was a son of Charlie's but could have been a nephew, was a born laborer. His body was hairy. I know this because he seldom wore a shirt. He wore Levi's held up by a leather belt with a big silver buckle and dusty work shoes. That's all. Rain or shine, cold or hot, windy or foggy, he let his hairy chest stand up to whatever was out there. If it were raining he wouldn't put on a shirt. If it were freezing he wouldn't put on a shirt. If it were hailing, he still wouldn't put on a shirt. We wondered if he even had one. But Jimmy loved to move earth. With a pick, shovel and wheel barrow, he could move earth faster than any one I've ever known. But the thing he liked most was moving boulders by himself.

Along the way he got his blasting license. There aren't many people licensed to do blasting. We called Jimmy! I told Sam, OK, but I didn't want to know and I didn't want to watch. I imagine Jimmy drilled into the boulder, backed everyone off, pushed on the detonator and the boulder went WWHHOOMPH! When the dust drifted slowly up the hill following the Pacific's westerly winds, Jimmy'd leap down the hill, bare-wasted and check his work. He'd move the debris out of the way, drill another couple of holes and detonate with another WWHHOOMPH! By the end of the day the boulder and debris were gone and the site swept up and ready for the young builder to continue.

Sam finished the job and Kathy and Jim Moule and their children and Karon and I became friends. We loved to picnic with them at their boulder house on the side of the mountain and talk. The Moule's are still close friends. They only stayed in their house for a few years until Jim was transferred to Phoenix, Arizona, but they didn't move before Jim Toland published their house in the Los Angeles Times Home section.

FLIGHT TO OAKLAND

John and Mary Dorr invited us to visit their home in Oakland across the bay from San Francisco to see furniture intended for the Malibu house. This time we flew a plane John owned jointly with his IBM executive friend, a four passenger Beech Bonanza, stored in Santa Monica. For Karon and me, flying here and there was the furthest thing from our minds, but we were flexible enough to allow whatever happened that seemed reasonable to happen.

Over wine country this side of Salinas we were flying through the skies at 8,000 feet with the roar of the engine and nothing under us but a seat attached to a slim piece of aluminum. John was to my left flying the plane and to his right I was sitting co-pilot.

I say I was *sitting* co-pilot. I was in no way *flying* co-pilot. If John became incapacitated, we'd fall like a stone and I'd be screaming all the way to impact. I pretended nonchalance with blood pressure pounding through my veins and praying for the flight's end and a safe landing.

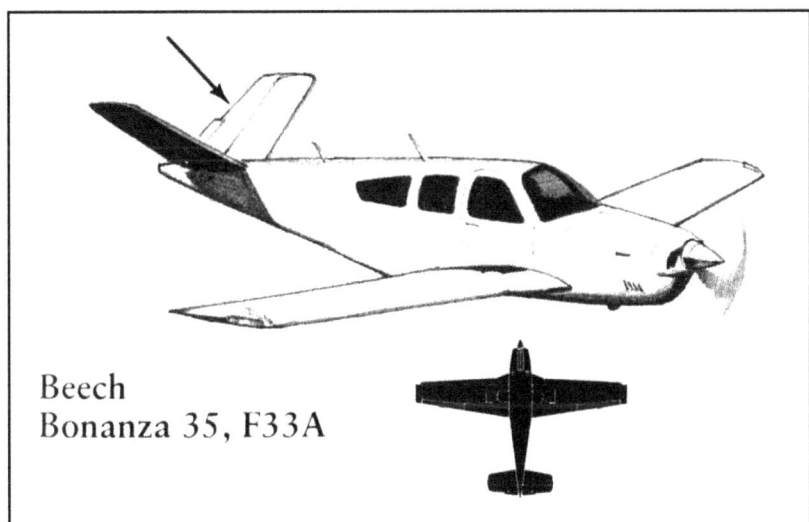

Beech
Bonanza 35, F33A

119 - John and Mary's Beech Bonanza.

It was a clear flying day with a few scattered high clouds. Conversation was at a minimum because of engine noise. Even so, Mary and Karon seemed content making loud girl talk in the back seats. John conspired with me through slim, mischievous eyes and nodded back over his head toward the girls. He pushed the stick forward and the peddles to the left and the engine whined. Orientation was garbled as the plane went into a steep diving turn and the swirling colored squares of earth below me recalled old combat movies with smoke trailing from the back. I forced myself not to scream *AAAHHH!* as

John pulled back on the stick after a two thousand foot drop. I felt the pressure of 3 G's on my back and my cheeks sagged to my neck as the little plane straightened out, becoming quieter and more normal sounding.

This was John's way to a break up the boredom. He scared the girls! *"Well, God bless him!"* Immediately after the dive, John climbed to our former height and joked with the girls about getting their attention. John thought he and I were doing it together. I was kissing my life good-bye but feigned good humor and restrained hugging the ground when we landed.

PREGNANCY

*W*ith the certainty of Karon's pregnancy we had to get real. Between my attempts to start a practice in Malibu and Karon's UCLA job doing private secretarial work for the head of the Theater Arts Department and getting her Master's Degree on her lunch hour, we began reading childbirth books. The most helpful was the Fireman's Emergency Manual. In 1960 most women went to the hospital, had an epidural, and while they were more or less knocked out, had their baby and stayed in the hospital for a week before coming home. It was a successful method and one I could easily have accepted. However the idea of having a baby naturally was a new idea in 1960 and few doctors could be found who would be willing to assist the birth without use of drugs. If the patient wanted to have the baby at home, there was almost no doctor to be found. Karon not only wanted to have the child naturally, but at home, too, with the husband *(me)* present at all times, theoretically assisting.

Karon considered herself a modern young woman and was going to do it the modern way or the hard way using no anesthetics and not being knocked out! Basic woman gives birth to basic child. I was distantly intrigued by the idea.

I felt comfortable with Karon because she lived and loved the contemporary life. This suited my temperament. I saw myself as a contemporary person doing contemporary architecture and thought we were well matched. She loved the newer composers like Stravinsky, Shostakovich, Copland and Ives, as well as the proven composers like

Beethoven, Bach, and Brahms. She loved all the artists of the Bauhaus Period, Kandinski, Klee, and Feinenger, and the new art of Henry Moore, Lichtenstein, Warholl and Pollock, and the earlier modern artwork of Picasso, Braque and Kandinsky. Though she sang in the church choir, she did not believe in organized religion and considered herself agnostic, or even atheist. In my life with her, I understood what she did *not* believe, but never knew what she *did* believe. She loved contemporary architecture, Wright, Le Corbusier, Mies Van der Rohe and the later works of Neutra, Soriano and Ellwood and strongly identified with the new Woman's Movement, N.O.W., begun by Betty Frieden. Considering these strong contemporary sides of her personality, it made sense she would follow the contemporary movement and have our baby naturally.

THE DOCTOR

During early pregnancy, Karon, with motivation and patience, was able to find a 60ish, zaftig, German woman, Doctor Behne, who claimed considerable experience assisting in natural childbirth. She was one of three Doctors who were willing to help in the home.

The latter portion of Karon's pregnancy was spent going to weekly La Maze classes, the two of us no less, and practicing breathing and birthing exercises. I read eleven childbirth books. Karon was sufficiently reassured reading eight. After all, she *was* a woman.

Karon liked to be pregnant. She liked the swelling of her breasts and the glow of her pregnancy. I liked how she looked and felt good about our marriage because she was carrying our baby. She stopped drinking alcohol, limited her smoking, and ate healthy foods while trying to keep her weight down. She continued working at UCLA and began painting the interior of the house, nesting. We'd tried for a whole year and this was our deserved prize, a wanted baby. I was happy about our coming new addition and am pleased to say that for Karon, pregnancy was a happy experience.

When the pregnancy was about 7 months, Dr. Behne began changing her mind about the idea of Karon having the birth at home. In a German accent she said, *"Sometimes da first childt iss more difficoouldt."* Her examination showed conditions less than suitable and urged Karon strongly to go to the hospital. In the last month she was adamant.

BIRTH PANGS

Karon's water broke in the afternoon of September 11, 1960. We notified Dr. Behne who again advised us to go the hospital. Karon refused and we began preparing the bed for a birth at home. Dr. Behne said she no longer would be responsible for the outcome of the birth. Karon was so determined to have the baby at home; she said she'd do it without a doctor if necessary. Of course where does that leave me? What Karon was unconsciously responsible for was that *we* were going to witness whatever happened *together*, no matter what.

We each had put in a hard days work and were getting drowsy and hoping for another good nights sleep when at ll:00 P.M. regular contractions began. The nine-month wait was over. Anticipation was becoming a reality. The thing for which we'd prepared was going to test us. I might say having my first baby was extremely difficult for me. Think of how it was for Karon or little Viveka.

I did what was expected. I rubbed Karon's back for a couple of hours. About two o'clock, totally exhausted with my hard day and the reality of what was happening, I tried to rest and relax between contractions. Karon did the same. About 4 o'clock, while I tried to doze, Karon started the fast breathing she'd learned in the Le Maze class. At first it seemed to help, but by the time Lois Conan, Karon's mother arrived at about 4 A.M., she seemed at the same time, tired and compelled to continue the rapid breathing. In retrospect, she started fast breathing too soon, well before the more painful contractions were to occur when the technique would have been most helpful. This is what is learned with a first baby.

About eight o'clock Dr. Behne arrived and she and Lois had a private talk in the living room. In a short time Dr. Behne entered our bedroom with a paper to sign. A disclaimer saying that Karon had not followed her recommendations and if she lost the baby, she *(Dr. Behne)* would not be responsible. Karon signed it.

While I supported Karon's desire to have the baby naturally at home, I was more than concerned about her refusal of the doctor's repeated recommendations to get to the hospital as fast as possible. She continued the contractions until 6 A.M. Dr. Behne examined her and found that, though she was beginning to open, it wasn't happening fast enough. The baby was stuck. Dr. Behne determined the final abnormal position of the baby was face up instead of face down. The bony crown of the babies head was jammed and fitting firmly into the cradle of the tailbone. This produced a prolonged, painful, and apparently futile effort with each contraction.

The two older women seemed at a loss as to what to do. They stood together in the doorway and shook their heads as we continued to have the baby. At 10 A.M. Dr. Behne clearly announced she feared for the life of the child. As I observed, Karon, exhausted as she was, clearly heard her words. She realized her determined efforts were not something she alone was doing, but involved two human beings, herself and the baby. The words, *"feared for the life of the child,"* brought it home to her. She got it and decided the Doctor might be right. Her special effort to have her child her way, which I admired and considered a wonderful trait, yielded to common sense when it came to the life of her child.

She thought she had been doing it right, but if her child were to die, she'd never forgive herself. I've asked myself why this thought didn't arrive earlier. It would have saved us all a lot of agony. Her child's and her own, especially.

We lifted her off the bed, threw a bathrobe around her shoulders, and between contractions and with much difficulty, were able to get her into our white Volvo station wagon. It was an hour or more drive to Dr. Behne's tiny, but more progressive hospital that allowed fathers in the birth rooms.

BIRTH

Dr. Behne was driving and Lois was sitting in the front seat. I was in the back, trying to be there for Karon. The getting up and moving was good for her. Her difficult walk to the station wagon, the climbing in, the re-situating of her body in the station wagon, redoubled her contractions. She strained and relaxed, tried to flow with the curves and speed and braking of the car. Strands of dark hair stuck to her forehead. She seemed better. Color returned to her cheeks. When I announced I could see the small round circle of the baby's dark hair, we gained hope.

At the hospital, attendants dressed in green, rolled her on a gurney and pushed her to a waiting room. According to Dr. Behne the birth was imminent. I stayed with her while the nurses gave her a shot of some kind and in a few minutes I was asked to leave as she was taken into the birth room. I was relieved to have what I considered my job taken over by the professionals.

Lois and I walked down the hall. No one in the hospital seemed to care. We found the birth room. The door had a small glass-viewing panel near the top. Lois and I took turns looking in to see Dr. Behne, Karon and a nurse or two assisting with and attending the birth. We could hear Karon's efforts and cries. Then the baby was born! She was born with a cry from Karon I'll never forget. It was a cry of relief, happiness, joy, and pleasure at having created a miracle. Who can explain the cry of a mother who has just given birth to her first-born? It was miraculous!

Lois and I saw Dr. Behne when she took the baby from Karon. The baby was blue. Dr. Behne held it face up and folded and unfolded it until after an agonizing minute we heard a tiny cry, and then another. The baby was breathing on it's own. They wheeled Karon into the recovery room for a good rest, while they cleaned the baby. Karon was falling asleep. Duke, Karon's father, had arrived and the two of us thought we'd drive home, leaving Lois to attend her daughter. I enjoyed our drive, happy Karon had delivered a 7 pound, 2-1/2 ounce little girl into our lives and the world. At home I fell asleep for a long time.

AFTERMATH

Before Karon was allowed to bring the baby home, the hospital required a name. Karon had seen the name Viveka on the program of the Royal Danish Ballet and liked it and asked me if I liked it too. I thought it a fine name. For a middle name, Karon chose to honor the baby's heritage and her father, Duke, by giving Viveka the middle name of Duke's mother, Sarah.

NOW APPEARING

1st TIME ANYWHERE

"I'LL CRY TONIGHT"

(AND SLEEP TOMORROW)

* * * * * * * * * * *

STARRING

VIVEKA
SARAH
RUCKER

THAT 7 LB. 2½ OZ. 19" CHARMER

* * * * * * * * * * *

PRODUCED BY DOUGLAS & KARON RUCKER

CURTAIN TIME....4:55 P.M.

MONDAY, SEPT. 12, 1960

*120 - Cartoon by Karon's girl friend, Marcy, a wife and neighbor with
the house with a contemporary addition by Bill Reid.*

   Viveka Sarah Rucker was a delight to have at home. Her
emergence, however, as would with the entering of any first baby,
changed the parent's normal one-to-one relationship into something

totally different. I felt like any new father would feel coping with work and a new baby. I was missing Karon's personal attention. The baby's needs obviously came first, the mother's second, and mine a poor third. Karon's attitude toward herself also changed. Friends and relatives laughingly said, *"By having a baby she automatically became a Saint."* She was as perfect in raising the baby as she was perfect about her studies or singing or performing and it seemed to me the baby got her complete attention.

I had convinced myself I was going to be in love with Karon forever. I would power through monogamously with whatever life chose for me. I wanted kids. This was my first. I did my part. In the morning I cared for my wife and child. During the day I continued my architectural practice and in the evening I again cared for my wife and child. I changed diapers so much I could do it sleeping and at some times thought I had. Since the baby was breast fed and had a unique schedule, she'd wake up at night, be fed, then Karon would fall asleep and I was left to guard the baby and see she was not rolled upon or covered with too many or too few blankets. Interminable sleepless nights and continual exhaustion became our norm for a seemingly unending time. We were brave.

We came to love Viveka and her distinct personality. Karon and I were proud to show her everywhere and talk endlessly about our brand new baby girl.

BUSCH

I had known Louis Busch for a number of years. Louis was a personal friend of builder, Harry Heckendorf, and may even have recommended me to Harry for the Zenn project, one of the first houses I designed in Malibu. Harry worked with a pipe-smoking associate named John Diefenderfer. Many couldn't help but smile when the combination of names, Heckendorf & Diefenderfer, were recommended as good builders. As time went by, Harry and John were to build a number of my client's homes, including our own Malibu house.

Louis also appreciated the friendship of Malibu's first and only surveyor, Mario Quiros, the person with whom I shared my office.

Louis was an active Chamber member and was not only a booster of Malibu's growth, but of great assistance and encouragement to the Chamber's and my ill-conceived Boat Harbor Committee.

Louis Busch's father had been notable in Malibu as working with Dave Diefenderfer, John's uncle, and the Adamson family to affect the first mandatory land sales along the twenty-five mile coastal strip.

121 - Screen for Busch Office Building unchanged since its construction in 1961. Photo: DWR – 2000.

Louis and Dave operated in competition with Art Jones and Dave Duncan, also one of the first firms to lease Malibu property. Louis Busch Junior was a true Malibu native, married with four kids and respected in his profession and by buyers and sellers for being honest and forthright.

Louis asked me to remodel his office on Pacific Coast Highway. He didn't want to spend too much money, but understood his office, which was a poorly proportioned two-story plaster box with nail-on windows, demeaned the honorable work of he and his associates. Architecturally his building wasn't much, and I advised the best and least expensive way to improve the building was to cover it up. Get rid of the building. Put something in front to hide it. If he did some minor entry and front window work and let the rest of the building remain for economy's sake while covering the whole thing up with a screen, he'd be better off. Louis realized this was true.

I designed horizontal wooden louvers around all four sides suspended on metal supports that held the vertical screens three feet away from the building.

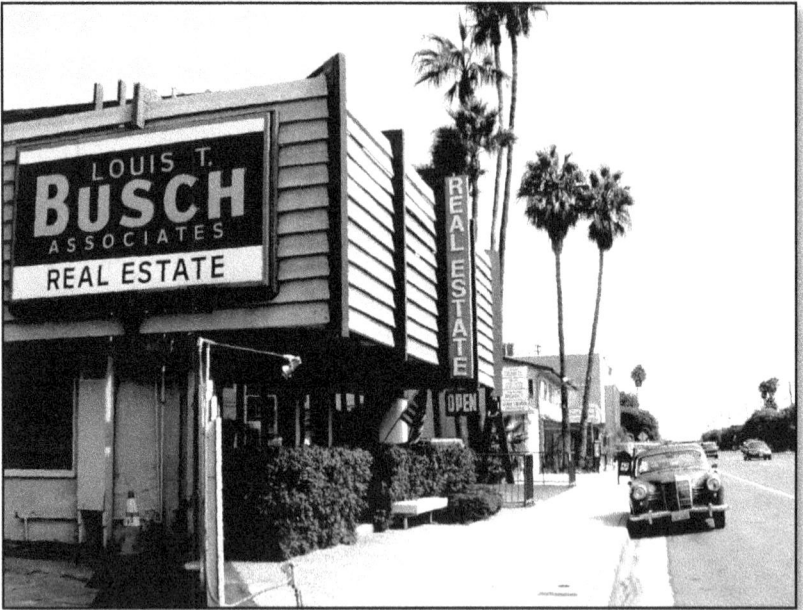

122 - Busch office remodeling seen from Pacific Coast Highway.

The wood stained louvers produced a handsome shadow line and simplified the structure. The plaster box with nail-on windows had now been replaced with an attractive screen. Louis's friend and contractor, Bob Zukin, efficiently built the low cost remodel job. The design allowed Louis to gain a large advertising space for his firm, *LOUIS BUSCH, Associates, Real Estate*. With a fresh coat of interior paint he now had an attractive place to work that complemented his style.

It wasn't much later that Louis invited Mario and me to rent his second floor at a very attractive rate. The business location and the fact that my remodeling of Louis's building might be an asset; I thought it a good idea to accept. Within a short time I found myself moving out of the Chris-Craft building and away from Cap, Pat, Tom the Surfboard Man, and the proximity to the ocean and my beloved window. Soon I had made two, three-foot long signs from a six-foot piece of clear heart redwood and plaster stick-on letters. They said, Mario Quiros, Surveyor and Douglas W. Rucker, architect. *(Still with the small "a" for architect.)*

THE MOVE

*L*ouis showed a particular caring for Mario, not only because of his superb Costa Rican education, honesty and direct dealings, but because he needed a surveyor for his own business and wanted someone to recommend as a reliable surveyor. It was the same in his thinking about renting to an architect. Renting to a surveyor and architect gave him a stronger hold on Malibu's building and real estate.

Mario and I were compatible and I've been proud to have been associated with such a steady, dependable, well-meaning person and family as the Quiros's. I admired Mario and his family and, since he is still in business with his son, at the time of this writing, I stop in to see him whenever I feel the need.

I handcrafted screens made from sheets of unbleached muslin and one-by-four redwood to screen off the entry from the drafting room. I bought another couple of hollow core doors and used them for layout tables and arranged my oak door conference table near one of the windows. My income was slight as were my office embellishments.

CHAMBER, WORK & PLAY

THE WORLD

John F. Kennedy succeeds President Ike Eisenhower in the 1960 election.

Gary Powers is shot down over Soviet territory.

Hitchcock releases the suspense thriller, *Psycho*.

Fellini directs *La Dolce Vita*.

The first LASER *(Light Amplification by Stimulated Emission of Radiation)* is developed by physicist, Theodore Maiman.

Birth control pills are first made publicly available.

Population of the United States is 179.3 million people.

East German Communists build a wall dividing East and West Germany.

The war in Vietnam continues despite American moral outcry.

France explodes its first atomic bomb.

The X-15, experimental aircraft, is flown at 2,196 miles per hour.

UN Secretary General, Dag Hammerskjold is killed in a plane crash in Northern Rhodesia. *(Now Zambia)*

Henry Miller Publishes *Tropic of Cancer* and *Tropic of Capricorn* in the United States, after being banned in the U.S. for obscenity for 30 years.

Alan Shepard is the first man in space reaching the height of 115 miles for 15 minutes, aboard Freedom 7, a Mercury Mission capsule

President Kennedy accepts full responsibility for the unsuccessful

Cuban invasion.

Arthur Miller writes *The Misfits* for his wife, Marilyn Monroe.

Virgil *(Gus)* Grissom is the second American in space making a 16-minute flight in Mercury Missions Liberty Bell 7.

Wilma Rudolph breaks the woman's world indoor record in the 220-yard dash in 25 seconds, flat.

THE CHAMBER

One thing I dreaded each month, yet tried to put on a happy face, was going to Malibu Chamber of Commerce meetings. One of the main purposes of the Chamber was to promote business. Why? To get your name in the paper, which eventually increases your income. How? By doing something that benefits the community, like being on a committee. Except for being on a committee, I attended the networking place for the above reasons.

It was not that I had anything against the members of the Chamber. In fact I liked most of them. I think the Chamber was *(and is)* beneficial to the community in many ways. They sponsored talks by the Malibu Board of Realtors. They listened to spokesman from the State Highway Patrol talking about crime and traffic control. They invited the Fire Chief, Harvey Anderson, to explain his methods and give safety advice, and heard an opinion or two from a Santa Monica Unified School District Supervisor on Malibu's eventual High School. The Chamber was a public place for groups to state their case, whatever it was. My case was to get known. This was the way.

I had arrived at a philosophic point. *A visible architect gets work. An invisible architect doesn't get work.* It was my choice either to be a good or bad architect. I saw bad architect's work going up all the time. The bad architect usually had no trouble getting work. He was visible because he was cheap. He didn't charge enough to do a good job. It seemed a waste of my valuable time to become a *bad* architect. What was it Mother said? *"It is important to be the best you can be."* To be my best meant I'd have to refuse jobs and explain my point of view going in to the Chamber. After two years of being in business, I hadn't yet thought out my approach.

I remember the Chamber installation dinner of sixty or so nicely attired men and women at the Sea Lion Restaurant's *(now Duke's)* gathering room. The Chamber President sat at the center of a formal table with his Vice President, Secretary, and Treasurer, flanked by important suited and gowned guests. I attended the occasion with eight or ten newcomers and their wives. After a three-course dinner, the clinking of glasses and the buzz and hum of the crowd, some members perhaps having had drink or two too many, and while the members were being served coffee, cobbler and cookies, the President, tapping his water glass with a spoon, stood up, welcomed the Chamber to the gathering and presently it was time to announce the new members. New members rose and thanked the members and President. As one of the last on the list, I stood and beamed at the sound of my name and the short exhortation about *there being a new architectural service in town.* The guests gave me polite applause to the delight of my spouse. My work and I had been announced in front of everybody and I nodded and smiled and mumbled a modest thank you and sat down. Fortunately, I didn't have to say anything. The fear of speaking in public was left over in me from my high school and college experiences. After the newcomer's were sworn in and seated, the Assistant to the County Board of Supervisors complemented the Chamber and promised us our Supervisor, Mr. Hayes, was particularly familiar with Malibu and would work tirelessly to achieve whatever Malibu desired. The assistant knew how to please the Chamber and was clear in voicing common opinions, especially so, since the owner-reporter from the Malibu Times, Reeves Templeman, was quietly taking notes in the back of the room. The Assistant was well aware that his and Mr. Hayes names and pictures would soon be on the front page.

I attended meetings held a few weeks later in the conference room on the second floor of the arched commercial building on Malibu Road. The building constructed by contractor, Nick Schiro, was seaward of the then popular circular drug store and restaurant on Webb Way.

A noticeable community leader, Henry Guttman, owner of the building, donated the use of the conference room. He attended Chamber meetings and I felt his donation-of-space enabled him to keep appraised of new community ideas that served him in his business dealings. Members would gather about 7:30 P.M. on the last Friday of the month and as preliminary exchanges of diverse opinions and experiences were winding down, about twenty-five members assembled themselves around the long table. At 7:45 P.M. the President would rap his gavel and the meeting would come to order.

He'd welcome old and new members, make an announcement, perhaps about the Chamber spring party at the Adamson Ranch below the Serra Retreat and introduce the local female Real Estate person selected for her consistency and community knowledge who read the minutes of the last meeting. After a seeming eternity, we'd discuss old business, to which there were numerous members who were not quite done with it yet. Next would be a guest speaker, the County Fire Chief, Harvey Anderson, for instance, who'd give a 20-minute talk, then call for questions. The members would disagree as to the size of water mains, where certain streets were, and be informed of new widening of certain firebreaks. Deliberations on former fires would take up time. Discussions were held on the availability of out-of-town departments coming to the critical aid of Malibu and where they'd be assigned. The issue was never *if* there was the next a fire, always *when* there was the next fire. Harvey would discuss how we could prepare ourselves, such as clearing volatile brush 200 feet from the house, assembling plastic trash cans to contain fire-fighting water with enough mops to extinguish smaller flames. Harvey was good speaker, a good Fire Chief and ran his department compassionately with firmness and authority.

During discussions, I would occasionally have something to add. I'd wait until the present speaker was done and tentatively raise my hand. At the same time my heart would increase in tempo, my face would flush, my blood pressure would begin to rise and I'd think, *"What if these leaders of the community actually gave me their full attention? I'd be on the spot!*

Now my heart pounded in my temples and my blood pressure threatened to gush out my ears and still the speaker spoke. About what, I don't know. Then I'd forget *how* to say what I wanted to say and get confused about the whole idea at hand. Instead of thinking about the subject, I was thinking about myself. Once given the chance, I was afraid I'd not be able to get my idea out and *I'd stumble over my words and freeze like the legendary deer in the headlights. Everyone would stare at me in embarrassed silence. I would have made a fool of myself. If I were a fool of an architect, only a fool would hire me.* Eventually so many speakers spoke before I could get called on, the subject had developed into something only vaguely related. What I had to say was now no longer appropriate. I had given up adding my thoughts. Only then would my heart and blood pressure return to a more normal condition, the tense state of, *I don't want to be here in my Sunday clothes but I have to,* would continue until I was home.

One time I became particularly self-consciousness when a majority of the Chamber members were voting *against* the idea of Synanon moving into the community. Having been to this self-help facility and having seen the good that was being done, I felt passionately that it had to continue. I was compelled to *support* the idea of Synanon moving to Malibu. Numerous times I tried to voice my thoughts, but because of my ardent interest, my heart beat too loudly and my face felt too flushed and my blood pressure rose to dangerous levels. Though I could have *written* my viewpoint and submitted it in essay form, I was unable to tell the group to which side I belonged. I felt a failure at my inability to express myself on what was to me such an important issue. The Chamber voted *against*. I was the only *for*. I felt it would have been important for the Chamber to hear another viewpoint, even though all were against the idea. They didn't think it would promote Malibu's business, nor be good for Malibu's residents. In light of that thinking, I had to ask myself, was I a loyal member?

MALIBU BOAT HARBOR

Early in my two or three year involvement, the powers of the Chamber of Commerce, knowing my passion for the ocean and my addiction to body surfing and skin-diving, thought it would be the right thing to put me in charge of the Harbor Committee. This was a new idea for me or for anyone to consider a Malibu Boat Harbor. Was it true the Chamber, looking out for the future of Malibu, thought as a man this would be a good idea? Apparently so! Santa Barbara had one. Why not Malibu? Caught in the holiday mood, imagination saw it beneficial for sailors on their way to Santa Barbara from the slips of San Pedro, to tie up at the new breezy Malibu dock and catch a lunch before sailing out. Santa Barbara seamen on a southerly run to San Pedro, Newport Beach, San Clemente or San Diego could stop at Malibu Harbor and do the same. And of course the Malibu Yacht Club, which numbered about thirty owners of Hobie Cats, *(small wet, fast catamarans with big sails)* was delighted. The Yacht Club, with a full stomach, could sail leisurely in either direction.

It is probable the members who were Real Estate agents in the Chamber felt a boat harbor would sell land and later, houses. The rank and file Chamber members saw it as a way to create business in Malibu. They foresaw a thriving enterprise for restaurants and stores, for fishing and boating gear, a bait store and construction of piers, and public bathrooms. They would need a huge parking lot, boat launch ramp, Fire Department, Police protection and a private Guard Service for the boats. Instantly the Edison Company would be involved and later, gas would be needed for a nicely humming and running Boat Harbor.

Dave Duncan, an elderly real estate agent from one of the original firms involved in the Malibu leasing and property sales with the firm name of *Jones and Duncan*, had in his possession an old Army Corps of Engineer's 300-page typewritten review of California coastal waters. He generously gave it to me to read. It discussed tides, beach building and erosion, rainstorms and draught statistics, seasonal water temperatures, scientific plotting of heights of waves in relation to the ocean bottom, direction and force statistics on storms, and coastal protection offered by islands off-shore like Catalina and San Miguel. They thought it would be good for me to be in a self-study program with coastal maps to inform myself so that my committee and I could determine the best location for the Harbor.

I accepted, of course. What else was I supposed to do? *If you're in the Chamber, you're on a committee.* My associates showed up for a couple of meetings at a subcommittee member's house on the Point and we put our feet on the table and discussed private matters. Occasionally the Harbor would come up and then we'd decide we needed more information someplace. We didn't know anything anyway, so we adjourned. Every month I'd have to stop my essential duties to make a progress report. I felt like I was still in school.

"*Yeah! We looked at Leo Carillo Beach, Victoria Point and Latigo and found pros and cons were such that ..... then returned our thinking to Little Dume ..... If only it weren't for those high cliffs, then ..... But that's only if ..... ? and so on.*"

I didn't have time to pursue a future Malibu Boat Harbor. I thought it was a bad idea anyway.

During monthly discussions with the more vocal members, it came about the Chamber, while unconsciously leaving me out of it, agreed as a man, the best place for the boat Harbor was easterly of Point Dume. Who was I to argue? In other words, the location for the new Boat Harbor would be Little Dume cove. Next was brainstorming on what to do about the *outrage* of the Point Dume landowners. *Was the Chamber helping destroy Point Dume's beach by bringing the public and all their boats through a residential neighborhood?* Next subject, how to get a breakwater? One of the suggestions was to bulldoze fifty feet or so off the top of Point Dume, thusly, knocking down the Point of Point Dume.

123 - Point Dume. Little Dume was suggested as the location of the new Malibu Boat Harbor. Photo: 2000.

Knocking down the 40-million-year-old heretofore-ancient landform, the former homeland of the Chumash Indians, knocking down that prehistoric geological miracle that forms nothing less than the northwesterly extremity of Santa Monica Bay. The idea was to bulldoze the point to smithereens; to sink it's broken boulders in 10-fathoms of seawater to form a breakwater for the Harbor. They had it on good authority the point was made of good hard rock. It would stand up well to the ocean's forces. After all, it had stood up well since the turn of the century and probably would even longer. It was a *point* wasn't it? Then there was the dredging to consider. Santa Barbara suffered from sand infiltration and it was likely a Malibu Boat Harbor would as well. I can say, so much for kelp beds and conservation.

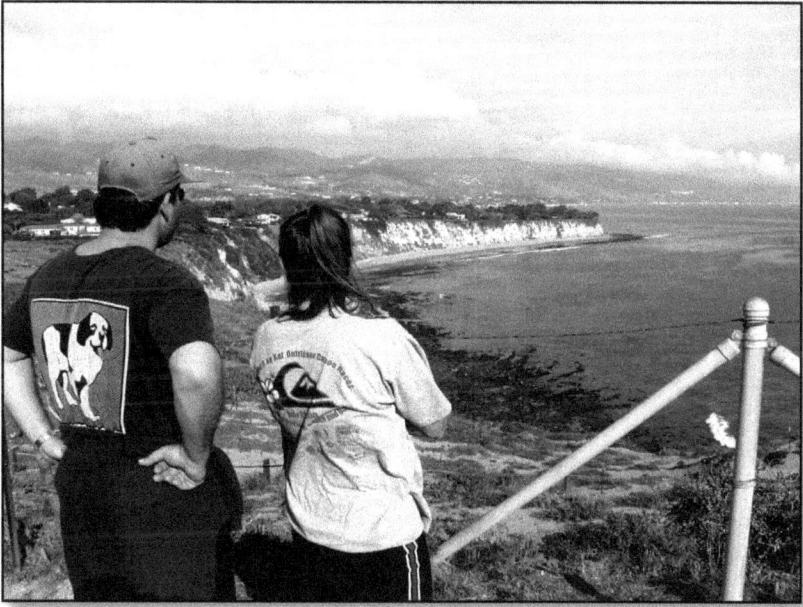

124 - Chris and Katy observing proposed harbor site.

Fortunately, the idea of bulldozing the Point and winding a public right of way eighty feet down the hillside to the beach through a quiet neighborhood died like a beached whale. Everybody got tired. Especially me. Nobody had the money anyway and everyone agreed, though it was not said, that it was a pie-in-the-sky project created to keep members busy. I thought the Chamber thought itself dramatic and grandiose for dreaming up something dramatic and grandiose for the community. I thought the Chamber, in this singular instance was, at least, self-deceived.

Being a Chamber member and agreeing to be involved in

something so preposterous, I'm embarrassed I had anything to do with such a bad idea. That and anxiety in expressing myself in public, colored my attitude in continuing with the Chamber. I realize I have unjustly condemned the whole organization based on one bad committee, or perhaps I have done so through lack of confidence in expressing myself in a group. On the whole, hindsight is better than foresight. Sometimes what seemed correct before doesn't seem so now.

From Dave Duncan's Army Corps of Engineer's Report I am happy to have learned the words, *littoral drift*. Littoral means shore or along the shore. Littoral drift means the direction of shoreline current. A *littoral drift* along the west coast moves either northerly or southerly. In Malibu the *littoral drift* is southerly about 80 percent of the time and northerly 20 percent of the time. *Littoral drift* carries sand. That means, if there is a wet season in the north, for instance when the Russian River floods and carries tons of sand and debris into the ocean, the *littoral* drift will distribute that sand and debris 80% along the southwesterly beaches. The wet weather in the North eventually builds up beach sand in the South. If Washington, Oregon and northern California have dry seasons, southerly beaches shrink.

WALKER

I was minimally settled in my new office over Busch's Real Estate building when an attractive, newly married young man walked into my office.

He had two adjacent parcels at the top of Bellagio Road in Brentwood Village. This portion of Brentwood Village is a lush, well-cared-for mountainous area bordering UCLA northerly of Sunset Boulevard and in the secluded and shady hillsides of many wealthy people.

Joe Walker wanted to build two houses. He and his new wife would live in one and sell the other. He gave the impression and visualized himself as an idealistic writer, and as I came to know him later, wanted to show the world by his novels his own point of view. I found his view of life extraordinarily similar to Ayn Rand's.

125 - The two Walker houses designed in 1961. Photo: DWR 2000

126 - The entry to one of the Walker houses.

I showed him architectural work already under progress. When he saw the Dorr House and grasped that Bob Butte, the respected contractor lived in Brentwood, he was completely sold and knew he had found his architect and builder. I designed two post-and-beam houses with decks cantilevering northeasterly high over the edge of one of the Brentwood Mountains. Both originally built with horizontal natural cedar siding they harmonized without being totally the same.

I returned one year to see how they were doing and got a couple of pictures. The photos do not show the mountainous drop on the other side of the houses, but just the street elevations. Joe and his wife seemed happy with the work and I wasn't to see the last of them.

WRIGHT APARTMENT

The Wright project has always bothered me and continues to bother me today. Though I have no cause to blame myself, yet it was one of my jobs I was not especially proud to show. It might have been said the owner didn't finish the job in the spirit in which it was designed, yet it could also be said I gained.

I had been discussing designing an apartment building with Loran Wright for several months. In my opinion, Loran was an unsophisticated client who seemed set on selecting me probably because my office was in Malibu and almost next door to his site. He'd seen my *Douglas W. Rucker, architect* sign and said to himself, *"Here's a young architect, recently in business, somewhat inexperienced, therefore, probably cheaper than anyone else I could hire. He knows Malibu. His office is practically next-door. He'll be fast and cheap.*

My problem with Loran was that he wouldn't pay me enough money to do a good job. I was beginning to learn that, as a young man with financial responsibilities, *I had to do a good job and make money*. That's the way my world worked. I didn't ask for it. If I wanted to be good at my work it was going to take more time than if I did poorer work. Therefore my first choice on how I wanted to live my life was, *"Yes, give a little extra, but at least make enough money to pay your bills."* I was eager to work for Loran and add my first apartment building to my list of accomplishments and willing to work cheap. But not that cheap!

Time after time, he begged me to work for him, but always offered me less than minimum wages. Finally, over a period of six weeks and after about the fifth request, I wrote him off. If he asked again, I'd *shine him on!* I'd antagonize him sufficiently to close the discussion once and for all. He did ask again and I offered to do plans and supervision if he'd allow me to design my own office over the existing Tom the Surfboard Man's store, which was part of his site and which he intended to keep, *and also give me free rent for four years.* He said he'd think it over. I calculated my rent would have been $100.00 per month for four years or a total of at least $4,800.00, twice what he'd offered to pay me in real money. That deal was definitely in my favor and I thought now he'll leave me alone, and returned to other projects.

A short time later he called me and said, *"OK, draw up the contract!"* I was shocked! He'd called my bluff! I drew up the contract and accordingly we signed the papers. Since Loran knew nothing about how many apartments would fit on his property or anything about design, I was free to work out as many apartments as I thought appropriate. Twelve units fit nicely including remodeling Tom's store and a new Doug Rucker architectural office on the second floor. Tom, of course, would go elsewhere and the remodeled store would be rented to others.

Working at home in the evenings and on Saturday, I finished the plans between money producing jobs and got a permit. Loran hired a contractor whom I thought was reputable, and lo and behold the following year he finished the office and apartment.

I will finish the Wright story in the next book because the follow-up didn't happen until the building was completed and I'd moved in. In the meantime I was working with Mario Quiros as a roommate on the second floor of the Louis Busch Real Estate office.

HOME LIFE

*V*iveka, whose nickname was Vivi, was nursed about three or four months. Karon loved nursing and was disappointed when she no longer could do so. Nevertheless, the mature look in her eyes, her radiant smile, her full, rosy cheeks, and appearance of health continued well after Vivi's birth. We took baby pictures and changed diapers and spooned baby food, and the healthy youngster, to the best of my knowledge, seemed to be doing quite well. Of course she was *far* more *intelligent* and *beautiful* a baby than we'd ever seen. We looked at our little miracle person and our eyes shown with joy. We doted on her. I was immensely proud of our baby, Viveka, as was Karon. Even so, Karon was extremely tired from the exhausting duties of baby care.

127 - Karon and Viveka. October 1961

When Vivi was willingly and comfortably placed in her bedroom crib, Karon insisted on closing the concealed door between the living room wing and bedroom wing, so Vivi couldn't be awakened by our noise. Karon needed rest from being with Viveka all day and I could understand this. It was her requirement we talk in soft voices, play the radio in subdued tones, and be watchful of making loud noises so as not to wake the baby.

To visualize the house, imagine an L shape. The three bedrooms and two baths occupied the vertical part of the L and the living, dining, kitchen, one wall practically all glass, occupied the horizontal part of the L. Opposite the glass was a wall of vertical interior siding that separated the living room from the bedroom wing. I had installed a concealed door, cut into the vertical wood paneling, so that persons while in the living room would not be able to see or be aware of the bedroom wing. The concealed door was of double thickness heavy vertical wood paneling nailed to a solid core door. The concealed door was almost soundproof.

128 - Doug and Karon. Concealed door to the right of post.

While Vivi was sleeping behind the relatively soundproof door we could not hear her cry of distress. I have questioned myself. Did she cry out and think she was forsaken, or did she *not* cry out and

Karon's scheme for her *(and our)* solitude was the perfect one? I'll never know.

After the baby came, I felt like all new husbands do, *abandoned*. While I had been receiving *all* of Karon's attention before the birth, I received about *one fifth,* afterwards. Karon loved Vivi, but was exhausted after 16 hours doing baby things. She'd recently been meeting the demands of musical, theatrical, and other creative activities, but now this energy was used in daily baby care.

129 - Doug, Viv and Karon. 1961

Though her cerebral friends, Ina Nuell, secretary to Debby Reynolds, Eric Armstrong, prestigious landscape architect, and electrical student, Tom Pincu attended her, a complete day of adoration and giving to a much-loved daughter can be exhausting. Attention to a husband became a low priority. Like all new father's, I felt discarded. I have learned since, *"So what? Don't be selfish! You've got a miraculous baby!"* I admit I was self-centered, but it is true I was affected.

RAUDIXON

In 1961 I was struggling with the long hours and emotional difficulties of a new practice. Since Karon was no longer working, it was up to me to maintain mortgage and car payments, health insurance, new pediatrician bills and property taxes. I disliked my involvement with the Chamber and despite the wonder of a new baby, felt less wifely attention. The combination of all this produced *stress!* My blood pressure was high! Having had a long history of high blood pressure, I decided to seek medical help.

Doug and Karon, Lois and Duke, Dick and Ana Rae.

Lois Conan, Karon's mother, had been a registered nurse and presumably knew about such things. She recommended an elderly doctor located in Santa Monica whose office was packed. As many as twenty people of all ages and nationalities sat in rows on worn couches reading tattered magazines in his waiting room. I thought, *"He's popular, he must be good."* Ten minutes per person was his motto. He'd ask your symptoms, prescribe a pill, and *you're out'a there!*

When it was my turn, he took my blood pressure and it was high.

He prescribed Raudixon. I was out of there. At that time I was aware drugs lowered blood pressure, but didn't understand, nor was I told of the side affects. Three years later in an appointment with Malibu's, Dr. Dan Hillman, I learned Raudixon was one of the drugs derived from the Rauwolfia plant. It's side affects were slowed thinking, dampened energy and mild to heavy depression. During my monthly ten-minute appointments with the elderly doctor, I had the satisfying feeling I was, at least, doing something positive about my health. Later, Dr. Hillman told me the *sad* story. I had conducted three years of my life while slowing myself with a destructive pill. Sort of driving up hill with the brakes on. Three years later, with many tough tests and great personal relief, Dr. Hillman took me off the *downer* pills.

I suppose in those days Raudixon was the favored treatment. I knew of no other drugs then available for the treatment of high blood pressure. Looking back, I can see the red *"downer"* pill affected my creativity. I wonder how much better I would have done for three difficult years *without* Raudixon.

SECOND FLIGHT TO MIDDLE FORK

The year after Viveka was born and while the house was just completed, John asked me to go with him on another Middle Fork rapids run. He'd be bringing his eight year old twins, his two older boys, John Junior and Lennie, and John's executive friend whom I'll call Bill. Mary and the rest of his family would stay home, as would Karon who would be tending Viveka. He wanted me because I was a good sport to have along and could be a lifeguard for the young twins. Again we took the twin engine Beech.

John was a good flyer and his passengers felt safe. Again I found myself sitting in the co-pilot seat flying over the dry mountains and plains of Nevada. John said we were flying at ten thousand feet, just low enough not to require oxygen. He said sometimes flyers and passengers can feel sleepy at such an altitude and if he were to doze off, I should be sure to wake him. I forced myself to stay awake. He had my attention. I had acquired a *responsibility*. Now and again John's head would fall on his chest and he'd jerk himself awake, then I'd watch his eyelids, which were momentarily OK, but then with every blink they'd stay closed a little longer until his head would hit his chest, again, and he'd awaken. I didn't say a word, but watched him from the corner of my eye while I scanned the slowly changing terrain below and observed the different shapes and ground colors. He never fell asleep long enough to lose control of the airplane.

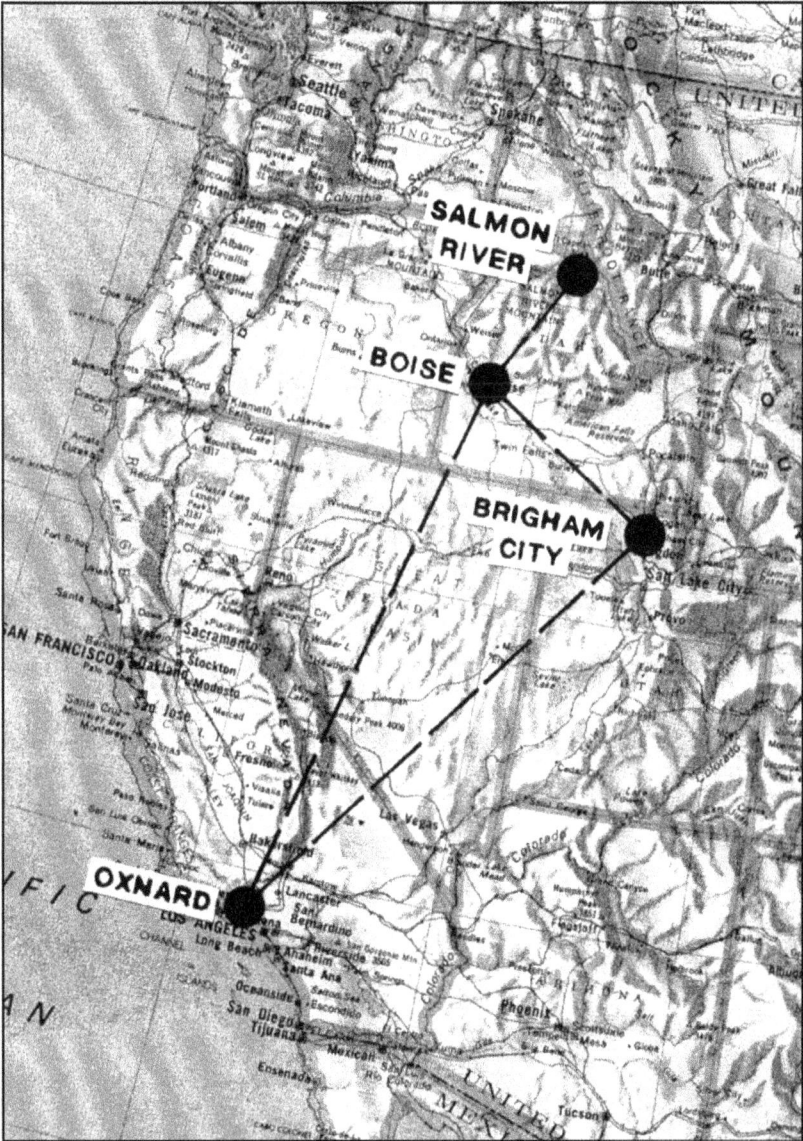

131 - Map of Western United States showing relative locations.

As we flew farther north I discovered long horizontal canyons sometimes cut the flat, sandy planes. We flew over the green curving valley of the Snake River until we saw Boise picturesquely framed by the dark green Sawtooth Mountains.

After picking up supplies, the runway was soon flashing before us as we gained speed for takeoff. Once leveled off for the relatively short hop to the Middle Fork, John pointed out the Grand Tetons in the distance. With the multiplicity of shark's teeth they scraped the sky and with the confidence of eternity they resisted the devilish winds, blustering snows and drenching rains of every season.

We approached the Middle Fork of the Salmon River at dusk. In a deep valley behind two steep mountain ridges, I could barely see the landing strip. The strip, thin, lighter colored line overgrown on each side with trees and bushes. I was thinking *"The hell with it! Let's bail out!"* Getting ready to land, John informed me the size of the Beechcraft was such that he could circle only once and then he'd have to land. The mountains were too high on each side of the strip and there was no room for error. If he overshot the runway he couldn't push the throttle forward and power up again for another try. His turning radius was so wide he'd plow into the side of the mountain. It wasn't as if the 911 number was available, either.

I was in the hands of fate and those hands were John's. However, he put 'er down like a bush pilot. Then we had to hurry to get the rafts set up before light faded and follow the river on foot around a forest of yellow pines that grew to the banks. The quiet was deadening. *The trees must have been surprised to see this little band of sophisticated foreigners, so far out in the wilderness traveling in their midst.* In a quarter mile or so we came to a tributary and followed that for a hundred yards up-slope to where John and William had buried two Navy inflatable rafts, with paddles, ropes and rudders for front and rear. The rafts were under tarpaulins, further hidden by logs, brush and leaves.

River rafting was seldom done in 1961. It was not done commercially and was certainly not as common as it is today. Floating down a river in an inflatable raft was still something foreign to the imagination. Because of their Naval experience with emergency rafts, their availability through Navy surplus, and because they had the money to reach a remote area, John and Bill were two of the first to do so.

I was taking life as it comes. Next to a small fire, we ate, rigged our sleeping bags and went to bed early for the following big day. I slept fitfully and awakened often to find myself alone, and with the exception of the sound of the river, in a very dark, quiet place. In deep silence, the stars quietly punctured the night between the jagged tops of black trees.

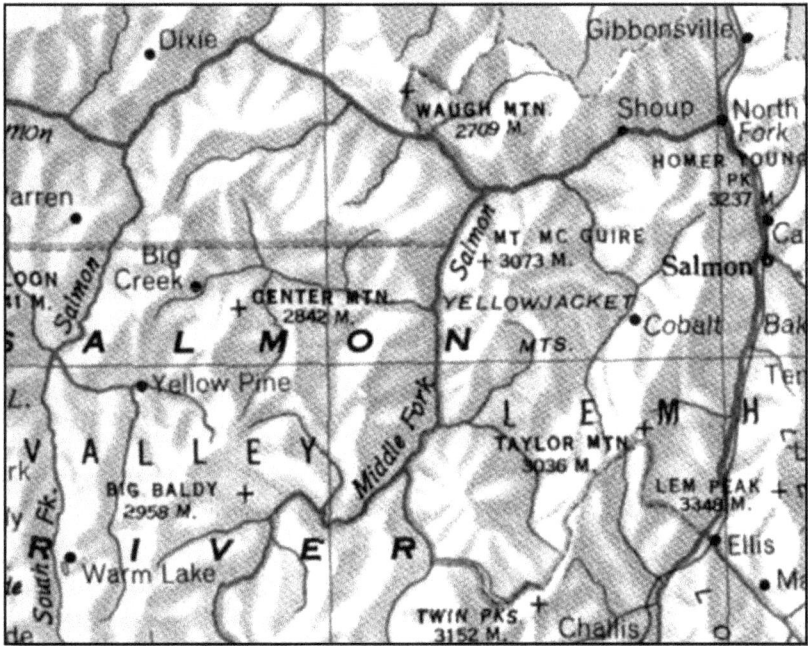

132 - Map of the Salmon River.

Before dawn and after a luxurious breakfast of bacon, eggs, toast, jam and camp-coffee brewed over an open fire, we dragged the rafts to the water's edge and packed our gear. John and the twins and I would be in the second raft and Bill and the two older boys handled the first raft. I was surprised to learn the Middle Fork ran *north* from the Salmon River Mountains into the Salmon River that ran east west to join the Snake River.

I put on my life jacket and climbed in the front of the raft to handle the front rudder. John had assigned himself to the rear rudder.

I thought I knew the philosophy of an inflatable raft front rudder but had no experience. A front rudder can be used to fend off rocks and rapids in an emergency and is positioned such that if the raft were to reverse itself, it could act as a rear rudder.

The twins in their orange life jackets were on each side of the center of the raft being excited and good. With a thrill in my stomach and a deep breath, John shoved us into the cold river and leaped in behind. The river's current seized the raft and we slid like grease into the center of the flow. Trees and boulders, sun and shadows, slipped by as we caught the main force of the river and began drifting at a rapid pace. The Middle Fork curled and bubbled around the rocks. The brush, branches, and shadows, dipped and played in the curling water.

The front rudder man didn't have much to do because there was nothing to dodge and I sat, front rudder drawn back and relaxed, enjoying the scenery. I was taken with the whole idea of where I was and what I was doing. Soon, several huge boulders seemed to block our path, the water being sucked around them with leaves and twigs bending and flowing with the water's forces. We had to turn the craft more rapidly. I dipped my front rudder in the proper direction, which thankfully I seemed to know, and avoided a collision. When we hit faster rapids I had greater difficulty.

There were huge boulders to avoid, magnificent pines and tumbling mountains to see, as well as exclamations and humor in conversation. During the two days water rafting, the twins, with five or more hooks on a line, trolled for Dolly Vardens, a singular trout in Idaho, and caught them on almost every hook. In addition to our luxurious store food we ate fresh trout.

When everybody was hungry we'd look for a sandy beach and dip into our luxurious lunches. The beaches were inviting with yellow sand and gray rocks surrounded by rich, untouched, pine forests and embellished with a diversity of water-sculptured boulders lying in odd positions evolved through geologic time. When we'd finished eating, it was difficult to leave. The longer we stayed, the more I'd see and the more I'd see, the more I'd marvel.

At dusk we'd pull our rafts onto shore, get a fire going, clean our fish and dine without shame on delightful foods thoughtfully purchased. At dusk we'd retire in our sleeping bags on the sand, or on a little grassy spot next to a tree, and as the night deepened, stars would appear in great quantity and brilliance, I was again humbled at one of God's supreme gifts. All that could be heard was the rushing river, a kind of white sound that I could easily forget unless I paid strict attention. There were bear and wolves, but I don't remember worrying about them. Possibly there was safety in numbers.

On the second day we came to the intersection of the Middle Fork and Big Creek rivers. Big Creek runs eastward from the Center Mountains and T's into the north-south Middle Fork. The combining of the two rivers resulted in a double flow northward and the muddy juncture swirled and eddied and foamed in the lee of large boulders. The water was so violently sucked around and between the boulders; it was no place to get caught in a raft. We gave this danger spot a wide berth.

I saw pines and river and mountains and stars, tasted fresh trout and cool, clear mountain water, smelled the pines in the fresh mountain air, felt the sun, breezes and cold sting of nightfall and the camaraderie and excitement of the river run. I was aware of the silence in the mountains beyond the rush of the Middle Fork or the roar of rapids at day or night. I was there!

How did I feel about it? I took it as it came. It was an adventure. Why shouldn't I take it? I did my job on the trip. I was pleasant. I had plenty of work upon return. I had a wife and child in Santa Monica Canyon. I will remember it always, like I remember my trip to Canada with Don Patton when we attended the University of Illinois.

TAKE-OFF

I remember taxing down the bumpy, narrow runway that snaked between the pines and how short it looked and how high the trees were at the far end. John was no help. That morning he'd told me the runway had been graded for single engine aircraft, which were lighter than planes as big as our twin engine Beech. He said he'd have to jam the throttle forward to gain as much speed as the plane was capable. The air was cold, quiet and still in the early morning, not ideal for takeoff. The rare, higher atmosphere was also a detriment. I wished there was *thick* air with a strong head wind, then I'd remembered we'd just stored 15 or 20 sizeable river boulders, significantly adding to our weight. The twins were in the back, the older boys were returning with Bill.

To me the runway seemed about two hundred yards long. I looked out when we were a bouncing along, wings waggling, at about a hundred and twenty five yards and we seemed to be traveling about 15 miles an hour. *This was full throttle?* I couldn't open the door and jump out of a moving plane, but I thought of it. There were no chair arms to squeeze or hardwood stick to bite. My seat belt was so tight I couldn't breath. The trees got closer and closer and looked higher and higher and I thought I saw John crossing himself and saying, *"Come on, Lord, just this once!"* Then with the thunder of two Beechcraft engines giving their final thrust and with the smell of airplane gas and smoke we jumped forward with the plane and cleared the tops with a roar and feet to spare. *I could see the needles!* In another fifteen minutes, I was able to talk. John looked over at me with his narrow eyes and grinned.

FLIGHT FROM BRIGHAM

Returning from the Salmon River, John had to stop in Brigham City that was not only named after Brigham Young and famous for the Mormon Church, but was also a commercial center for Bing cherries. John was to give a presentation to IBM employees on how to sell their newest equipment. I wasn't interested in his talk, nor was I invited to come hear it. The Brigham stop seemed an annoying interruption of our non-stop flight to Los Angeles. I would have a couple of hours to kill taking care of the twins. John glided to a perfect landing, rented a car and left the twins and I to follow our needs. A short walk took the twins and I to the edge of town. I was hungry but there were no restaurants and I had little money but we discovered a small grocery store. I was surprised they carried the biggest, blackest, firmest, juiciest, Bing cherries at two and a half pounds for a dollar fifty. I bought a dollar fifty worth and shared them with the kids. They ate a half-pound and without thinking, I finished the remaining two pounds before we met John again at the airport a couple of hours later. John, in a hurry to beat the light, rushed us into the plane and we hurtled into the sky for the three-hour flight.

I sat for the first hour rather comfortably, enjoying the flying experience, but soon I felt an ominous rumble in my bowels. As far as I knew there was no bathroom on the plane. I would just have to hold it. I kept silent, loosened my belt, holding gas and squirming in my seat for another half hour. Fifteen minutes later I was still quiet on the progressively uncomfortable flight when my forehead broke in sweat as I realized it was impossible for me to hold it another minute. I was going to explode! There was going to be an embarrassing and messy accident in the close quarters of the twin-engine Beechcraft at 10,000 feet.

I blurted out, *"John, I've got to go to the bathroom, now, I can't hold it!"* This was not what John wanted to hear. After an interminable time, perhaps thirty seconds, he admitted there was a porcelain enameled potty he kept for such emergencies in the recesses at the rear of the plane. I should creep back there slowly, go through a narrow door and handle my problem in there, however, it was his rule and my duty to clean the facility when we got back to the Oxnard Airport. Well, of course, it was an instant deal.

When we reached the airport, I did my duty, hosed off the potty, dried it and returned it to the plane. The next day I broke out in a rash all over my face, arms, legs and stomach that diminished over four days. It is in this way I learned never to eat two pounds of Bing cherries on an empty stomach and take off on a three-hour flight in a plane with no bathroom.

CLARK PUBLICATION

After a few years the former Clark house came up for publication. Since he had published the Larsen houses and the Halliburton children's room, I had come to know Jim Toland, the Home section editor at the L. A. Times fairly well.

I was delighted when he asked if I had any more post-and-beam houses. I remembered the Clark house and Dick and I visited the owners to see if it was properly finished. Dick agreed he could make something out of it.

Since early morning or late evening light is considered the best for dramatic architectural photos, the two of us arrived before dawn with lights and 4 x 5 Polaroid camera for test shots, tripods, and a duffel bag of lenses, cases and film. We climbed down the slope carrying all our equipment for a long exterior shot from the creek, battling stickers and watching for rattlesnakes. Dick would set up the tripod and camera and frequently hold up his hands and squint his eye to square off a composition. He'd usually lift his 4x5 camera and tripod to a more advantageous position, set the legs firmly into the bank and focus the lens. After doing this a number of times to get his composition perfectly arranged, he'd snap a few Polaroid test shots to check lighting and composition. Sometimes he'd adjust his camera so many times, he'd begin to lose the light and quicken his actions. He'd hurry me to remove a last minute trashcan, or hold back an intrusive branch, or move a wheelbarrow sneaking into the frame.

133 - Former Clark house. Home section photo, June 30, 1963.

When everything was ready, Dick would stand for a minute or so, his hand on the remote switch, *"To let the magic creep in,"* he said. *"To affirm his decisions."* And during that long moment, things were silent, the quiet, soft light would slip into his work, the composition would heighten and take on an otherworldly reality. While radiating that spirit and during that precise time when Dick could feel in his bones the timing was perfect, he'd press the remote button and with a silent click, the shot was over. We could *"Tear down the set."* I was saddened to see the magic disintegrate, but reminded myself we'd have the magic of the picture.

Interiors were similar except for hiding his photographic lights and rearranging furniture. He'd eliminate glare with a handsome, well-placed bowl or add a potted plant taken from the terrace, or pick up every last intrusive straw that could hinder the shot. The same intensity, nevertheless, arose at the end, Polaroid trials, waiting for the magic, pressing the remote, and tearing down the set.

134 - Former Clark house view of living room.

135 - Former Clark house entrance interior.

136 - Former Clark house Later the Mary Buchanan house.

1962 – LILIANNE

APARTMENT AND DUPLEXES

Next to the University of California at Santa Barbara, in the adjacent student town called Isla Vista Pacific, Ada Marie Bowers had completed her eight-unit apartment, the Mulberry Tree, and Bob Olshausen had finished his two duplexes.

137 - Ada Marie Bowers eight-unit apartment building in Santa Barbara called the Mulberry Tree. Photo: December 2000.

Though I didn't supervise the construction on any of the Isla Vista projects, we had many telephone calls and clarifications and approvals of minor changes so that I did not feel out of touch. In fact the idea of building apartments and duplexes seemed like such a good idea that Karon and I decided to invest a little of our own painfully saved money.

138 - Duplex in Isla Vista next to the University of California at Santa Barbara built by Bob Olshausen. Photo: December 2000

We asked Ada Marie if she would look for a commercial piece of property so that we, too, could build ourselves an income-producing apartment. She found one on the next street farther inland and close to her own apartment. It was only one hundred feet away from the landscaped University property and cost twelve thousand, five hundred dollars. It was perfect! We bought it! Without time or money to pursue its development, we decided to sit on it for the time being. In the meantime mischief was brewing at home.

RHEINGOLD

Pat Ahern, the young cousin who worked with Cap at the Chris Craft building, walked up the stairs to my office above Louis Busch's and asked if I wanted to make some big money for one day's work. I'd be a photographic model for a Rheingold Beer advertisement working with Tom the Surfboard Man and two beautiful models in swim suits. The pay was a hundred-fifty a day. In those days, I thought one hundred fifty dollars was a lot of money for one day's work. The pressure in my temples increased suddenly with a familiar push as I heard an inner voice mumbling, *"I'll consider it."* I put down my pencil, turned off the radio and replied in a breathless voice, *"What do I have to do?"*

"It was simple, he said, *all you have to do is go boating in a Sail Fish around San Pedro Harbor with a young girl in a skimpy bathing suit. Cameramen in a big rented launch would take your picture while you're sailing and publish them on billboards across the Eastern part of the United States. The model would smile and wave and I would look cool, mature, and nonchalant like this happened every day."*

I blurted, *"But I don't know how to sail!"*
"Sailing the Sail Fish is like sailing a surf board. He replied.
"When can I practice?" I said.
"You don't have time to practice, the gig's Saturday!"
Was this going to be an adventure? Was it different from doing architecture work? Was I flattered by being chosen as one of four models that would be on billboards across Eastern America? Would I be able to sail the damn boat? What if it got windy and we were blown over in the corner, cold and wet, sloshing against a steep wooden pier, unable to be saved. I'd be responsible for another life! The model didn't sail! Could she swim?

I met Tom the Surfboard Man next day who really did exude the cool, maturity of a slightly older young man. I asked him how he felt. He lifted a bachelor eyebrow and said he thought it was a great way to pick up easy money. Since there was no other sailor available and my vanity had been solicited, I began to think, *"Yeah. Picking up some easy money might be good for me, too."* Self-conscious and as ignorant as I was about sailing, it wouldn't be that easy.

Saturday came. Karon, interested in anything theatrical, decided to come along. A few officiators were sent to help us and we met two enchanting young ladies, one taller for Tom, and one shorter for me. The officiators told us Tom and his starlet would be the main focus of attention and my glamorous person and I would play supporting rolls. The sun was gingerly emerging from a mist hanging over what looked like an abandoned lake adjacent to the larger San Pedro Harbor. The shore revealed a floating plastic cup or two stuck in the weeds while a scored concrete boat ramp sloped steeply into the brackish water.

A quarter mile or so across the lake and on the other shore was a line of dark buildings. I presumed the ocean was beyond. To the left, a multistoried residential complex broke the skyline and to the right, a slim low breakwater dividing the harbors. In such an early morning, we were the only ones on the bay. It was going to be a nice, still day. Pat had brought the two large sailing surfboards *(Sailfish's)* down in a truck and we got busy assembling them. The red, white and blue striped sails hung loosely about the masts.

Tom inquired about the photographers. One of the handlers pointed out in the harbor and there, fat, black and still as death, was a forty-foot power launch that could sleep and feed over a dozen workers and crewmembers. There was a suggestion of dark, shadowy figures moving quietly about.

The handler said, *"When you get out there, they'll tell you what to do while they take photos."*

Soon, all was ready, me with my new blue trunks and Tom with his red. Since they'd obviously spent an hour or more with the make-up man, the ladies were meticulously groomed and stunning. This would be a bad time to tip the boat over. I might ruin their hair. I've got to sail this boat perfectly. Tom and I noticed the sails were hanging limp and lifeless from the masts. The wind was still sleeping, apparently caught in the trappings of the mist. The sun was well up. It was time to shoot. The launch sprang to life and with a low fluttering of the engine, moved in a parallel path leaving a fat wake that spread in V-shaped courses across the still water. Coming about, power off and gliding like grease across the face of the dark water, one of the dozen or so photographic men using a megaphone and a wide-arm gesture gave us mechanical sounding instructions to *"Sail out!"* I considered the thousands of dollars per hour the launch and photographic crew were costing as against my responsibility at one hundred-fifty dollars per day. I was ready to be responsible. Their cameras were fully loaded. They were ready to shoot!

Tom gave Pat a questioning look and with his anxious model lounging attractively in the bow in a posture photographically correct, gave his Sail Fish an enormous push into the harbor, partially wetting his trunks. This enormous push was so he'd coast as far as possible. I immediately followed, also with a magnificent push, also getting my trunks wet. After fifty feet our little sailboats drifted quietly to a stop. The sails hung like wet sheets. Tom and I clung to our tillers as if we fully expected to use them. We drifted arbitrarily and directionless just off shore, the only movement was that from our bodily adjustments. We wiggled the tiller's to get some kind of forward motion, but alas, the Sail Fish just jiggled, sending miniscule wavelets of it's own. The two sailboats, forty-feet apart and motionless in the quiet water, sat there.

Considering I was worried about their being too much wind perhaps too little was worse. If there had been a moderate wind, I think I could have handled this first experience of sailing in over 20 years. Without wind, what was I to do? I can't sail without wind. We were in the doldrums. Numerous people on the launch boat waved frantically and called through the megaphone, *"Sail down the harbor! Sail down the harbor!"* We understood their directions. We were at a loss to implement them. They apparently had visions of two sailors expertly commanding their sheets and tillers, with cute girls, hair ripped by the wind, the small boat knifing through rolling waves on a windblown reach. Such was not the case. We couldn't move. Sailboats were sometimes becalmed. We were becalmed. No wild waving of arms or loud calling through the megaphones could change that. They flailed their arms. We could hardly see them. We were unresponsive. Tom lifted up his shoulders and spread his hands signaling helplessness. It took the photographic team an hour or two, but eventually they thought it out. No wind! No sailing!

As the mist lifted, short-lived zephyrs moved us from time to time farther from shore. Our boats would pick up a puff of breeze and our hearts would sing for a while, and then our hearts would die as the zephyrs died. The full sails would begin to hang limp and listless again and our little boats would glide to a stop and float there, dead. The zephyr's and unpredictable breezes, of course, would excite the launch's crew and they'd aim their cameras like big guns and a man would call through his horn and gesture to me to catch up or gesture for Tom to fall back, neither of which was possible because of the capricious wind. We continued this for another hour and a half. It seems the photographer wanted his stars, Tom and the model, in front heading toward the camera, and me, my boat and model, comfortably sailing in the background. This was impossible. We were wasting costly time.

After four hours I felt myself squirming. There are no bathroom facilities on board a fourteen foot Sail Fish and yours truly felt the call to nature. It looked like we were going to work through lunch or not have any at all. It became an urgent priority to relieve myself. To heck with the shoot! But I couldn't jump overboard and let the Model sail the boat. She didn't know how. I couldn't go in front of the crowd on the launch, especially while being photographed.

But there came a time when the breeze was a bit steadier and the launch, excited by the activity, left a rolling wake as it moved down the harbor towards Tom's boat. They were more interested in a single shooting of his boat than mine. Perhaps they could superimpose the two boats for the final shot. I saw my chance and slowly fell back out of range. Perhaps they thought I didn't know what I was doing. Perhaps I was acting unconsciously. Perhaps, I wasn't a model anyway or didn't understand something. Soon the launch and Tom's boat were large and small dots well off in the distance. I quickly sailed for an island of low rocks and told the lady my problem, then pulled the bow high up and jumped to the other side of the rocks and relieved myself – *in full view of an apartment complex staring down at me.*

Embarrassed but feeling my old self again, I pushed off and sailed back to Tom's boat and the launch. The rest of the day was spent in the whimsical breezes until 5:00 P.M. and time to quit. The launch got their costly Rheingold Beer pictures and realized the day had probably not been what they'd expected. I didn't hear about the Rheingold people until about a year later when an acquaintance thought they'd seen a billboard ad with sailboats somewhere in the Eastern or Middle Eastern States. A month or so later a check came for a hundred and fifty dollars.

SECOND PREGNANCY

Shortly after Viveka's first birthday, Karon and I were surprised to learn Karon was again pregnant. Karon felt it was too soon for her to be pregnant. She wanted another child but was so involved with Viveka at one year old that having another was far from her thinking. Things don't always go as planned and there is no choice with pregnancy. Fortunately Dr. Behne was still in place and was thrilled with the news. I had always wanted four children and despite Karon's inconvenience, I thought we were getting off to a good start.

139 - A tree reflecting our unconscious mind during desperate times.

WORK

Work was slim and sporadic at the end of 1961. I had the slight possibility of picking up a two-bedroom and bath addition to a post-and-beam house in the Hollywood Hills for a client whose last name was Gordon, but he hadn't called back. Then I met Gordon Ewert, a thirty-six year old former sniper in the Marines who had done heavy fighting in the South Pacific. He wanted to do an eight-unit apartment in Santa Monica. He was good with his hands, creative and enthusiastic. He planned to build the apartment himself. But this job, too, took a while to generate.

Then the holidays struck. Our Christmas tree was expressive. I found an old dead tree and under the theory that Karon and I were *creative* and *avant-garde,* decided we could make a thing of joy out of a piece of destitution that expressed anything but a celebration.

JOE WALKER AGAIN

Joe strode into my office on the second floor of the Busch Real Estate building followed by his attractive wife carrying their newborn girl in soft blankets. The couple had just purchased a long and gorgeous promontory on the coastal hills off Trancas Canyon Road. It had three beautiful sites, stair-stepping as it descended with magnificent views of the Pacific Ocean, Palos Verdes Peninsula, Catalina, Point Dume and Zuma Beach.

Sitting across from me, tall and impeccably dressed for a Saturday morning, Joe, his combed hair low on his forehead, sat with his shy and lovely wife with her baby snuggled against her shoulder. He seemed quietly proud and had a special glint in his eye. He had a surprise for me. I was to do three house projects as a harmonious group. I would start with the lowest and best, the one nearest the ocean, the most private, and the one with the uninterrupted view. It would be two bedrooms and a den and I would have complete control over the design. The deal was that I could do anything I wanted with an *unlimited* budget. Joe would stay completely out of the design. He would not interrupt me in any way. Convinced of his hand's-off viewpoint, Joe would produce the building, pay for the permits, hire the contractor and pay all the bills and that's all. What did I think?

Even if I wasn't, I acted flabbergasted! Never had a client said that to me. Having complete control over design with an unlimited budget was the architect's dream. There was nothing I could do but take him seriously. No arguing with the client, no budget to worry about, nothing to do but have fun with architecture on one of the most beautiful pieces of property in Malibu. How come I was so lucky? I was to be limited by my own talents.

After he left and I had collected a thousand dollars for a retainer, I had to ask myself why Joe would give me such a job. He was obviously happy with the two houses we'd done in Belle Aire. He was a creative guy and liked to see the three-dimensional beauty of his investments. Also it helped that he had a private income of his own. But I wanted to learn more. Before I got started I invited myself to see Joe's office.

LUNCH AT THE BERKELY

*J*oe Walker and I were to have lunch at a restaurant on the penthouse floor of the multi-story white marble-tiled Berkeley Building on Sunset Boulevard near UCLA, the most beautiful and at that time the only high-rise building in the area. I took an empty elevator to the seventeenth floor, got out at a small lobby, and walked alone down a thickly carpeted hallway to a heavy walnut door with an embossed gold *Joe Walker* and number. I knocked and sure enough Joe opened the door. While it seemed totally unoccupied, there really *was* somebody in that new and lonesome building. I followed Joe into a small reception room with reception desk, but no receptionist, and into his main office. It was about twelve feet wide and sixteen feet long with a large window at the end of the north-facing wall. Joe's desk was along the east wall and I sat opposite him with the window to the left.

I asked him about his writing and he produced a fifty-page manuscript and said I could read it later if I wanted. We had small talk and then went to lunch overlooking UCLA and Westwood Village from the penthouse of the Berkely Building. I had the hot vegetable plate and we discussed the philosophy of Ayn Rand.

When I had a chance to read the manuscript, I found it less professional, but similar in idea to the writing of Ayn Rand. Joe, having just read *The Fountainhead,* was convinced of her philosophy and wanted to do more with her idea.

The Fountainhead, of course, was the reason he insisted I have complete control over the architectural design. In his mind I was another Howard Roark. Would that it were so!

DIGRESSION

In part, Ayn Rand's book discussed the right of those who think they are intensely creative to demand, to the point of blowing up millions of dollars worth of construction and risking innocent lives, that their work be completed exactly as designed. What if a self-centered but less talented architect should blow up his poorly completed work? Would that be acceptable? Rand's philosophy is not and was not my philosophy at that time. Certainly Howard Roark was not acting from a position of power when he relinquished his roll as architect to his friend. We might give him the benefit of doubt and say Howard couldn't foresee his work would be compromised, but this shows supreme naiveté.

I would never knowingly give my work to an incompetent because I'd know it would be bastardized. Without my personal attention to the end, I could never be assured of its proper completion. If that fateful fact should occur and I found myself in Howard Roark's position, I am too much of a humanitarian, and I might say a deeper, less self-absorbed person, not to take all facts into consideration. I would consider the somewhat designer-destroyed building useful to thousands of people who wouldn't know the difference anyway. I would consider the loss of millions of dollars to pay for the nasty building, clean up the mess, and do it over again, and think about counting the innocent man-hours already spent and the irreplaceable time lost from hundreds of people's lives. Does that mean I would say, too bad, and go on to the next project having learned a vital lesson? Yes, probably. After all, my name would not be on it.

THE REST OF THE STORY

I took Joe at his word that was diligently backed by his check. I saw no reason not to accept a gift from God so genuinely offered. With sketchpad, I spent a full day circumnavigating the property and drawing it in its natural terrain from a multitude of angles. *If I knew my site I could design my house.* At the University of Illinois I had learned to get the plan right then allow the elevations to follow. After that, my job was to make the elevations as beautiful and as sculptural as possible. This was a dramatic site. It would be in a view driving all the way up Trancas Canyon Road as the central part of the landscape.

It was visible for a mile traveling in both directions from Pacific Coast Highway. Coming down the driveway called for an especially creative approach. This time it was important the *exterior* was good and the *interior* worked second.

Back at the office I came up with Frank Lloyd Wright's old but new idea of making the house a completion of the promontory. I would make a niche in the end of the hill and stick the house in it. Rounding off the copper roof, top and sides, the all glass house would be like the *point of an arrow completing what the promontory always intended.* Its foundation would be poured in place concrete friction piers supporting grade beams, slab and slate floors running inside and out. The finished design was completely natural, as if the coastal slopes had remained untouched except for the outcropping of a spectacular copper-colored jewel bursting silently forth in the most prominent position. This design would *not* be the standard ill-conceived, poorly proportioned, sore thumb on the primordial hillside. It would harmonize, it would blend, and it would be part of nature. It would speak silently and eloquently of it's unusual sensitivity. Its deck was perfectly designed so it fit the slopes. Though I'd never studied with him, Frank Lloyd Wright would have been proud.

I was so proud of my design, I decided to draw a perspective to show how it might look from a helicopter, how it blended in with nature, how it grew out of the hillside like a stunning natural formation. I was so happy that instead of using pencil I decided to ink the project on vellum and make striking prints in dark brown sepia tone.

The day of the presentation Joe and I were excited. Joe sat down, ready for the happy surprise, fully willing to build what I had drawn. I spread the three large drawings in front of him and waited for the reaction. Joe's enthusiastic look of expectation faded over a short period of time to one of genuine concern. It became obvious to me he couldn't grasp the design. It was too foreign to him. Either that, or I'd made a colossal mistake. I don't think he had any idea of the design's worth. I began to question if *I* did. He was full of guarded praise. He would pay me the rest of my preliminary design fee and take the project under advisement.

I rolled and filed the drawings and heard little from Joe for a long time. Eventually, he and his wife went back east.

WATER BROKE

*L*ate evening in early January, our surfing friend, Gene Grounds, Karon and I were having a quiet conversation over coffee when Karon noticed a warm liquid spreading through the sofa and onto the carpet beneath her. She thought at first she'd spilled her coffee, but excused herself and upon returning announced her water had broke. Blood and water was now soaking in a thick pool under her chair. We called Doctor Behne instantly who said Karon should go to bed immediately and made an appointment to see her at our house the following morning. That evening I remember Gene, our six-foot-four-inch guest scrubbing blood and water off our carpet and my thinking what an intimate thing to do and what a true friend.

The next morning Dr. Behne told us losing water so early was *not* a good sign, but there was apparently no immediate threat to the baby. Since Karon was not having contractions, it would be best for the baby if Karon could continue to carry it as long as possible. She said she didn't expect the baby to go full term but made us realize the baby would have a better chance if it were more mature when born. She advised Karon *in no uncertain terms* to go straight to bed and stay there for the next three months, if necessary, so the birthing could try to complete its natural process.

This was an exacting direction to give someone like Karon, who had energy to burn and had much to do taking care of Viveka who was only a year and four months. Karon's mother, Lois Conan, who had recently returned from Mountain Home Arkansas, became a willing and necessary asset.

I thought Karon did a superior job of staying in bed for almost five weeks, particularly since the baby and Karon both apparently felt healthy as a horse. *I feel devastated now when I let in the fact that for five weeks, the baby had little room to float around in the womb and ready itself for a healthy birth. I question what detriments to physical and emotional health may have occurred during that time of extreme confinement.*

During the latter weeks, little by little, Karon chanced getting up more and more often and sometimes staying up with the multitudes of activities surrounding her care for the house and Viveka. It was necessary to make preparations for the new baby's arrival. By the sixth week, much to the dismay of Lois and Dr. Behne, Karon became overcome by her own vigorous self and undiminished enthusiasm and got up, almost, to stay.

SECOND BIRTH

I had been coming down with something for about a week. I didn't know if it was the flu or a cold or something else, but I felt out of sorts and over-tired. On the evening of April 7th, 1962, I was glad to go to bed early. Karon stayed up a little longer and came to bed at her usual time, eleven o'clock.

Shortly after midnight Karon woke me up announcing definite contractions about four minutes apart. Because she felt she had become overly anxious and had reacted too early during her early contractions with Viveka's birth, this time she decided to relax and cool it. She assumed the new birthing would match the last. This time she would try to sleep between contractions and save the rapid breathing for when it was absolutely necessary. Our appointment with Dr. Behne was set up for eight o-clock the following morning and Karon felt her contractions would certainly last that long.

But the contractions continued to occur on a regular basis and on an ever-quickening schedule. A restless three hours later Karon was fully awake and the contractions were close and severe. I examined her and could see the baby's hair, something I certainly never had seen after four hours of contractions with Viveka's birth. Somebody was trying to tell us something. I began to panic! We decided to be calm! What would a calm person do? *(1) He would call the Doctor! (2) If the baby were to be born at home the drama might be too traumatic for Viveka! (3) No hot water, no clean towels, no clean sheets, a husband with the flu, we weren't ready!*

In sweat-pants and T-shirt I rushed to the adjoining bedroom, lifted Viveka in her pajamas from her crib, ran out the sliding door off the kitchen, noticing her wide eyes with a questioning look. I ran next door to the sliding glass door of Milt and Mania's master bedroom, ripped aside the screen, flung open the door, and to the astonished looks of Milt and Mania, tossed Viveka on Mania's side of the bed and said, *"We're having a baby?"* then fled back to the house.

In the kitchen was the telephone book with Dr. Behne's number. I dialed the number quickly, then hearing Karon's crying out, dropped the phone and ran to her aid. She was having the baby at that moment and was in the last stages of pushing. I scooted around to help the baby out while cradling the phone Dr. Behne had just answered. The baby was coming out and Dr. Behne was saying *"Hello? Hello?"* I cried out, *"We're having the baby! It's coming out! I have the head! I'm holding the baby! It's here! It's here! I'm holding the baby!"*

I was experiencing a stupendous event, the most wonderful miracle of my life, delivering my own child. Now you might think I confidently grasped the child as it emerged and maturely placed it on Mother's breast. That didn't happen at all. I'll confess to an intimate thing. When the tiny baby was squeezed out of the womb on Karon's final effort, it rolled on the bed and came to rest against the covers. I instantly and gently picked her up before I cried out, *"It's here! It's here!"* I'm sorry Lil, but that's how it was on April 8, 1962. The baby was long and slim with dark hair and cried out immediately. I asked over the phone, *"What do I do? What do I do?"* Dr. Behne said, *"Put it to breast."* I put little Lili to breast and she bit down with what seemed to be such determination and emphasis as to let her mother know there was definitely a new life to consider. I was excited, gratified, and happy to see the new child with its umbilical cord disappearing into its mother. There was the primordial sight, our new baby lying warmly atop Mother's tummy.

Observing the wonderful event and thinking there must be something very important to do during such a magnificent affair, Dr. Behne brought me to earth. She said, *"What is it a boy or a girl?"* Of course Lilianne was a wonderful girl.

NAME

After Lili's birth Karon and I were deciding on her name. Karon asked what I wanted to name her. I confidently said, Lilianne.

Looking back, I seem to have known exactly what name she should have. Karon had selected Lili's older sister's name, Viveka, from the program of the Royal Danish Ballet. I liked Viveka as well. Karon asked me how Lilianne would be spelled, Lili Ann, two words, or Lily Anne. Or Lillian. Or Lilli Ann. Or Lillianne. *"No, I said, Lilianne, one word, one "l" and 2 "n's."* We'd call her Lili 'til she grew up. Karon and I agreed and we were both happy. Lilianne looked like a Lily. Though her personality sometimes evoked the gentleness of a Lily, at other times this was not so. For her middle name we both thought the mother should have a choice. I suggested Karon and Karon was pleased and we selected Lilianne Karon Rucker.

140 - Karon with Lilianne Karon Rucker, May, 1962.

AFTERWARD

I called Lois, Karon's mother, and while Dr. Behne and Lois were on their way, we enjoyed our baby. Lili was trying to nurse while lying on Karon's stomach. Suddenly Karon had another contraction and the after-birth was born. Now we had a baby, free and loose in the world, still attached to the afterbirth.

Lois and Dr. Behne came in shortly afterward and took the baby to the bathroom and put it down on Viveka's changing table. Then Lois, much to my dismay, had the honor of cutting the cord. I wished I had had the honor of cutting the cord. Perhaps I was a little afraid of cutting the cord and perhaps fathers at that time were discounted when it came to birthing. Dr. Behne cleaned Lili up while I comforted Karon.

Karon seemed immensely happy after the birth. She was smiling from the center of her being. It could be she expected the birth to be as difficult as Viveka's and was pleasantly surprised the labor, instead of taking twenty-two hours, had only taken a not so severe four. But things seeming momentarily easy were not to be.

I became severely ill the next day and it was decided, for Karon and the baby's health, I should be removed to my studio and be separated from the house. The baby weighed four pounds, eight ounces when she abruptly had to face the world. Afterward she was to go to the hospital and be separated from her mother and placed in an incubator for a day or so where she continued to lose another four ounces. Lili was seven weeks premature and hadn't had time to complete her full development before entering the world.

A bunk was fixed up and I was banned to my separate architectural studio to recover from whatever I had. I lacked energy to work and didn't want to infect Viveka. I was so tired for two weeks I couldn't even read. I felt disheartened but was less aware of Viveka's problems than my own. My attention was on my own illness, the newborn baby in the incubator and our severe shortage of money. Now, when I think of what happened to Viveka after Lili's birth, I am distressed. Intrigued and looking forward to the birth of her new sister, she was forced into a neighbor's bed in the early morning hours, with no explanation, and the next day removed to her grandparent's house in the Palisades where she stayed for about two months. Viveka, at the critical age of eighteen months, had been separated from those she loved and who loved her. She had been left in a state of wonder for two months without a soul to explain what happened or to further comfort her. Unconsciousness was happening. This circumstance is unthinkable, but it took place.

For one week we fended for ourselves until my mother, Evelyn, arrived from Denver to take care of Karon and the premature baby. She took care of me, too, and brought me orange juice and cereal, soup and crackers, and a nutritious dinner every evening for a month.

ILLNESS

In about seven days, Lilianne came home from the hospital, weighing four pounds, four ounces. Viveka, to my knowledge, was OK with grandma in the Palisades. Mother was living in Karon's sewing studio in the main house, which she had converted into a guest room. I was lying on my back all day under the covers staring at the ceiling on a narrow cot next to the window and behind the hollow core I'd used for a drafting table.

141 - Doug seen through the window in home studio.

During the three weeks that followed, I showed no improvement. I was bone tired and slept all day and all night. I couldn't seem to shake what I had. Lilianne, however, was steadily gaining weight and so far had shown no signs of catching my illness. She was marginal for the first couple of weeks or so but improved with time. As the weeks continued and they settled into their routines, Karon, my mother and Lois began to worry less with Lili and more about me,

Lois recommended I see an Eye, Ear, Nose and Throat Specialist she knew. I don't know what it was about her recommendations, but after I struggled to get to his office in Santa Monica, I discovered he was what I'd call an *Old Codger.*

Thin, about eighty, in an office that smelled of years, with pince-nez glasses and a white coat, *Old Codger* sat me down in his medical chair and said, *"Open wide!"* He stuck a fat piece of wood on the back of my tongue and I went, *"Ahhhh!"* He poked far up each nostril with a microscopic light, his nose almost rubbing mine. He examined a fluoroscopic image of my forehead and had me honk mucous into a cup that he sent out by nurse for analysis. Then he left the room and I sat in a weird chair and looked at the curious things in his office. I assumed he conferred with his associates, if he had any, and returned. With a quick explanation and palming some small equipment, he said *"This won't hurt a bit."* and shoved something black with the tube up my mouth to the back of my throat and rotating a black plastic disk and my feeling a resounding crunch, said, *"There!"* I thought that was it and it was over but he did it again on the other side. Then tilting my head to the side, turned a switch and water blew up one side of the back of my nose and forced itself through the sinus cavities in my forehead and snot and yellow gunk and honkers spewed into a cup in front of my face. He did this a couple of times until he thought he'd removed all the mucous.

Did it hurt? Yes, I was tortured for a while. I would prefer to have a cap put on my tooth but that's as bad as it was. He was force-cleaning the mucous from my sinuses. He gave me antibiotics and an appointment for the following week. Thankful and exhausted, I went home to bed.

The sinus cleaning seemed to help. Within a day I had the energy to read. I read Alan Watts, *Book of Zen* all week. My next appointment with *Old Codger* showed I was healing. He said I had a *bad sinus infection.* I read all the following week until I felt good enough to get up and move around.

I had been in bed well over six weeks. Mother was exhausted from taking care of Karon, the baby and me. She missed her husband and was anxious to leave. We gave our hearty thanks and she flew off home to Golden, Colorado.

Within another week Viveka was happy to return home and our little lives could now continue with four in the family. Viveka was intrigued by the baby and helpful and loving. She may have another story, but I felt she got along well in the first year with her new sister.

LILI WALKS

I remember when Lili was almost one year old and she was beginning to walk. It was January or February in the corner of our living room near the fireplace hearth. Karon and I were delighted with Lili's first steps. We wanted to be there and participate in the great event. It meant a lot to us to catch her as she took her wide-eyed and faltering steps.

142 - Viveka, Doug, Karon, Lilianne.

But Viveka at two and a half was also intrigued and emotionally taken with her new little sister being able to walk. She wanted to have Lili walk to her. Lili was willing. Viveka held out her hands, like Mommy and Daddy, for Lili to walk to her, but Mommy and Daddy were too self-absorbed. We weren't big enough to do that. Viveka, at two and a half years old, might not be strong enough to catch Lili. If Lili fell, how would that influence her future walking? What if Lili fell and bumped her head? If she had a disagreeable first experience, would she ever walk again? We wouldn't let Viveka catch Lili during the miracle of her first steps. More likely, we were selfish and probably wanted the experience of Lili's first step for ourselves.

I regret participating in stopping Viveka. It meant so much to her. What possibly could have happened? If they both fell down, so what? How could they possibly have injured themselves? They would have plumped to the ground like the millions of times before. Viveka, I apologize to you for not letting you catch Lili. I should have let you. Your mother should have let you. You were right. We were wrong. I wish I had it to do over again.

EWERT AND BEYOND

RECUPERATION.

*W*hen I finally got well and tiny Lilianne seemed to be thriving and Viveka returned to her routines and Karon was where all young mothers are, overworked by the miraculous and relentless little ones, we had some decisions to make.

Though I went to work every day to supervise a job or two, our income was insufficient to meet our bills. Like everyone else, we had a house mortgage, a car payment, insurance bills, taxes, and living expenses to pay.

The commercial lot we owned in Isla Vista was our ace in the hole. It seems money, which had been available to construct new buildings built for speculation, had vanished. Property was now over-built. Banks and Savings and Loans discovered a large percentage of loans were un-collectable. The spec house buyers were not there and the surplus of apartments more than filled the need for the now few tenants. Money had gone *bye-bye* with no sign of returning.

Karon and I could have struggled to hold the commercial property in Isla Vista for a few years before building but we decided to sell and pay our debts. Building an apartment seemed like a good idea. We were ambitious and smart enough and had the additional benefit of my architectural abilities, but looking back, I don't think Karon or I would have been happy apartment owners. Owning an apartment is selling space and making continuing repairs. It wasn't what either of us was about. We were creative and forward thinking, not landlords. Neither of us could imagine getting tough and demanding payments, which was standard in the apartment game. We were not *get-tough* kind of people.

This is to explain why we sold. The property was ideally located and appealing to a landlord type of person. It sold quickly for enough to pay the remaining $6,500.00 owed and Ada Marie's Real Estate fee and gave us a profit of $3,000.00. With $9,500.00 cash in our pockets we felt rich, paid our debts and put five thousand in savings. Money bought time.

EWERT APARTMENT BUILDING.

Though we now had financial breathing room, I was thinking I was never going to get another job. Karon began the first of her many suggestions. I get a teaching job. She said I could apply at Southern California University or Moorpark College or UCLA, Northridge. If I got a job on my own, I could do it at home after teaching. However private teaching was *not* what I wanted to do with my life! Teaching was the farthest thing from my mind. My personality did not sing when it came to teaching. I was afraid of getting up in front of a class feeling I didn't know my part. I didn't want to prepare for classes. Teaching. Bad idea! If I taught I would surely get stuck in a job abhorrent to me. The phrase, *"Those that can, do. Those that can't, teach."* repeated itself in my mind. I would be in the category of *"Those that can't, teach."* I understood Karon liked the scholarly life. If she couldn't be a teacher herself, she would have enjoyed telling friends her husband was on the Staff at S. C. or some other fine University. *(If I could have gotten a job at a fine university.)* I wasn't a professor. If I taught, I'd have to get a teaching credential and work toward a PHD. I wasn't going to do that!

Then one day Lady Luck smiled when a handsome, athletic young man opened the ugly chocolate-brown-painted-door that matched Louis Busch's office building and announced he had an R-4 property in Santa Monica near the Junior College. He wondered if I did apartments. Gordon Ewert was five feet ten and a half, wore jeans, open shirt and Marine boots. He spoke directly with eye contact and gave me the impression he could do whatever he chose. I enthusiastically showed him the twelve-unit practically across the street and was delighted to make a Saturday date with him to show him the recently completed eight unit and two duplexes in Isla Vista.

Gordon and I thought we could work together and made our agreement. I did the necessary preliminary work, getting the survey and checking with the building department. We wrote the program together and I came up with what we both thought was a good design. Gordon was enthused and I made the working drawings and specifications. Within a few months Gordon was ordering material, hiring sub-contractors and, with carpentry belt dangling from his khaki shorts, was making foundations.

WRIGHT APARTMENT BUILDING

In the meantime Loran Wright's twelve-unit apartment was progressing. My new office design had been framed over what was to become Johnny Fain's Television Store. During the design I made an attractive private stairway to the small office surrounded by glass. It had a natural plank ceiling with open beams, bathroom, storage, and a separate room fronting the Highway to be used as a conference room. When my 4-year agreement was up, the separate room would become a bedroom. I looked forward to, and was thrilled with the prospect of having an office of my own design on the Malibu Beach rent-free for four years.

MR. GORDON'S TWO-BEDROOM

While doing Ewert's working drawings, Mr. Gordon, appeared again to me in my office. He was a somewhat overweight, middle-aged man, neatly dressed, and obviously a successful businessman, probably with a teen-age family. He had heard I did post-and-beam work and wondered if I would be willing to do plans for a two bedroom and bath addition to his contemporary home in the Hollywood hills. I was delighted to work that out for him and was able to recommend Harry Heckendorf and John Diefenderfer for construction. I remember the job harmonized well with the original post-and-beam design but didn't find the time after completion to make a visit. I'd like to return now, though, to see how it has weathered the 40 years of storms.

Selling our Isla Vista property, securing the Ewert apartment job, and getting the smaller Gordon job, I was able to work us slowly out of our financial hole.

HOW WAS HOME LIFE?

Karon and I had the two babies, Viveka and Lilianne. Being a stay-at-home mother must have occupied all of Karon's time at home. Obviously, during the day she shopped, cleaned, visited, made dinner, had other children over and I don't know what else. I presume if she had any time after caring for the children, she read or did creative work.

We continued singing although it was a more difficult time because rehearsals required baby sitters. Occasionally we would have a picnic with Jim and Kathy Moule and their little ones.

Lois Conan, Karon's mother, needed to be involved with our family. Her husband, Duke, went along with whatever Lois required. Lois seemed to be the boss of her own family. Though I would have liked my family and our in-laws to return each other's visits, our neuroses conflicted. To me it seemed Karon had a love-hate relationship with her mother. Karon knew she, Karon, was intelligent and a special sort of person, and should be accepted for her differences from other people and even lauded for them. Karon was artistic, musical, athletic, a superb actress, seamstress and amateur artist and art historian. Lois, except for singing as a young adult, was none of those things. Instead she needed to be needed. To fulfill this desire to be needed, she had been a nurse during World War II and apparently a good and hardworking one. If her mother complemented Karon, Karon knew her mother didn't know what she was talking about and would always tell her that. Neither female was capable of not saying what they thought. Sometimes the complement became the source of argument.

143 - Kathy Moule, the twins and older girl. Dad, (Phil),
Karon, Lilianne and Viveka.

Lois continued to repeat her opinions over and over, apparently without learning or changing, much to Karon's and my dismay. This may seem strange, but I became angry and tired of Lois being needy after six years. It seemed to me when I married Karon I married Lois as well. I was probably guilty of being a *"stuffer"* one who stuffs his anger until one day it bursts all at once.

One day I told her off using swear words. She'd brought us food. I told her not to bring us food any more. She'd been making a habit of it and today's gift caught me when I was feeling particularly helpless about our poor financial situation. It was too much. I cracked and slipped from my normally optimistic attitude of accommodation. *(1) I was supposed to be the breadwinner. (2) We didn't need her gift. (3) Food gifts especially made me feel inadequate. (4)The meta-message was I was unable to feed my family. (5) It forced me to see I couldn't meet my family responsibilities.* Am I sorry now? I'm moderately, but not really.

On the brighter side, we'd invite Milt and Mania Black with their three kids, and Jim and Kathy Moule and their three children, and Grandmother Lois and Grandfather Duke, for Viveka's and Lilianne's birthdays. We had family celebrations of the children's first Christmas's and video taped them all. We enjoyed and were proud of our children. They gave Karon and me a sense of maturity it would have been impossible to attain otherwise. Grandmother adored her new grandchildren. The kids loved Grandmother, partly because she was an accomplice and secretly fed them cookies, pie, cake, candy and ice cream. We were hesitant on the sweets for our children, but gramma, to the delight of our little ones, continually broke the rules. Looking back, I guess that's what grandma's are *supposed* to do.

FREAK-OUT TIME

Sometimes Karon would become so frustrated with the continuous crying, whining, and discontent of our little children, she'd be about ready to explode. One day she locked Viveka and Lilianne in the closet with the heavy concealed door off the living room. When I returned from work, she told what she'd done. I was struck dumb. I was so shocked as to not know how to feel. I was so stunned I didn't know how to be angry enough. The thought of her locking my kids in a dark closet, insulated so their cries could not be heard, was so reprehensible and unanticipated; I didn't know how to react. I began to think I'd married someone mentally unbalanced, that my original discontent had been correct. What if there had been a fire? What would have become of our precious children if she had become incapacitated? I told her *never, never, never* do that again, and I thought to myself, if she were to do it again, I would have to seek a divorce and custody of the children. I said, *"If things get so bad you can't cope, call me! I'll come home and take over!"* Karon probably knew she had behaved badly and felt guilty. After all, she did tell me what she'd done. Fortunately, she never did that again and I didn't have to face my *"what ifs."*

I have learned that mothers frequently get into Karon's state and many have had to find a way to ease the discomfort. They somehow have to affirm their own life belongs to them. I think it's never a good idea to lock children anywhere. The idea of being confined in a dark, narrow, closet is child abuse. One with a concealed door is particularly heinous.

UPS AND DOWNS

*H*ome life had its ups and downs. On the whole our kids were a big plus and every bit worth it, but a chore as well. Life with the in-laws also had its ups and downs. Our physical place to live was supremely accommodating. Our friends, Ricky Volkman, Tom Pincu, David Rheil, Ina Nuell, Gene Grounds, Eric Armstrong, were close and real. We had an interesting and intellectual social life. Though there were some adjustments to be made, I'd give our home life a big round B for Better than average. *(Hindsight suggests, maybe I'm wrong.)*

DUTCHER

*M*y contractor friend, Nick Schiro, invited me to his office that was in a building now replaced by the 76 station at Webb Way and the Highway. I was to meet Scott and Marianne Dutcher. We were to discuss a house to be built on their recently purchased 30-foot lot on Malibu Colony Road.

When our talk was finished, we inspected their lot. An ancient one-story cottage would have to be removed to make room for a new three-story, three bedroom and den house. The Dutcher's, who had four children in age from middle teens down, lived permanently in a 6,000 square foot house in Phoenix. *(Read: Family well to do.)* Mr. Dutcher was either president of his own big firm or in business and investing his own money. The Malibu house was to be a vacation house and was an architect's delight. I though it similar to the Dorr house. It appeared the owner's were cultured and educated. They liked Schiro. They liked me. They had money. They were in a hurry to enjoy.

I was overjoyed! They asked how quickly we could write the program. They were vacationing only for a few days. I answered immediately and pencil and notebook in hand was ready the following day. During the meeting I guessed at a few sketches, which they liked immediately. I thought to myself, *"These are dream clients."* I told them I would order a survey from Mario Quiros and check with the Building and Health Departments to verify the exact Colony Road code requirements. I would send a preliminary by mail and if they liked what they saw, could approve it from Phoenix. In that event, neither of us would need to make a long trip for my personal presentation. They thought the idea superb.

The survey done and Nick removing the old cottage, I did my Department checking. *On a lot as narrow as 30-feet an architect must study the parameters; verify the limits of his design.* Three-foot side yard setbacks were required, forcing the house to be only 24 feet wide. The leach field for the sewage disposal system would have to be eight feet below any other structure. *(Like a second floor.)* A ten-foot separation between buildings was imperative. *(Such as that between the garage that fronted Colony Road and the seaward main house.)* The Home Owner's Association would only allow a one-story *"tea house"* structure to project thirty feet seaward of the main house setback line.

With so many restrictions and wanting to do my best on a ridiculously slim lot, I discovered the new house filled out and matched the setback lines. Forget proportion and design, the new house was blatantly dictated by governmental agencies. How could I design a meaningful house if I was stuck with a predetermined shape?

I accepted fate, finished my designs, explained things to my clients by phone and to my great joy, they liked the design and told me to proceed at once with working drawings and construction. They intended to occupy in early spring.

Nick began construction. When the third story was framed and plywood shear walls added, but prior to plaster, I made a trip up the stairwell by ladder to the top floor which contained only the master bedroom, dressing room and bathroom. From the third story it was thrilling to see the views of the Malibu Mountains and the wide expanse of the beautiful blue Pacific. Only one or two other houses were three stories high in the Malibu Colony and they were on wider lots. But the Dutcher house was a slim 24 feet wide and the third floor projected like a tower. Its narrow height dwarfed everything around it. It was a bright afternoon and the wind was whistling between the open studs. I adjusted my baseball cap firmly on my head as the carpenter casually asked me a leading question, *"Was I sure the building was properly engineered?"* I was taken aback and asked him why? On the top floor, he grabbed an interior open stud wall, squatted for leverage and rocked back and forth. The house rocked back and forth with him, all three stories of it. If he kept it up, he might have rocked the building out of alignment or even rocked it down. I felt warm with anxiety but remembered I *did indeed* have the building properly engineered by a well-known structural engineer, Robert Marks. We had all the permits. The plans had been plan-checked. But I had to ask myself how such a tall, slim building might do in the Santana winds or in a rumbling earthquake? How would I like being awakened by the building shuddering in the wind and threatening to topple? Would I feel safe in the tower?

The building was plastered which apparently stiffened it sufficiently that I never heard another word about a shaky top floor.

The yard between the garage and the main house was to be used for an underground sewage disposal system. Over the top of the system, I designed a landscape using a brick platform, low brick retaining walls which could also be used as a bench, succulents, washed aggregate concrete, sand and well-placed sandstone boulders that interlocked with the walks, patios and landscaping.

Jimmy Decker, my friend who worked without a shirt even on the coldest, rainiest days, wrestled the boulders into selected places. I liked the landscape design when it was done.

We got the house practically finished and were installing the three-story steel circular stairway that had been ordered two months in advance. Under my present supervision I considered it properly installed, however a rule surfaced that hadn't entered my mind. There was an ordinance that required a height of six feet six inches between the tops of any stair tread, and whatever construction there was above. This was a safety rule intended to allow sufficient head room in hallways, stairs and passageways. I measured the steel stairs and found head room of only six feet five inches. Headroom was an inch too low. The stairway did not conform to the ordinance. If the inspector caught our mistake, the stairs would have to be taken down, adjusted and replaced. That might have been impossible since the height of the floors couldn't be changed. In that case, Code compliance would be impossible.

We dreaded the inspection day and when it came we followed the inspector on his rounds. He approved everything then paused at our ten thousand dollar stairway, took out his tape and measured the bottom step from it's top to the construction above. It measured six feet six and one half inches. He so noted and we moved on. We passed inspection! Afterward, Nick and I measured the stairs again and found *only* the first step, the one the inspector checked, complied. The rest, for two stories, were illegal. We got away with it! Someone up there was looking out for us.

As I remember the Dutcher's didn't make one trip to the site to inspect the work. Of course we were in touch by phone and letter and Nick and the Dutcher's had their necessary communications. Finally, the glorious Friday arrived and I was there to greet the owners and proudly walk them though their new vacation house. They were delighted with the architecture, but complained the house looked bare. Evidently they had come to play and thought they were entering a furnished hotel that provided a place to eat, sleep and relax between trips to Malibu Beach. The Dutcher's wondered if I was doing anything Saturday and if I knew a good furniture store.

Fortunately, getting a resale license to sell furniture was easy for architects in 1963 and I had one. I took them out on Saturday and between 9:00 o'clock A. M. and 6:00 o'clock P. M. we bought four beds, a dining table and chairs, sofa's, living room chairs, chaise lounges, coffee tables, game table and chairs, end tables and waterproof outdoor furniture. We spent over $12,000.00 dollars in one day buying furniture with a re-sale license at 40% discount. Today I would guess the cost to be well over $48,000.00. It was delivered the following week. On Sunday the Dutcher's made another trip to the Beverly Boulevard area without me and spent another $6,000.00 on artwork to put on the bedroom walls, in the living-dining areas and stairway. Within a week the Dutcher's had a fully furnished house. I presume they enjoyed it. I never saw them much after that.

Eventually, Dick Gross, using me as his photographic assistant, came to make professional photos of the Dutcher house for the Los Angeles Times Home section.

VACATION TRIP

Karon and I planned to get away from it all and drive north up the California Coast, possibly to Eureka, and back. We'd be giving our new black Volvo station wagon its initial outing. We'd never seen California north of San Francisco. The first day we drove up Highway 101 to Atascadero and visited Karon's sculpture teacher who was now retired and doing wonderful stone sculptures. His work was similar, but smaller than Henry Moore's. Seeing and talking to him gave us a breath of fresh air. It was inspiring to see him living with his creative wife in the country, far from his academic life, doing exactly what he and God always intended.

We continued through San Luis Obisbo, King City, Salinas, and stopped for the night in Santa Cruz. The next day it was marvelous to cross the great Golden Gate to Sausalito. The children, little Viveka (3), and Lilianne (1-1/2), were as peaceful as can be. We marveled at the redwood forest north of San Francisco, then moved west to Highway 1 where we passed seaward of Santa Rosa. We loved the bluffs and winding rocky shoreline all the way to Mendocino and Fort Bragg where we decided to stop and sleep. Little one-year-old Lili had not been feeling well all day and when we awoke in Fort Bragg she was down with a major cold.

Lili's cold dampened our spirits along with the chilly, overcast weather. We worried that we wouldn't be able to provide her with the comfort she would receive at home. We were strangers to northern California and far from Lili's pediatrician and appropriate medicines. We would not make it to Eureka. It was time to go home. We had lunch in the home for artists, Mendocino, and admired the sea bluff setting and local paintings and the apparently carefree nature of those who would spend their lives devoted to art in spite of poverty The Mendocino idea appealed to both of our artistic natures.

We may have reached Santa Cruz before finding a motel and food for the evening. The next day Lili had a significant temperature and sore throat. She was miserable with coughing and sneezing. Her nose was a mess. Karon thought we should get to Highway 101 immediately because it was faster. I had the idea I wanted to see the exquisite Highway 1 between Carmel and San Luis Obisbo. We had a long, serious argument and I won. We didn't rush home to take care of Lili, we saw highway 1. We took the long, arduous, but supposedly beautiful way that was three hours longer. We raced up, down and around the treacherous but gorgeous curves on an overcast day. Lili's illness cast an additional pall that made the experience nearly morbid. Karon and I didn't speak to each other the entire way. It was a break in our more-or-less harmonious marriage.

I feel guilty for forcing my way and prolonging Lili's discomfort. I feel guilty because Karon was right! We should have rushed home. I had only seen Highway 1 along that coast when Karon and I drove my mother five years earlier to San Francisco in the Black Beauty. Mother in the back seat with the top down, was windblown and freezing, another instance of my, and possibly Karon's, self-centeredness.

Lili recovered. Her cold lasted the usual time for young children. The coastal Highway 1 trip was not severely injurious to her. Karon was angry with me and it took a month for full equanimity to return.

JACK WARDEN

When the Dutcher house was under construction, Jack Warden, an actor and neighbor adjacent to the east, was a frequent visitor to the Dutcher construction job and a close neighbor. Jack was a strong Irish looking redhead who claimed he'd been a former boxer. He loved to run on the beach and exercise to keep his body in shape as well as look good in the movies. He befriended the Dutcher's contractor, Nick Schiro, then me, and before long I was invited to see his house and talk. Vanda, his gorgeous young French wife, spoke English with a captivating French accent. She probably had been a former European model and would-be actress. My first impression was that she and Jack had little in common except, of course, a strong physical attraction.

Jack wanted to do a separate guesthouse over the garage, probably for Vanda's mother who would soon be arriving from France. Afterward it would become a den. I told him I could do that. I came up with a fine looking guest room and bath with a generous landscaped deck over a work area below. The guest room design was post-and-beam with slim, high continuous windows on all four sides. The deck was made from 2x4 clear heart redwood boards laid flat with 1/16" space between. We countersunk screws into the finished redwood to attach it to the sleepers below and protected it with a natural clear finish. On the deck's two sides were wood benches interspersed with planter boxes filled with grow-mulch and foliage.

Forming a shield for nearby windows and as a backdrop and for the landscaped deck was a semi-obscure, white plastic, curved screen. Appearing suspended in the air, the semi-circular privacy screen was about seven feet high and formed a point of particular interest from below. Supporting the screen on the top and bottom were two, twenty foot long, curved, wood beams each made of six, ½ inch x 6 inch wide plywood strips glued together. The built-up beams were made by assembling the six plywood strips in form of the desired beam on the patio, bending and staggering them to the proper shape by holding them in restraints, then gluing and screwing them. When the glue dried over the weekend, the result was two, 20-foot-long, curved, laminated beams to support the top and bottom of the screen. Three coats of clear spar varnish gave them a nautical appearance. It was unusual in those days for an architect or builder to make glued, laminated beams, especially in a curve.

Jack had studied acting in college and had attended various acting studios and apprenticed by doing several years of Shakespearean Repertory Theater in New York. I found it strange that a man of such wide experience seemed so non-verbal. To me he seemed the macho-man. When I'd show up for supervision, he'd invite me in and ask if I was hungry and did I want a sandwich. I'd usually say, no. Then he'd ask if I wanted a beer and motion for me to have a seat in his living room. There we'd sit and unless he was responding to a question of mine, it was as if he had nothing to say.

Later, after Vanda had a boy child, she and Karon and Viveka and Lilianne used to have lunch together. We were fringe-friends. Eventually, Jack divorced Vanda and moved to New York where he acted on the stage. Perhaps twenty years later, after he'd been in Woody Allen movies and was a respected performer, I met him in the Malibu Bookstore on Cross Creek Road. After a *hail-fellow-well-met* greeting, we ran out of things to say. I felt dismissed and went elsewhere. Jack continued looking through stacks of books.

JOHANSEN HOUSE

*H*arold and Millie Johansen, 28 and 33 years old, owned a moderately sloping ¾ acre on Busch Drive. They lived in Santa Monica with a girl and boy of two and five, a dog and two cats. They wanted a new house within a limited budget.

It would be a three-bedroom house, with kitchen, dining and family rooms. A forward thinking couple, to save money, they intended to put less emphasis on the living room. Building magazines in 1963 questioned the need for a big living room if the house contained a family room. Living rooms usually sat empty, they argued, while family rooms buzzed with activity. A bomb shelter was also to be built separate from the house to alleviate the soul-shattering dangers of world annihilation that pervaded the cold-war years.

I began my designs. After a day or so I was stumped and thumbed through architectural magazines until my brains were fried. During my early practice I frequently tried to find solutions by looking elsewhere than my own brain, but found this never worked. A published answer never fitted my special problem. I think it is wonderful to look through magazines to find a personal solution if only to learn that *looking for the answer in magazines has no redeeming benefit whatsoever!*

Resolving the Johansen's program continually resulted in a house too big for the budget. I fooled myself by cutting every room to the bone to achieve the proper square footage and multiplied that by the going rate for houses in an attempt to show my clients I was within reason.

Cost is thought to relate to the size. The theory was if I cut size, I cut cost. But it is also true that shapes relate to cost. A square building is cheaper than a U-shaped building. But a square building looked terrible on the acre lot. As an inexperienced designer I based my estimates on square footage only and presented a long thin U-shaped house that harmonized with the lot. Unfortunately it had a major problem. A permanent passageway was designed inside the family room that traveled diagonally across the center. *A room with a diagonal traffic pattern is a room with a failure.* I had violated one of architecture's greatest principles. Either my own talent limited me, or the owners had written me a program that forced me to make a mistake.

I felt guilty about that house for almost thirty years until new owner's had me do a remodeling and I was able to fix this error.

144 - Johansen house remodeled in the 80's. Photo shot while house was being used to photograph a motion picture.

RECAPITULATION

QUESTIONS

Where had I been? What did I do? How did I feel about where I'd been and what I did? Had I learned anything? What did I learn? Had I gone backwards? Did I grow? How was my home life? Had I fixed my social problem? How did I feel about the world situation? Was I OK? Did I have hope for the future? Was life good? Would I do it all over again?

RECAP

I went alone to Denver and was able to sustain a living with oval-dome architect, Eugene G. Groves and found an enduring friend in Chuck Hazlewood. Shortly after, I took a vacation in the East Stadium Dormitory in Tucson with football brother, Dave, and enjoyed campus life without study. Thinking it would never happen; I looked for a job and was surprised to be offered an excellent one. Feeling immature and foolish, I immediately rejected it!

In San Diego I lived with adopted parents, Dona and Tom Rutkowski, and honed my tattered social skills with 15-year-old Georgia Rutkowski. I was able to hold a job with the architectural firm of Kistner, Curtis and Wright doing schools for almost a year while trying to find my undeveloped self. On weekends, I escaped to skin diving.

In Altadena I worked in several architectural offices and met my mentor, Kenneth M. Nishimoto. Dating Karon and meeting her family changed my life. I became married, worked for Ray Jones in Glendale doing the Kenter Avenue School while having strange, weird and unpleasant feelings that forced me into nine months of psychotherapy. Deciding I couldn't lick 'em, I joined 'em and took up smoking. I joined a musical group doing the Gondoliers and sang and danced at the Pasadena Playhouse for a month of performances. This was all I could think of to do to grow up. Oh yes! I got my architectural license.

Moving to San Vicente Boulevard in Santa Monica, I enjoyed doing houses in a railroad tie building in Brentwood where I was being educated to the life philosophies of Hap Gilman, Frank Young and Willie Moore. In my final year I became chief designer of contemporary houses in Hap Gilman's office and learned more about the business of architecture.

While working at home I designed and built two spec houses in Santa Monica Canyon, the first of which became our own home when it came up for sale a year later. After moving in I began having my first architectural experiences with clients. We joined the Pacific Palisades Civic Chorus, did the musical Girl Crazy, and Karon worked in a play called *Blind Alley* at the Ebsen Theater with Harvey Korman.

In the Palisades I tried my luck with partner Dwight Pollock and was unexpectedly presented with another partner, Bob Hess. We planned big buildings for which we were never paid until I dissolved our partnership and took a drafting job with Dick Irwin. Dick led me to my dream office in Malibu and experiences followed with Bruce Koch, John Dorr and my early jobs. I joined the Malibu Chamber and in my practice, began to learn by doing.

At home, I discovered the difference between real talk and superficial talk by attending the Saturday night meetings of the addict's self-help group called Synanon. After four years of marriage, Karon and I were delighted with Viveka and eighteen months later, Lilianne. I changed offices from the Chris Craft building to the top of Louis Busch's Real Estate Office sharing both with surveyor Mario Quiros.

SOME ANSWERS

Where had I had been and what I did are answered but how did I feel about those things. I felt OK about my actions. I was in my early career building stage and it was not supposed to be easy. I had my own house; a couple of kids and what I thought was a good marriage. I was proud of Karon's abilities in acting, singing, set design and art and found her a tireless worker. She had some fixed ideas about life, but how could I deny her those. I had some, too. On paper, my life looked fine. Sure, I had problems to overcome, but I felt I could solve them.

Learning took place because eleven years can't go by without learning. I learned, not only about architecture, but also about myself. I could handle an architectural project on my own and could hire help and be boss. I could do schools and large and small houses and additions. People tended to like me. They didn't know my high blood pressure bothered me or that panic attacks lurked just under my skin during most of my projects or that my adrenal glands were squeezing competitive juice most of the time. I learned I could stay married and could deliver a child. I was not yet on a quest for self-knowledge, but it occurred, nevertheless. I had not gone backwards. Time and life always go forward – to the death. *Did I grow?* I couldn't have helped growing. *Was it easy?* No, but not impossible. *Had I fixed uneasiness over relationships to the opposite sex, my self-consciousness in large groups, and my inability to hold a cigarette and pour wine and be mature like Humphrey Bogart?* Marriage put that task on hold. Being married, I was obviously heterosexual and with a steady job I was maintaining the normal state. I was normal! No questions asked! To complete social growth, I would have had to date other women. This was not only unthinkable, but never entered my mind. Karon and I were showing the world how to live. We would be the perfect family in the perfect house. We were educated, musical, dramatic, artistic, philosophic, literary, hard working, wonderful young athletic people who had the most delightful, talented and mindful children. We were the couple who knew how to live. My unconscious was running amuck. It had done nothing with social naiveté.

Was I OK? I'd have to say yes. Things were difficult, but I was OK. *Did I have hopes for the future?* I was hopeful. *Was life good?* I didn't think about it much, but I'd say yes. *How did I feel about the world?* Prejudice and injustice to the blacks and women was rampant and disgusting to me. Designing bomb shelters did not give me a good feeling. Mankind knew how to blow up the world. We might all die. This thought robbed our hearts, sapped our strength and exacerbated feelings of futility. Nevertheless, indomitable people were alone and achieving little things of which I was proud.

STATE OF THE NATION

Police in Birmingham, Alabama arrest 1,000 civil rights protesters.

Four Birmingham black girls die after a bomb explodes during a church service.

A sniper in Jackson Mississippi kills Medgar Evers, civil rights leader.

Martin Luther King, gives the speech of a lifetime to over 200,000 people assembled in Washington D.C. on August 28, 1963.

"I still have a dream. It is a dream deeply rooted in the American dream. I have a dream that one day this nation will rise up and live out the true meaning of its creed: "We hold these truths to be self evident, that all men are created equal.' When we let freedom ring ... we will be able to speed up that day when all of God's children, black men, and white men, Jews and Gentiles, Protestant's and Catholic's, will be able to join hands and sing in the words of the old Negro spiritual, 'Free at last!" Free at last! Thank God Almighty, we are free at last!' "

On November 22, 1963, president John F. Kennedy was shot in the head twice as he rode through Dallas with Jacqueline, his wife. Evidence pointed to Lee Harvey Oswald as the assassin, but before police could obtain information on Oswald, nightclub owner, Jack Ruby, shot him. Vice President Lyndon B. Johnson was sworn in as president.

(Where was I when John Kennedy was shot? I had just finished a morning of drafting in my office over Louis T. Busch's Real Estate office and had walked to a little luncheon cafe at the Malibu Sands where I

joined friends. We decided to sit outdoors in the shaded and landscaped rear patio beneath a Malibu foothill. I had almost completed my Malibu Burger when the calamitous news spread from table to table. I was shocked and felt I had been delivered a mortal blow. I couldn't assimilate the facts all at once. It would take time to digest such an American tragedy.)

Betty Friedan published *The Feminine Mystique*, stating there had to be more to life than raising children and running a household. She hit a nerve with women and in 1966 co-founded the National Organization for Women. *(NOW)*

The Beatles, Paul McCartney, John Lennon, George Harrison and Ringo Starr release their first album, *Please, Please Me*.

Sylvia Plath describes her various suicide attempts in her morbid autobiography, *The Bell Jar*.

Popular TV Series included, *The Twilight Zone, Mr. Ed, Perry Mason, Dr. Kildare, Gunsmoke, Leave it to Beaver, Bonanza, The Beverly Hillbillies* and *The Dick Van Dyke Show*.

Cassette tape recorders and touch-tone telephones debut.

Color TV is relayed by satellite for the first time.

Elizabeth Taylor and Richard Burton starred in the motion picture, Cleopatra. At 37 million dollars it was the most expensive movie to date

British author C. S. Lewis died at 64.

Jack Nicklaus is the youngest man to win the Masters golf tournament in Augusta, Georgia.

Motown releases the first album of the 12-year-old genius, Little Stevie Wonder.

John Pennel was the first to pole-vault over 17 feet. Using a fiberglass pole he cleared 17 feet, ¾ inches.

Rudolph Nureyev and Margot Fonteyn dance the ballet, Marguerite and Armand.

OFF PILLS

Doctor Daniel Hillman had formerly headed the Malibu Medical Emergency Hospital and had done work on crash victims or severe contractor's accidents, or others who needed immediate medical care before being rushed to Santa Monica or St. John's hospitals for additional care.

In 1963 the good doctor was one of Malibu's first General Practitioners located on Malibu Road close to Webb Way. I decided to use Dr. Hillman for annual check-ups and he discovered my continuing blood pressure problem. I told him I had been taking Raudixon pills under another doctor's direction for the past three years.

Subsequently he said Raudixon was made from a species of the Rauwolfia plant and was one of the old snake-oil ingredients effective in the old days to lower blood pressure. Its side affects included repressed libido and chronic depression.

Hillman decided he'd do an exhaustive check-up and gave me a cholesterol test, urine test, blood tests, tread mill test, x-rays to determine heart size, and a kidney test where I had to drink some awful tasting stuff, Barium I think. My kidneys and urinary tract were photographed at five-minute intervals. After a few weeks I saw him for his final diagnosis, which was, *I didn't have high blood pressure.* Tests indicated my kidneys were perfectly healthy and my heart showed no enlargement. He said my blood pressure may increase, temporarily, when under stress, but during normal times, such as when sleeping or relaxing, I was quite normal. Frequent check ups without *"downers"* revealed moderate elevation, but not in the danger zone. He had done exhaustive research and found he could recommend taking me off pills, altogether.

Later it came to me that I'd been taking *"Reds"* or *"Downers"* for three years. I was an unconscious addict. Though I thought myself adequate sexually, I slowly realized downers had prevented me from reaching my full potential. I'd been trying to build our house, open a practice, maintain a relationship and have two children while being chronically depressed and amorously inhibited.

Now I experienced an upsurge in energy like I'd never felt before. I was alive! I was vital! I was strong! I was invincible! I was inspired! Nothing could stop me from any quest I might make. I suddenly wanted to do art, singing, board surfing, architecture, writing, cartooning, poetry, and adventure. I was on my way without having started. I was inspired by possibilities of where I could go.

MONEY AVAILABLE

To add to my feeling of well-being, the banks and savings and loans were lending money again and several jobs were milling around here and there ready to hire me as their architect.

NEW JOBS

Russcor and Associates, a tract development corporation handling the Roy Roger's Ranch property in Chatsworth, were seriously thinking of having me do a pilothouse design for a 180-house tract development. *(A pilothouse is the first house built in a tract and is used to show prospective buyers a fine example of what could be built).* My house would be that fine example. To get it I had to compete with the head of the Architecture Department at Southern California University, the renowned, Quincy Jones. When I was awarded the job the manager of Russcor told me I had out-Quincied, Quincy.

Ada Marie Bowers, my old apartment house friend and client from Isla Vista next to the University of California at Santa Barbara had spoken to two of her dear friends, Charlotte Anderson and Bessie Smith. They had purchased a three-acre property on top of a hill off San Marcos Pass in Santa Barbara and wanted to split it into three legal parcels and have me harmonize three homes, one for each of them.

In Malibu, Jerry and Ellie Hauffe, who had three small children, purchased a hillside property with a sweeping westerly view down the beach to Point Dume. They hired me to do a three thousand square foot house on Sea Vista Drive.

NEW OFFICE & PUBLICATIONS

Good news for 1964 was occupying my new office on the beach, rent free, for four years, thus avoiding the tenant's relentless financial burden.

I would be published again in April and June of 1964 in the Los

Angeles Times, Home section. *Dick Gross*, with me assisting, had already photographed the three-story Dutcher house in the Malibu Colony and *Richard Fish* had photographed the Ewert apartment building on Pacific Street in Santa Monica.

GOOD HOME LIFE.

Karon surprised me by telling me she would like to have another baby. I was delighted. I'd always wanted to have four children. I wasn't sure about asking Karon, but having a third would get me closer to my original hearts desire of four.

Viveka was a little over three years old. Lilianne was a little under two. Both seemed happy and healthy and progressing normally. Each accepted their trips to our valued pediatrician without too many tears when their shots were due, and to their dentist when their teeth were regularly fluoride-treated. Karon had learned what she needed to handle stay-at-home work with children. Our relationship was steady. Karon was locked into an adamant home routine as I with my Malibu practice.

Lois and Duke Conan and their son, Dick and his new wife Ana Ray were constant parts of our lives. My mother and dad visited every year and Dave and his new bride, Ellyn, came to sunny California now and then. Sometimes cousin Gene and JoAnne Kennard and their five children visited.

Our best friends were Ricky and Art Volkman, Ina Nuell, David Rhiel, Tom Pincu and Gene Grounds. I had just met architect, Rick Davidson, who was to become my best Southern California friend, one who shared his personal self with me and one from whom I learned much.

To be continued.

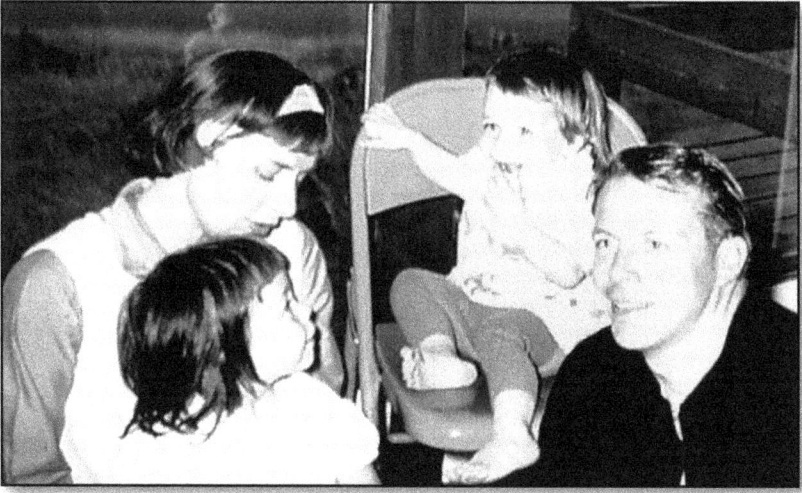

145 - *Viveka, Karon, Lilianne, Doug early in 1964.*

END

Acknowledgments

I'd like to express my love and deep caring to Marjory Kron Lewi-Rucker, *(deceased)* my life friend and spouse, for her intelligence, understanding, and patience in editing this work.

Thanks to Helane Freeman, computer expert, artist, editor, and all-around creative force, for her InDesign work and beautiful covers.

I would like to express my gratitude and deepest appreciation to Ron Munro, who guided me with tireless enthusiasm through the intricate complexities of my computer.

Thanks to Jack Birdsall *(deceased)* artistic giver-of-all-time who freely tackled the job of getting a proof-copy of this book published.

My thanks and love go to my daughters, Viveka, Lilianne and Amanda and to my stepchildren, Jenny, Katy, Christopher and Marggy and their spouses and children for their continued encouragement in my writing.

To my relatives, friends and acquaintances of whom I've written. Please know I appreciate every one of you for being part of my only life. After all we were together and shared this lovely planet until the year, 2018. I think of all of you with love.

www.ingramcontent.com/pod-product-compliance
Lightning Source LLC
Chambersburg PA
CBHW041828090426
42811CB00010B/1138